The Future of
Volunteer Fire and Rescue Services:
Taming the Dragons of Change

Kenneth B. Perkins,
Longwood College, Farmville, VA
and
John Benoit,
Dalhousie University, Halifax, NS

Published By:
Fire Protection Publications
Oklahoma State University
©1996

Edited By: Carol M. Smith
Design/Layout: Connie Burris
Graphics: Connie Burris,
          Don Burull, Rick Arrington

ISBN 0-87939-131-6
Library of Congress #96-85567

First Edition
First Printing, August 1996

Printed in the United States of America

Table of Contents

Acknowledgements

With the inevitable risk of omission, let us acknowledge the contributions of a number of individuals who have greatly aided our task in writing this book. Gene Carlson played a central role as a substantive editor. Indeed, it is probable that the standards dragons might have escaped our attention without his input on this subject. Despite international assignments, Gene unfailingly read and commented in detail on the drafts of each chapter, often reading the material while sitting in economy class airline seats flying at over 30,000 feet.

We would like to acknowledge several individuals and organizations based in the United States. Gus Welter, Jim Monihan, and Red McKeon of the National Volunteer Fire Council have been strong supporters of academic research on volunteers and volunteer fire departments. Carl Milofsky, Alexander Thompson, and Ram Cnaan of the Association for Research on Nonprofit Organizations and Voluntary Action (ARNOVA) along with its journal *Nonprofit and Voluntary Sector Quarterly* have been very good academic resources. Garry Briese of the International Association of Fire Chiefs has been very helpful. Susan McHenry formerly of the Virginia Office of Emergency Medical Services provided considerable insight to the complex dragon of EMS. Finally, we acknowledge help from the National Fire Academy and Sue McCauley at the Florida EMS Clearinghouse.

In Canada, several members of the Canadian Association of Fire Chiefs have provided much insight into the issues addressed in this book. In particular, we would like to mention Marcel Ethier, Executive Director; Gary Greene, Past President and Fire Commissioner of Halifax, Nova Scotia; and Bill Hewitt, President and Fire Chief of Saskatoon, Saskatchewan. We would also like to thank Jim McDavid of the University of Victoria whose pioneering research on combination fire departments inspired much of our thinking. Moving east, we thank Terry-Dawn Hewitt, an Albertan lawyer who has studied Canadian law in relation to the fire service, greatly aiding the legal chapter. More locally, we would like to thank Harold Richardson, Past Chief of the Hubbards Volunteer Fire Department; Ed Rees, Executive Director of the Nova Scotia Firefighters School; Mike Eddy, Chief of the Sackville Nova Scotia Fire Department; and Ken Kelly, Chief of the Yarmouth Nova Scotia Fire Department. The years of conversations with these individuals have helped academic outsiders to learn the issues.

Finally, we would like to thank Ramona Ryan of Four Eyes Unlimited who typed some of the chapters, word processed all of them, and copy edited the text in preparation for Fire Protection Publications of Oklahoma State University. Despite the erratic work schedule and sometimes failed deadlines of the authors, she responded with professional aplomb, humor, and efficient action.

Foreword

The Volunteer Fire Service Leadership program at Dalhousie University had, in 1989, a lesson on organizational change that is very telling. In that lesson, volunteer fire departments were portrayed as slow-moving organizations responding to a calm, placid environment. Of course, conflict would arise both within a department and with a local government, but such conflict was as much a response to boredom as anything else. The challenge presented to the students (many of them chiefs) was to change their own departments without raising the ire of their memberships. An angry membership can reject a chief at election time. (Unfortunately, one student was "turfed out" by his membership before we even started the organizational change lesson.)

Six years later, in 1995, our perception of the environment of a typical volunteer fire department has changed entirely. Now that environment is turbulent. Fiscal restraint by local government has made fund-raising more difficult. The rumor of civil litigation has increased the anxiety of fire chiefs. Recruiting difficulties have introduced a more diverse volunteer membership. Differences in race, class, and gender have introduced new values and new ways of communicating. In many volunteer departments, an emergency medical service has been added to the repertoire of services. Each of these challenges introduces new players who begin to scrutinize what was once (and may still be) an "Old Boys Club." Such scrutiny no longer requires conflict to reduce boredom. The boredom will disappear even if there are hardly any structural fires to fight.

From our perspective, this change is partly attributed to the orientation of the Volunteer Fire Service Leadership program in 1989 compared with the orientation of this book written in 1995. In 1989, the perception of a placid environment was reasonable. In 1995, this book is as much about the future as about the present. As such, the difference in perception of the degree of turbulence in the environment may be exaggerated. Nevertheless, the trends we present in this book (we will call them dragons) are real. No chief we have interviewed, and few we have heard of, still believes that the environment of a volunteer emergency organization is a placid one.

We have chosen to concentrate on the relationship between local government and the volunteer fire department. We do this partly because local government often mediates between the volunteer fire department and its environment. We do this partly because local government is part of that environment itself.

I met with several kinds of
associations in America of
which I confess I had no previous notion; and I have often
admired the extreme skill with
which the inhabitants of the
United States succeed in proposing a common object for
the exertions of a great many
men and in inducing them
voluntarily to pursue it.

Alexis de Tocqueville, written in 1835

THE ARENA:
INTRODUCING THE HERO, THE VILLAIN,
AND THE DRAGONS OF CHANGE

The reader is invited to begin our introductory chapter with an examination of a dramatic, real-life story. Notice in this case there is fear of change, vicious behavior, and ambiguities of power and authority between the government and the fire departments.

THE QUEEN COUNTY CASE:
FROM RIVALRY TO SABOTAGE

Queen county is located in a southern Atlantic state and has a population of just over twenty thousand inhabitants. The county seat is a small town called Queen. History has it that another town, still in existence only ten miles away called Minerville, was in contention for the county seat. Queen prevailed since the sheriff (and his jail) and the local judge both lived in the town of Queen. The county's early economic and social history is one that centered around mining for minerals and precious metals. Mining played out in the middle 1800s, and now is only of interest to the occasional tourist.

The rivalry between the towns of Queen and Minerville, which was apparent 200 years ago, remains a well articulated part of contemporary county culture. Recently, for example, when a county water control authority was established, Minerville refused to participate. After the water authority installed an automatic check valve at the Queen County Public High School, (located in Queen — the Minerville High School was consolidated into Queen's in 1930), the Minerville Town Council installed its own manual valve citing that it could not trust an automatic one. "Each of these towns has its own sun which rises and sets," noted a government official.

One unit of the Queen County Volunteer Fire and Rescue Department, Inc. is located in the Town of Queen, and the other in Minerville. It will be a point of interest later on in this case to know that the two units are legally one corporation.

The county is home to a nuclear power plant. This facility had a major impact on the economy of the county because, among other things, it brought in considerable development, an increase in residences, more school children, and an increase in the tax base. The government has utilized this revenue for public schools and housing, and has financed the upgrading of the two fire and rescue departments' buildings and vehicles. Manpower for both departments has remained all volunteer.

Internal Strain

Queen County Volunteer Fire and Rescue is not unique in that it is common for one governing body to oversee separate units, such as those in the towns of Queen and Minerville. What is unusual is the way this arrangement is structured. From their founding in the late 1950s until 1990, the Queen and the Minerville unit, each on an alternate basis, elected either three or four of their members to serve as officers on the one governing board of directors. Of course, depending upon what year it was, one department would have a majority and each unit had its own chief. Since the chief is in charge of the unit on a daily basis, having two equally ranking individuals, each in charge of their units for the same formal organization, served to create a serious internal strain.

From the interviews, it seems that for the first few decades of the units' existence, there was a more or less healthy competition between them. Certainly, this would be expected in light of the historical relations between the towns of Queen and Minerville. However, the environment turned hostile in the middle 1980s when the Queen unit proposed to move out of its location in the Town of Queen and into a larger building half the distance to Minerville. The proposal upset the tenuous balance of power between the two units.

One version of the proposal was to consolidate the Minerville unit into the new Queen County Volunteer Fire and Rescue Department. Another was to make the Minerville unit a "satellite" station. The reaction of Minerville was to draw battle lines. The tremendous upheaval created by the proposal, coupled with threats by the Minerville unit not to relinquish any of its trucks and equipment, plus the unusual structure of the governing board, resulted in a protracted conflict.

An interesting story related by the emergency services co-ordinator serves to illustrate the strain experienced between the Queen and Minerville departments. It seems that a member of the Minerville unit was dismissed because of a traffic incident. The next day, this individual applied for membership in the Queen unit. Its board, apparently ignoring its own policy on a waiting period for new members, immediately granted membership. Subsequently, at least two Queen members resigned in protest of the policy blunder. Several months later, the new member was dismissed from the Queen unit for driving under the influence. The next day, he applied for membership in the Minerville unit and was accepted because, according to the emergency coordinator: "His stock was up. He had been kicked out of Queen."

The Ten-Foot Pole Standard

In all this conflict, the government had a minimal role. The emergency coordinator reported that he had "no big stick or big carrot" to control the threats to split or to reduce the "terrible beating" the public image his departments were taking. He related that recent history showed both units guilty of grievous behaviors that affected public safety. In one instance, he related that one of the units practiced patient abandonment. It seems that the unit was dispatched for a sick call, but left that scene to attend a knifing incident. Another time, after the senior dispatcher in the sheriff's office reassigned a unit in the field to respond to a serious automobile accident, another unit in the field reassigned the first one without regard to the dispatcher. The emergency coordinator said of all this: "They respond to **their needs**, not the county's." The coordinator reported that soon after the wreck, he bought every member of the county's governing board a scanner radio for their home in the hope that the politicians might see for themselves how the units actually behaved.

The government has a "ten-foot pole rule" when dealing with the departments. The coordinator reported that:

The Board of Supervisors wants me to oversee these organizations, but will not back me up. I am full of piss and vinegar because I have to sit back and watch the departments be negligent and make fools of themselves. There are a lot of people in the county that listen to everything on their scanners. There is not a person on the board that wants to take on one of these groups. They use the old ten-foot pole rule...they keep a safe distance away...and give me just enough authority to irritate the volunteers.

Mediation, Litigation, And Sabotage

In 1990, the emergency coordinator had an idea about how to break the tension between the units. He brought in outside mediators. The mediation team was invited to meet with groups from both units to find some compromise. There was still the threat from Minerville to appropriate equipment bought by the government and form their own independent department. The Queen unit still wanted to set up a new and bigger shop halfway between the two towns but wanted Minerville to cooperate and not become a separate corporation only five miles away.

The only idea from the mediation effort that took root was the suggestion of a completely external board of community leaders from both towns and other communities in the county. No volunteer from either unit would be on this new board. Indeed, the board was formed with the president as the county extension agent. This occurred with little overt dissension.

The new board arrived at what the old proposal of Queen essentially had suggested. The best thing for the county, it found, was to move the Queen unit out of the town and into new facilities at the industrial air park. This new site was only five miles from Minerville. The Minverville members unit could either join the Queen unit in a consolidation, a word that struck horror with Minerville, or maintain a scaled down version to operate as a satellite station, which would be another form of disgrace and loss of their community identity.

Minerville's chief (a captain) filed suit against the new board. His position was that the new board was illegal. He cited the original constitution and by-laws that had not been duly revised to make for a new board and, thus, argued that Queen did not have the authority to make any decision about moving a unit or consolidation. The suit persisted in the courts for three years. In August of 1993, the state supreme court upheld a lower court's dismissal of the suit as frivolous. It ordered the captain to pay $10,000 in legal fees.

According to the emergency coordinator, the morning following the Supreme Court's ruling a call was given to the dispatcher that the Minerville department was "on an indeterminate leave of absence." The coordinator responded by recruiting volunteers from another nearby department to work temporarily out of the Minerville building. Upon arrival, they found that all the vehicles had been disabled and would not start. The following Tuesday, Minerville called to report that they were again responding to calls. There seems to have been a secret deal struck between the unit and the governing board about who would have to pay the $10,000. The emergency coordinator said that he had only been "on the sidelines during all of this."

The coordinator had had no direct role in any of the maneuvers by the Minerville unit. He said:

The only thing I could do was sit around and make contingency plans...I had an opportunity to shut down the Minerville unit, but no one would give me the green light. What they did to the trucks was really a criminal matter. Now they have a taste of real power. They will be even harder to control. Did you know that the Tuesday they went back in service, a state inspector from the Department of Emergency Services came and renewed their EMS license?

At the present, the new board's decision to alter the county's fire and EMS structure seems to be gaining momentum. The captain of the Minerville unit has resigned and several of Minerville's members have defected to the Queen department.

No doubt the foregoing story is an unusual way to begin a book about the survival of volunteer emergency service in North America. However, at the heart of the Queen County case are several themes we wanted the reader to notice early. In this case, we introduce the issues of fear of change, ambiguities of power, and authority among the players according to the emergency coordinator, and their unflattering behavior. We can point out some themes in the story that relate to themes in this book. There is the obvious theme of relations with government. There are also themes of consolidation and community identity; the demand on volunteers when providing emergency medical service; threat of litigation from clients and volunteers themselves; and recruitment and leadership blunders and challenges. In the background is the theme of training standards for volunteers, although this did not come up in the story. We call these themes "dragons of change."

The use of the term dragon is to suggest that there are elements in the environment of volunteer emergency organizations that represent serious threats to their survival. The discovery of these particular dragons has come from our research for this book and our experience in the volunteer fire service. This is not to say there are no other threats out there, but the ones we focus on seem to threaten most organizations. Each of these dragons must be "tamed" — they are never eliminated — by joint efforts with volunteer agencies and their local governments; these parties sometimes view each other as heroes or villains.

As sociologists with practical experience in the volunteer fire and rescue service, we recognize that a purely academic treatment of all this subject matter would likely fail. Therefore, we have tried to write for an audience of practitioners — chiefs, local government administrators, elected officials, and others who have real-world responsibilities for volunteer fire and EMS services. The reader will find in every chapter true stories, newspaper accounts, or legal cases that make it easier and interesting to read as well as make practical points. The discussion part of each chapter is also aimed at providing practical strategies to deal with the dragons that haunt one's volunteer service.

The book encompasses perspectives from the United States and Canada. There are obvious differences between these two countries. The basic political divisions in the U.S. are called states and are called provinces in Canada. National, state, and provincial governments differ in terms of titles of officials, functions associated with various offices, taxation policy, health care funding, and environmental policy, to name a few. At the level of local government (called the municipal level in

Canada), there are very similar patterns to such things as the way volunteer fire departments are constituted and their relations with local government. Most of the differences at the local level can be understood as different methods of dealing with very similar issues, such as education and public safety. Our interest is the local level of volunteer organization-government relations. With few exceptions, practically all volunteer fire and EMS organizations are local.

Both Canada and the U.S. have a vast volunteer fire service. It is estimated that there are about 25,000 all-volunteer fire departments in the U.S. and 5,000 in Canada. This does not include combination departments (volunteer and career firefighters in the same station). These numbers do not even include the hundreds of all-volunteer Emergency Medical Service (EMS) squads in the U.S. In the U.S., and less so in Canada, volunteers provide a considerable amount of emergency medical service. Hospital-based EMS is more the norm in Canada, but there does seem to be an increasing interest by the volunteer fire service and provincial and local governments in having some EMS provided by fire departments. Indeed, many rural volunteer fire departments have taken on EMS already. The U.S. has a variety of EMS providers: private ambulance companies, volunteer EMS organizations, EMS under the umbrella of volunteer fire departments, and, of course, career fire departments which provide a large share of EMS in urban areas. What is important is that the dragons of change can be seen in both the Canadian and the U.S. volunteer services. Although there are distinct differences in how these "dragons as change agents" have come about, have been met by local government, and inspire volunteer organizations, these differences make interesting reading and inspire good ideas for survival strategies.

WHY SURVIVAL IS IMPORTANT

The backdrop for our work is the survival of the volunteer service. By survival we mean successful adaptation to change. It is our position that the next decade presents some difficult "dragons" to be confronted and "tamed." Without a positive relationship between volunteers and local governments, serious threat to volunteer service provision can develop. We are firm in our assumption that this service not only should survive but must do so if we are to continue at current levels of service provided in many areas of North America. Fully paid services, typical in the majority of urban areas, are not options for many communities, towns, and suburbs in North America. Simple economics, such as tax bases and revenues, support this assertion.

There is another reason we see as important to the survival of the vast volunteer sector of the fire and EMS service: the dependence of citizens on government. The famous and often cited observer of 19th century America, Alexis de Tocqueville, observed in the 1830s that when any country allowed government to assume more and more provision of services, there would be increasing dependence of citizens on the government. We certainly do not see government as bad, but there are limits to what it can do, and perhaps should do. We agree with Tocqueville that voluntary associations have an important role, not just in the specifics of what they undertake, but in the health of civil life in general. Allow us to include his exact words:

> *It is easy to foresee that the time is drawing near when man will be less and less able to produce, by himself alone, the commonest necessaries of life. The task of the governing power will therefore perpetually increase, and its very efforts will extend it every day. The more it stands in the place of associations, the more will individuals, losing the notion of combining together, require its assistance...* (1945; p. 116)

Historically, as Tocqueville noted even in the 1830s, people in North America have had a love for voluntary associations — from associations that might be considered trivial to those that allow individuals to volunteer together to address very serious issues. Volunteer fire associations are some of the oldest, most numerous, and serious associations in terms of what they do for their communities, and, thus, their nations. These organizations are part of something rather unique and, if one believes Tocqueville, quite valuable.

BACKGROUND FEATURES OF THE VOLUNTEER SERVICE

What are the background features of the volunteer fire and EMS service? This question should be addressed, however briefly, so that we have a starting point from which to outline what the reader will find in subsequent chapters. "Vast," "varied," and "unique" are words that come immediately to our minds in any general description of the volunteer service.

We noted above that the volunteer fire and EMS service is made up of thousands of local organizations. These organizations are varied in how they are constituted and how they relate to local government. Many are like Queen County — fiercely independent, non-profit corporations which have as little to do with government as possible. Others are actually formally part of a local government, provided for in the government's charter, and do not enjoy any legal independence, but often act as if they were legally independent. Some are devoted to one mission alone — fire or EMS; while others provide both services. The oddest of all, often found in suburban areas, are what commonly are called combination departments (composite in Canada) with paid personnel and volunteers in the same department. This patchwork of "types" of volunteer emergency organizations (VEOs) will be organized more systematically and discussed in Chapter Two.

Because of the varied nature of volunteer organizations, the terminology we use must be clear and consistent. We have already used the term **voluntary associations** to describe these organizations in a sociological sense. This term will be abandoned for more specific descriptions. Volunteer emergency organizations (VEO) and fire/rescue and emergency medical service (EMS) cover all of the configurations of volunteer emergency organizations, such as the traditional all volunteer fire department without any EMS mission, the fire department which also runs EMS calls, combination departments (composite departments in Canada), and the organizations that only provide EMS service. When the context is more specific, we will qualify the kind of organization under study. For example, Chapter Eight will be about combination fire and EMS departments. Chapter Nine will be about volunteer EMS squads (they are usually not called departments in the U.S.) as well as fire departments with EMS missions.

We should note here that just as volunteer fire and EMS departments are varied, so are local governments. We will use the term **local government** to describe such governments as counties, townships, local service districts, villages, towns, and cities. Invariably, the cities which interest us are suburban satellite cities of a major metropolitan area. And, from the perspective of this book, local government is an important, ever-present background feature for the volunteer fire and EMS service. Thankfully, the terminology is much easier to use. We do know that thousands of local governments in the U.S. and Canada are indeed far from being perfectly uniform in structure. In saying this, however, we note that the typical outline of any local government in both countries is a set of democratically elected individuals representing some form of voting districts. There is also a corresponding paid administrator (usually appointed but sometimes elected) with a paid staff of varying size constituting subordinate administrators — a bureaucratic hierarchy — that answer to the local governing body of councilmen, selectmen, or supervisors. Terminology of titles differs greatly, but in practically every instance there is a chief administrative officer (CAO). Town managers, county administrators, and municipal heads are examples of CAOs.

As one would expect, the problems the local governing bodies confront in Canada and the U.S. are quite similar. In addition to individuals struggling for re-election, the governing body itself is faced with figuring out how to deal with state or provincial mandates, settling disputes among citizen groups, establishing funding priorities, assessing property values, educating the young, and providing for public safety.

It is the public safety concern of government that involves volunteer fire and EMS organizations. Here, local government must communicate with their volunteer organizations. Government cannot ignore these organizations, if for no other reasons than: it has a mutual interest in public safety; it cannot rule them with an iron fist; and it cannot put them out of business and find another vendor for services. Volunteers can be very powerful political forces at election time. Yet, the bureaucratic tendency toward making policies and demanding compliance with them is always a temptation in dealing with any organization for which government may feel it has some responsibility. For our purposes, let it suffice to say that these relationships from both sides of the fence can have considerable ambiguity that can give way to misunderstanding, suspicion, power struggles, and conflict. If this were all there was to it, our book would not be very relevant. However, this ambiguity and misunderstanding take place in an environment of change. In other words, not only do local governments and volunteer organizations have to deal with each other, they have to identify and overcome some powerful forces that threaten the survival of volunteer organizations. As we noted above, we decided to call these forces "dragons." At times during the struggle to confront and tame these dragons, (we do not think they are ever slain), local government and volunteer organizations act like "villains" or "heroes." Sometimes in the contests with the dragons and with one another, volunteer emergency organizations can behave "virtuously" or "viciously."

What else is left to say about background features that cannot wait until later chapters? Perhaps we should mention where several dragons have come from. Several have come from forces of economics and demography. Both of these forces have been attended to by all kinds of technological advancements that have affected such things as how long people are expected to live, access to and cost of emergency health care, and cost of fire and EMS apparatus. Several dragons have their origins in another large force in our society: we have to take the risk of sounding too much like sociologists and say that volunteer organizations are caught up in a process of becoming more and more bureaucratic. We will explain below.

We have already noted that economic factors have not created bountiful funding for expanded government services in most areas of the U. S. and Canada. "Do more with less," seems to be the order of the day. Tremendous pressure is put on local government to allocate a pot of money that seems to be getting smaller in relation to the needs of many deserving service providers. This makes volunteer services take on a whole new meaning in what they represent in labor cost savings. At the same time, capital and operating costs have no respect for whether or not an organization is volunteer. And, as every government administrator and fire chief knows, in an environment of resource scarcity, the daily administrative routine tends to become politicized and plays for power are more frequent.

Most of North America has been affected by demographic change. Demographic change has to do with fertility (births), mortality (deaths), and migration (changes in permanent residence). Two dragons that are highly visible come directly out of demography. The first is visible more so to volunteer organizations than to most local governments: recruitment of volunteers. The local landscape around many volunteer departments has changed from an ample supply of friends and relatives of old-time members, to an abundance of newcomers that have no former ties to the organization. During decades of local residential stability, many volunteer departments developed an inward-looking culture which was suspicious of outsiders. This culture does not function well given the current need to attract new people.

The second dragon created by demography is EMS. This dragon, easily visible to both volunteer organizations and to local government, is partially the result of increasing life expectancy (how long the average person is expected to live). For example, infants born in 1992 in the U.S. are expected to live for 75.8 years (Kochanek and Hudson, 1994). Canadian life expectancy tends to be even slightly higher. In comparison, the life expectancy in the U.S. in 1940 was just over 60 years (Weeks, 1989). The implication is that while people now live longer, they are not immune from health problems, especially in their later years. Consequently, there are considerable demands on health care systems. EMS, in the form of firefighter/EMTs (emergency medical technicians) or EMTs from volunteer EMS squads, is sent via the three magic numbers of 9-1-1. As we will note in Chapter Nine, 9-1-1 is like a panacea, or a cure for all ills.

Bureaucratization is a term that carries negative connotations, such as impersonal officials, slow response to needs of clients, and excessive, trivial paperwork. However, we mean it in its purer conception of the increase of formal, written rules (agreed upon or imposed) that govern actions of an organization and the behavior of members (Weber, 1947). These rules grow to become familiar procedures, such as standing requests for written budget reports to the local government, standard operating procedures, written policies on recruitment, retention and expulsion of members, extended descriptions of duties and positions in the by-laws of departments, written training expectations, and even state and national operating and training standards. The fire departments of a hundred years ago would not be able to recognize many of the policies we take for granted.

The reason we mention bureaucratization is that we see it as one key to understanding the background to debates about professionalism and training standards (a dragon nearly invisible to local governments). We see struggles and tensions in the process of having more and more written rules, particularly when they are imposed upon departments by outside agencies, whether they be the local governments or some national policy making body. If all volunteer fire and EMS organizations were bureaus of a central office somewhere, perhaps the issues of bureaucratization (and a related pressure, for professionalization) would be uninteresting. We all know that the departments and squads in question are essentially locally based community organizations that have enjoyed a long history of doing things their own way without a lot of written rules. The fundamental changes in these organizations, which, we suggest, are happening due to bureaucratization, can be very disturbing to these groups. This is not to say that the changes will be bad. On balance, the organizations may be much improved.

We have said enough about demography, economics, and the familiar force of bureaucratization. We turn now to a brief overview of our chapters.

CONCLUSION: THE PATH OF THIS BOOK

In Chapter Two, we introduce volunteer emergency organizations in greater detail: we give the variety of types and examine their characteristics. We also introduce local government, particularly as it is found in small towns, rural areas, and suburbs, because it is in these kinds of communities where volunteer emergency organizations are found. We end the chapter by presenting a method of classifying volunteer emergency organizations.

In Chapter Three, we concentrate on the **relationship** between the volunteer emergency organization (VEO) and its local government. Central to this relationship is the notion of power. We examine what power is and what strategies are used to deal with powerlessness. These strategies often drive changes in the relationship between VEOs and local governments. We end the chapter by considering another way of looking at VEOs by identifying them as vicious or virtuous. This discussion helps to see how the dragons of change affect the power relationship between VEOs and local governments.

Chapter Four is a discussion of legal issues of immunity from tort litigation as well as the threat of civil rights suits. These two legal concerns will be approached by using actual cases. Our interviews and experiences have uncovered an erroneous belief, held by many volunteers, that, because their organization is volunteer, it cannot be sued. Local government figures into this belief because, in the United States, local governments in most cases can still "cloak" their volunteer fire departments with sovereign immunity extended from state government. This is not the case in Canada, and trends in the U.S. suggest an erosion of this immunity. There is no such thing as sovereign immunity for civil rights suits. The most complex lawsuits are the ones brought on by members or former members. The reader well may benefit from the final section of this chapter on risk management.

Chapter Five presents the dragon of training standards. This chapter analyzes the debate between the National Fire Protection Association (NFPA) and the Alliance for Fire and Emergency Management. The position of these two national organizations (which have ramifications for Canada and possibly other countries) are examined in light of the role that external standards have on locally based volunteer fire organizations. We speculate as to how local governments might be drawn into the issues surrounding this debate. The general concern about training standards, regardless of which organization sets them, can have an impact on a volunteer department's relations with government. If sovereign immunity has eroded in Canada and is eroding in the U.S., the tort of negligence will likely be judged in light of a department's conformity to standards of training and performance.

Recruitment and leadership are the subjects of Chapter Six. These dragons are highly visible to volunteer organizations. We agree with the National Volunteer Fire Council that leadership in volunteer organizations has a direct impact on retention and may be the more important of these two problems for many departments. As we say this, we do recognize that recruitment is a perpetual difficulty. This chapter does not try to give a "cookbook approach" to attracting volunteers. It does seek, however, to give the reader a vantage point for viewing his or her own organization's strengths and weaknesses.

The dragon in Chapter Seven is called consolidation. We use the term to refer to a variety of situations where "the ground shifts" for volunteer departments when they are faced with merging services with other formerly autonomous departments. The simplest level can be seen in the Queen County case, presented earlier, where one of the two units wanted to merge physically. There was no government involvement in this decision; however, the reader might remember it as not a peaceful process. At the other extreme, the most complex level is the combining of public services from two or more governments with an aim at cost-savings. This situation might involve a forced mixing of volunteer and career personnel. Regardless of the scale or complexity, consolidation is a delicate matter. As we noted metaphorically, the ground shifts in a way in which great uncertainty occurs.

Chapter Eight focuses on a very unusual entity called the combination (composite) department. Typically, such an organization evolves in suburban areas where demand for services has overstretched the volunteer department's ability to meet it. In a sense, this is a kind of consolidation where government employees are "consolidated" into an existing volunteer system. EMS is often the catalyst for this. These departments, with volunteer and career individuals sharing the same station, are very complex creatures, to say the least. Our view is that however unwieldy and complicated these arrangements may be, they are an attractive option to many governments. We do not claim to have all the answers on how to create lasting peace and prosperity in these organizations, but we do think examination of the contested issues will be worthwhile reading to anyone faced with this situation.

The last dragon is the biggest of all, and (to extend the metaphor) can thrash around. Chapter Nine examines EMS from the point of view of the present and future. This was the most difficult chapter for us to write. There are many changes underway in the field of EMS provision. We readily admit that this chapter is incomplete. Presently, EMS has created a great demand for services. We speculate why and we look at two cases where serious internal conflict among volunteers and government intervention has occurred, respectively. We suggest some strategies for the all-volunteer EMS organization to help them cope. The future, from our research, is one where EMS may "migrate" into something called managed health care. In the U.S., health costs are so high that attempts at cost containment has bred groups called health maintenance organizations (HMO) that have an interest in the provision of EMS. In this economic and organizational context, private providers are likely to continue to gain in the marketshare of EMS. Many volunteer fire and EMS organizations, including combination departments that have government employed firefighters/paramedics, may find that they no longer have a firm hold on EMS.

Chapter Ten invokes the thinking we used in Chapter Two. The reader may appreciate that this is the last chapter. It is here that some of the main points from previous chapters are summarized. We also go on to suggest some possible directions where the volunteer fire and EMS services are heading.

INTRODUCING THE HERO AND THE VILLAIN

TROUBLE IN RIVER CITY

River City was a newly incorporated city formed out of the towns and villages which dotted the banks of the Salmon River. As a newly incorporated city, River City faced many growing pains, not the least of which was the friction which arose between the Northbank and the Southbank fire departments.

The Southbank Volunteer Fire Department (SVFD) was 47 years old. Indeed, Horace Williams, honorary life member, was one of the founding members. He would often tell stories about the early days of scrounging and petty theft to maintain the department. Everyone knew that a Department of Highways grader was "borrowed" at 3:00 a.m. one summer night in the mid-fifties. The gravel in the SVFD parking lot was graded to provide an even surface for training exercises. Even the Department of Highways foreman knew about it, but he was a volunteer firefighter as well.

Many of the members of the SVFD grew up in Southbank, the more sparsely populated side of the Salmon River. Indeed, over half of the total volunteer membership (41 people) had one of three family names. If you were an adult male with the last name of Lutes, McQuiggan, or Shanahan, then chances were you were a volunteer firefighter in the SVFD.

The Northbank Fire/Rescue Department (NFRD) was older than Southbank. Indeed, the Northbank Fire/Rescue Department traced its origins to the late 19th century when the local lumber mills organized fire brigades to extinguish wood pile fires which were common at the time. Despite these older beginnings the NFRD changed more rapidly than its Southbank counterpart. As Northbank grew in response to the growing worldwide demand for pulp and paper, so the NFRD grew as well. In the 1960s, as the population expanded, the NFRD was assimilated into the local government of Northbank. Volunteers were still encouraged but the chief was now paid and jointly selected by the local government and the volunteer membership. Similarly, the NFRD began to take on a stronger rescue role as it grew from river rescue to include an emergency medical service capacity. Further growth in calls led to the hiring of more firefighters and even female emergency medical technicians. Volunteers were still welcome but they began to wonder if their days as volunteers were numbered.

Then in the late 1980s events began to change. It soon became clear that all volunteers were welcome. The local government in Northbank could not afford to hire any more firefighters or EMTs. Moreover, the provincial government began to pressure Northbank and Southbank to consolidate their local governments along with the other adjacent communities on both banks of the Salmon River. This would force the Northbank Fire/Rescue Department and the Southbank Volunteer Fire Department into a "shotgun marriage."

River City (the new name for the consolidated city) assumed the responsibility for fire protection for the Salmon Area Hospital, newly built in Southbank. In anticipation of the hospital construction, the Southbank Volunteer Fire Department had just raised $200,000, matching a provincial contribution to purchase a new aerial truck. The consolidation of River City, the construction of the hospital, and the purchasing of the aerial truck started a war.

Once River City was formed, the mayor said that the new truck would be moved to the Northbank fire hall. She argued that even though an alarm at the hospital would require this aerial truck to cross the Salmon River, only the personnel of the Northbank department were professional enough to handle the complex evolutions of a hospital evacuation. In response to this impending action, the volunteer chief of Southbank said:

> We may have engaged in petty theft to build our fire hall, nevertheless, most of what built this hall was volunteer sweat and hard work. But you, Madame Mayor over in Northbank, by taking our aerial truck, you and Northbank are committing grand theft auto! We'll quit before we see our aerial truck moved out of our fire hall!

This brief story helps to introduce several organizational actors to the book. The actors are volunteer emergency organizations on one hand, and local government on the other. In River City we have the new local government actor, River City, which has grown from the various river bank communities. (And it suffers growing pains.) In addition, we have two actors that are volunteer emergency organizations. Clearly, however, each one is somewhat different from the other. On one hand, the Southbank Volunteer Fire Department is a traditional rural fire department. On the other hand, the Northbank Fire/Rescue Department is no longer traditional. It embraces emergency medical service as a goal; it hires career employees and maintains a cadre of volunteers; and it hires female employees. All of these features are non-traditional and, indeed, characteristic of many suburban fire departments.

This chapter will first examine the traditional rural volunteer fire department, describing its features, its origins, and its functions. After this, the chapter will describe a more recent type of volunteer emergency organization, the suburban fire/rescue department. Neither of these two types exhausts all the types of volunteer emergency organizations, but these two types introduce the reader to the range of possibilities.

This chapter moves on to describe the other key actor in our drama, local government. In particular, we are interested in the rural, small town, or suburban types of local government because these types of local government deal with volunteer emergency organizations. Our description of small local governments will be simplistic. We will only describe these governments enough to understand how they relate to volunteer emergency organizations.

We will end the chapter by returning to types of volunteer emergency organizations, concentrating on how we might classify volunteer emergency organizations. After this, we will begin to explore the advantages of classifying volunteer emergency organizations. In Chapter Ten, we will elaborate further upon the classification scheme to make predictions about how volunteer emergency organizations evolve.

At this stage, the reader might wonder which organizational actor is the hero and which is the villain. There is no one answer. Sometimes the volunteer emergency organization is the hero; sometimes it is the villain. Similarly, sometimes local government is the hero; sometimes it is the villain. Figuring out which is which, when, how, and why is the challenge of this book.

THE TRADITIONAL RURAL VOLUNTEER FIRE DEPARTMENT: THE HERO AND THE VILLAIN

The following scenarios help to illustrate the motivation needed to be a volunteer in the traditional rural volunteer fire department.

Scenario One

A male volunteer firefighter is awakened from a dream at 3:15 a.m. by an alarm.[1] He dons turnout gear in the back porch and rushes over to the station, 100 yards (meters) away. He climbs into the cab and starts the engine. The radio reveals the nature of the call as a working house fire and the location of the emergency.[2] After a six-minute ride, he sizes up the fire, then directs the firefighters to enter the structure.[3] After another harrowing four minutes, during which he operates the pump, the fire is knocked down[4] and the slower process of salvage and overhaul begins.[5] By about 5:30 a.m., he has returned to the fire hall, returned the station to operational readiness with his fellow volunteers, and has trudged home to bed.

---

[1]This person is part of the classic rural volunteer fire department, which is elaborated upon in a few pages. This type of department is, among other things, almost exclusively male. Thus, the male volunteer firefighter is presented in these particular scenarios.

[2]A working fire: a structural fire in progress.

[3]Size-up: the act of diagnosing the situation and applying the resources available to extinguish the fire.

[4]Knockdown: the reduction of most flame and heat generation by a fire.

[5]Salvage and overhaul: protection of property from further fire, smoke, and water damage after the main body of fire is extinguished.

As he dozes off, the alarm rings. He has to get up to make breakfast, help his spouse get the kids off to school and prepare to go to work.

Why would anyone do this without pay? Typically, the obvious answer is a combination of satisfaction in putting out the fire, satisfaction in doing good for the community, prestige as the story of it is passed by word of mouth within the community, respect from fellow volunteers, and, finally, the camaraderie which results from undertaking a somewhat dangerous activity. However, before we expand upon these reasons, let us consider two more scenarios which are far more likely.

Scenario Two

A male volunteer firefighter is awakened from a dream at 3:15 a.m. He dons turnout gear in the back porch and rushes over to the station 100 yards (meters) away. He climbs into the cab and starts the engine. The radio reveals the nature of the call as a *chimney fire. After a six-minute ride, he sizes up the situation, directing two firefighters to the roof. He enters the house, throws ice cubes into the wood stove, hears the steam. Afterwards, the firefighters, under his direction, drop a chain down the chimney. They judge from the steam and the lack of smoke that the fire seems to be extinguished. By about 4:15 a.m., he has returned from the fire hall and has trudged home to bed. Angry at the fact that homeowners don't clean their chimneys often enough, he doesn't easily get back to sleep.* As he dozes off, the alarm rings. He has to get up, make breakfast, help his spouse get the kids off to school, and then prepare to go to work.[6]

Scenario Three

It is 3:15 a.m., several volunteers and their spouses are cleaning up the bingo hall above the fire apparatus floor. The Volunteer Department has just held a fund-raising dance. The volunteer firefighters present enjoyed themselves up until 2:00 a.m. At that point, the dance ended and one volunteer exclaimed: "I joined to fight fires. Now I serve this Department by mopping beer off the floor." The others grunted in agreement but continued their cleaning.

Both Scenario Two and Scenario Three lack the motivators present in Scenario One and yet volunteers (and sometimes their spouses) per-

---

[6]Scenario Two is identical to Scenario One except those words in italics.

form these activities as well. Why do they do this? In Scenario Two, the work may appear "glamorous" to the outsider but it is not to those who know it. In Scenario Three, nobody perceives cleaning up after others as "glamorous." To explain the motive, we must understand the values shared within a volunteer emergency service.

THE RURAL VOLUNTEER FIRE DEPARTMENT: THE HERO OR THE VILLAIN

The volunteer fire service has been long with us in North America. For a number of years, many of its knowledgeable members have feared its demise. Most recently, some of that fear has diminished. Nevertheless, we should try to understand how volunteer fire departments have persisted. First, let us consider the basic requirements for a typical volunteer department.

To **survive**, a volunteer fire department must:

1. attract a critical number of volunteers to the fireground in sufficient time to at least appear to extinguish the fire;

2. own or use a pumper which transports firefighters, holds enough water to knock down a one- or two-room fire, and has a pump and assorted equipment such as breathing apparatus, bunker gear,[7] hoses, axes, saws, etc.;

3. have a garage to park the vehicle and maintain its performance;

4. have the money to pay for the cost of the pumper,[8] the gear, and the garage.

To have survived more than 25 years the volunteer fire department must also:

5. recruit and socialize new volunteers to the social and functional structure of the organization;

6. upgrade the pumper vehicle.

To survive more than 50 years, the volunteer fire department must also:

7. replace or enlarge and modernize the garage.

---

[7]Bunker gear: the protective equipment worn by firefighters.

[8]Pumper: a fire apparatus with at least a 500-gallon water tank (2 000 liters) and a 750 gpm (3 000 L/min) pump.

These seven items are the minimum achievements of any long-lasting fire department. Of these, the most problematic remains the first; that is attracting a critical number of volunteers to the fireground.

Historically, this goal was achieved by recruiting white, able-bodied males ranging in age from about 17 to 67. In a rural environment, where most males are farmers, farm workers, fishermen, or miners, the influence of these characteristics remain. The historical legacy is significant because the volunteer fire department, until recently, has been in a placid environment resisting change. It could do so because standards of fire protection were low and citizens had no expectations of standards. As a result, the key requirements, except that of attracting volunteers, were easy to meet.

Attracting sufficient volunteers to the fireground required social bonds among the members. Thus, not to show up at a fire was to let down one's friends. Indeed, informal conversation at the fire hall reinforced the norms and values of volunteers for the traditional department. Nearly every traditional department has a creation myth. (Back in '03 the general store burned down and ignited the grain elevator next to it. That's when they decided our fire department was necessary.) Much of that myth includes tales of persistence, tales of "Robin Hood" type crime, (remember Southbank "borrowing" the grader), tales of heroism on the fireground, and occasionally tales of sorrow when a volunteer, or more likely a civilian neighbor, is a victim. The stories, the parties, and the fund-raisers all contributed to strengthening these social bonds. Why are these bonds so necessary? The social bonds retained the volunteer, which was desirable because many years were necessary fighting the few working fires needed to acquire competence on the fireground. Thus, the department needed to make an investment in its volunteers which had to be nurtured lest it be lost to some other interest.

Each working fire created peak emotional experiences which strengthened bonds even further. Unfortunately, until recently, these social bonds generally did not cross social class, gender, or race. Thus, the "culture" of the fire department was akin to a "red neck social club." In many ways, this "club" reflected the dominant values in the rural environment. Indeed, recruitment was by word of mouth: friends and relatives recruited friends and relatives. On one hand, aspects of that environment have changed more rapidly in recent years. The volunteer fire department, on the other hand, tended to resist change. It could do so because it was fairly independent of other organizations, such as the local government. Firefighting experience (not so much training) was valued, but firefighting experience could only be accumulated by decades of participation.

To illustrate this point, let us assume that at least ten working fires must be fought before assuming an officer role. (Undoubtedly, many readers would argue many more than ten must be experienced.) Recognize, however, that in many rural communities it might take **15 years** to accumulate this degree of experience. If this is the case, and a volunteer joins at age 20, then that person is not likely to be elected to the most junior officer position until age 35. Moreover, senior officer status is not likely to arise for at least another five to seven years. Thus, most senior positions are likely to be occupied by those males between 45 to 55 years of age. Should we be surprised that external change will be resisted?

Despite the control of middle-aged and older males, officers are elected. We should be heartened by the democratic behavior, let alone values, espoused by volunteer fire departments. Typically, even the most minor expenditures will await approval at the monthly meeting. Such a decentralized approach is part of the motivation to volunteer. More importantly, that same meeting is a forum to socialize the membership. It serves as a social and ceremonial function to enhance the commitment of the members. On one hand, it serves to orient new members into the department, helping to ensure the longevity of the organization. On the other hand, officer election leads to lots of politicking. Picking a fight with "city hall" becomes one strategy to ensure election, a point we will develop further in the next chapter.

THE SUBURBAN VOLUNTEER FIRE/RESCUE DEPARTMENT: THE HERO AND THE VILLAIN

In the Northern Virginia suburbs of Washington D.C., the **7-Eleven** stores display a large banner which can be read from any speeding automobile driving on the adjacent highway:

"Pork Rinds to Perrier...Is this Heaven?"

Part of the message is that a customer can purchase these products at **7-Eleven**. What is more significant, however, is the range of products that are available. Pork rinds have their origin as Appalachian food, stereotyped as the product made for "poor white trash." Conversely, **Perrier** is the quintessential yuppie product. Thus, an institution of the suburbs, the **7-Eleven** store appeals to these heterogeneous tastes. Note that the banner ends with "...Is this Heaven?" Perhaps **7-Eleven** and the advertising agency felt that an exclamation mark or even a period would be too farfetched. Thus, the statement ends with a question mark as though the heterogeneous tastes of the suburbs are an ambivalent feature.

It is this heterogeneous environment which makes its stamp on the organizations found within it. Thus, we should expect the suburban volunteer emergency organization to be different from the classic rural volunteer fire department we examined earlier.

The suburban department is composed of a mixture of those volunteers born in the community along with those who have migrated in recent years. As such, a variety of occupations is likely to be found among the volunteers. This variety results in greater heterogeneity in terms of social class. Even more evident will be the heterogeneity arising from differences in race and gender.

Many of these differences will be a reflection on the greater heterogeneity of the suburban community compared with the rural one; however, this is not a sufficient explanation. The mixed department engaging in EMS will also attract and select many more female emergency medical technicians (EMTs) than would occur if this suburban department was only a fire service.

Because the department offers EMS, and because the average level of formal education of its members is higher than in the classic rural fire department, then more application of standardized rules will be expected.[9] Experience, because it is more easily acquired, will be less valued.[10] Thus, the likelihood of rule by a clique of elders will be reduced.

Power within the organization will be based on technical and administrative expertise. Position power will prevail during the training for major incidents as well as at those incidents themselves. However, service delivery will be realized much more often by a **pair** of volunteers responding in an ambulance or rescue vehicle.

Cohesion within the department will likely be weaker but it is allowed to be weaker. Much more success will be based on individual expertise rather than on group performance.

---

[9]Higher educational levels are found in suburbs compared with rural areas. However, a department providing EMS will require many more hours of formal training to be an EMT compared with a firefighter. This necessity selects volunteers with higher formal education.

[10]Since EMS delivery leads to many more serious calls, then significant experience can be acquired in months or a few years at most. Conversely, the classic rural fire department might fight only one structural fire each year.

So far we have introduced two organizational actors, the traditional rural volunteer fire department and the suburban fire rescue department. Let us see how they differ by examining the following table:

COMPARING "THE TRADITIONAL" AND "THE SUBURBAN"

Characteristic	TYPE OF DEPARTMENT	
	Traditional	Suburban
Experience	Important	Less important
Education	Unimportant	Important
Cohesion	High	Low
Heterogeneity	Low	High
Power	With chief	In the ambulance
Call Frequency	20-80/year	500-2000/year
Call Type	Fire	EMS 70%/Fire 30%
Size	15-40	40-80
Schedule of Response	Respond always	Respond on shift
Likelihood of Responding to an Alarm	About 30 %	About 80% if on shift
Use of Rules	Low	High

FIGURE 2.1

At this stage we have **not** specified whether the suburban department is connected to government nor whether it is all volunteer or combination. We maintain that connection to government and/or the addition of career members accentuates the suburban characteristics even further. A suburban community demands greater evidence of worth as defined by rules, qualifications, and selection criteria. These demands will force the local government to make these demands, not only of its own organization, but also of the independent corporations implicitly contracted to provide the fire and rescue service. Failure to do so will lead to the pressures to hire (and thus be able to fire) personnel and even to control these organizations by contract if not by ownership. Thus, the culture of the suburban department described above is congruent with its environment and is thus likely to be as stable in its suburban environment as the classic rural department was in its rural one.

Despite these stable states, many other types of departments are far less stable for a host of reasons which were first introduced in Chapter One. We will describe these types later on in this chapter. The next chapter will explore how transition can take place within the volunteer emergency organization. The major result is not internal but external and is often resisted. This will force us to examine inter-organizational power between local government and the volunteer emergency organization.

LOCAL GOVERNMENT: THE HERO AND THE VILLAIN

Now let us consider the other principal actor in this book, the rural, small town, or suburban local government. The theory of government suggests that its role is to resolve the conflict arising from contradictory values present in the community. Whether it is voting on a law or approving a budget, government recognizes the expression of these different values in debate and resolves them through vote. Thus, conflict is deemed healthy because policy is improved by the debate. Rural local government is fraught with debate but the cohesive forces seem to be equally strong. The next few paragraphs will address those forces.

Many rural councillors grew up in the same area. Many have known each other for years. Similarly, they expect to know each other for years. The result is a certainty of the other councillors' personalities. Irrespective of the particular issue, there remains a strong belief in knowing the others at the council table. This knowledge will not necessarily produce harmony but it will generate a sense of predictability.

Most rural governments are divided into electoral districts. Usually, the individual receiving the most votes among the candidates is elected. (Occasionally, the top two candidates are elected.) As a result, on one hand, there is no need to compete with other councillors at election time. On the other hand, many rural councillors feel compelled to demonstrate how they have been successful in having more money spent in their own district relative to the districts of other councillors. Thus, competition arises in the awarding of contracts for the building of public works. Rural governments often have branch offices.

The location of the branch office in the district may mean more jobs for citizens of that district. Indeed, many councillors will campaign on a platform which promises to increase spending in one district as opposed to another. These divisive forces are cyclical in nature depending on the frequency of local government elections. Thus, the four months before and the two months after an election are more divisive.

Nevertheless, nearly all councillors have a strong desire to lower the tax rate. This leads to the common aphorism that local government should be "run like a business." The reasons for this are elaborated upon at a later stage. At this point, the key factors are:

1. the legal prohibition against budgeting a deficit[11];

2. the declining grants from provinces and states along with the downloading of expensive responsibilities[12];

3. the small business backgrounds of many councillors.[13]

The financial problems of local governments have dominated the concerns of councillors for the last decade or so. Energies are directed to finding new sources of revenue, particularly special grants from the senior levels of government. This is the equivalent of finding taxpayers from elsewhere to pay for a rural government's costs. Historically, this has been successful because many rural areas are poorer than their urban and suburban counterparts. Thus, grants to rural governments reduce rural-urban disparities. Once senior governments recognize these disparities they are likely to attempt to reduce them by providing grants to rural governments.

Irrespective of the cause of financial problems, the preoccupation with "coming in on budget" dominates the role of the councillor. Typi-

---

[11]A deficit arises when, in any given fiscal year, expenditure exceeds revenue. A surplus arises when, in any given fiscal year, expenditure is less than revenue. The sum of all deficits over all years (minus all surpluses) is the debt.

[12]Downloading is the transfer of debt from a higher level of government (e.g., federal or state/provincial government) to a lower level of local government. Often, this is done by reducing the grant to the lower level. This reduces the higher level of government's expenditures but also reduces the lower level of government's revenues.

[13]The councillor in a rural, small town, or even suburban area will receive little pay. Indeed, the job is not expected to be full time. Nevertheless, many candidates for office recognize that the role of councillor will perhaps require 20 to 30 hours per week. Thus, small business persons, who have an interest in the issues **and** have discretionary time, are likely to seek election.

cally, long meetings are spent planning and then approving the next year's budget. Debate often arises over expenditure. In effect, the rural government council is like a board of directors of a medium-sized company. Much hand wringing attends to financial matters.

Just as volunteer fire departments vary, so do local governments. Nevertheless, a number of features can be identified which apply to many rural and small town local governments. Let us examine a typical structure.

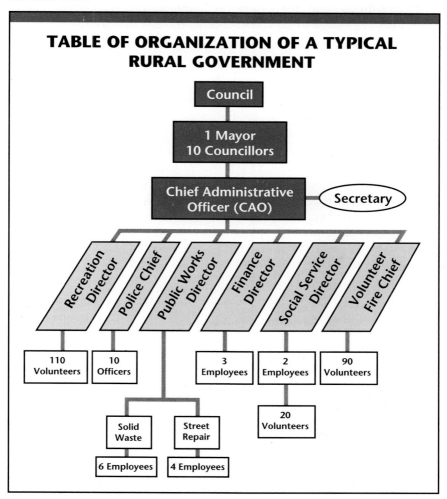

TABLE OF ORGANIZATION OF A TYPICAL RURAL GOVERNMENT

Council

1 Mayor
10 Councillors

Chief Administrative Officer (CAO)

Secretary

Recreation Director — 110 Volunteers

Police Chief — 10 Officers

Public Works Director — Solid Waste (6 Employees), Street Repair (4 Employees)

Finance Director — 3 Employees

Social Service Director — 2 Employees — 20 Volunteers

Volunteer Fire Chief — 90 Volunteers

FIGURE 2.2

This structure organizes 32 employees, 221 volunteers and 11 councillors (supervisors).[14] The apparent activity is to serve the property of the citizens of the local government. In fact, several personal needs are met as well. In general, this structure seems to be accountable as follows: Council is accountable to the citizens, particularly at election. As such, budget approval, setting the tax rate, legislating by-laws, and general budget management are its principal roles. In addition, council must hire, evaluate and, if necessary, fire the Chief Administrative Officer (CAO).[15] Finally, council provides its councillors to serve on a variety of committees which oversee the operation of particular departments. Similarly, council provides councillors to serve on various boards and commissions such as the school board, the hospital board, and the planning advisory committee. This latter role is to serve as liaison between the participating board and council. In general, the role of council is policy making; the role of staff is the administration of that policy. In fact, the distinction between policy and administration is not so clear, as will be discussed below.

The role of the CAO is to coordinate the various departments reporting to council. The CAO is probably the single most important individual in local government, corresponding to the fire chief of the local volunteer fire department. The CAO ought to be the liaison between council and various department needs. The CAO approves budget submissions to council from the department heads and he or she also evaluates the performance of the departments as well as the department heads. The department heads will ensure that the departments' functions are carried out by evaluating their own subordinates.

A typical operating budget might be as follows:

The finance department will collect the revenues from taxes. The chief elected official and the CAO will negotiate with the state or provincial government for some of the grants, but much will be determined by formula. The majority of the revenue will be derived from taxation, particularly commercial or industrial assessment. Although

---

[14]The term councillor is the most generic term. Other synonyms are falling into disfavor for being gender specific (e.g., alderman, selectman). Another common term is supervisor and, thus, a synonym for council is board of supervisors.

[15]The CAO is the highest appointed official in local government. That person's job is to liaise with council and oversee the various departments. Synonyms are City Manager, County Administrator, and Town Manager.

THE OPERATING BUDGET OF A TYPICAL RURAL GOVERNMENT

REVENUES	
Local Government Taxes	
Residential Assessment	2,500,000
Industrial Assessment	3,500,000
Provincial/State Grants	
Unconditional Grants	1,500,000
Conditional Grants	1,500,000
Federal Grants	500,000
Fees	500,000
TOTAL	**10,000,000**
EXPENDITURES	
Social Services	2,000,000
Police	800,000
Recreation	200,000
Fire	200,000
Public Works	2,000,000
Finance	200,000
Council	100,000
Debt Servicing	900,000
Boards and Commissions	
School Boards	3,000,000
Other Boards and Commissions	600,000
TOTAL	**10,000,000**

FIGURE 2.3

the assessment of property is often done by a third party, (usually government assessors), the **rate** of taxation on property and the differences between commercial/industrial and residential rates are determined by council.[16]

---

[16]For example, a homeowner with a $100,000 house might pay 60¢ per $100 of assessed values, resulting in a tax bill to the local government of $.60 \times \dfrac{\$100,000}{100} = \$600$ per year. The $100,000 is determined by an assessor but the taxation rate (60¢ per $100 of value) is determined by council.

Usually, a local government's revenue is threatened by several sources, including its own council. First, by facing its own greater debt, provinces/states reduce the grant to local governments as part of a general measure to cut their own expenditures. Lobbying against this trend are the CAO and the chief elected official. Second, many rural governments depend on a small number of large employers. Resource-based industries, such as mining, fishing, forestry, and more recently, agribusiness, are concentrated in rural areas. A local government may be dependent on the taxation levied on a few large employers. These employers may seek a tax break, threatening to close down on occasion. The impact of this threat is greater than the direct loss of the taxes. Layoffs of employees will lead to outward migration to find work elsewhere. This will lower property values. (The supply of houses exceeds the demand.) It will also lower the former employee's ability to pay property tax, (or the rent to the landlord who pays the tax).

The final pressure is the misconception, shared by most citizens, that they fully pay for the expenditures of local government through their own property taxes. Many citizens believe that a council forced to raise the tax rate is doing so in order to increase expenditures. Councillors know this and, fearful of the consequences at the next election, are far more inclined to reduce expenditures...but can they do so?

Local governments are incorporated bodies, suggesting that they have full autonomy to adjust their budgets. In fact, much of the expenditures are required by the provincial/state government, such as required grants to school boards, or are obligated by multi-year contracts, such as collective agreements with local government employees, and contracts with land developers. As a result, the local council has only limited ways to reduce expenditures. One way is to reduce grants to fire and rescue services.

We have already seen that intra-organizational conflict is common within any volunteer emergency organization. Local governments often exhibit intra-organizational conflict as well. For example, conflict is common within council. As mentioned already, councillors may be political opponents if they are elected at large. Conversely, if each councillor is elected by an electoral district then conflict arises over the geographic distribution of local government expenditures. However, conflict within council is seen as a norm. Politicians are supposed to debate and, indeed, are particularly likely to do so in open meetings rather than in camera sessions.[17] More painful, because it is not consid-

---

[17]In camera session: a meeting of council which is private. The public or the press are not invited. Most monthly meetings of volunteer emergency organizations are in camera. Usually guests are allowed to observe only with the permission of the members.

ered acceptable, is conflict between council and staff. In a small community, voters will often call councillors directly when they have a complaint rather than contacting the **appointed** official responsible. For example, a pothole in the pavement in front of a voter's house might lead the voter to call the councillor. The councillor, wanting to seem and even be responsive to address the complaint, will often contact the foreman on duty at the public works department directing that the pothole be filled immediately. The foreman is caught between the schedule of activities laid out by the local government's engineer and the directions of the councillor. The obvious resolution to the dilemma is to balance the needs of the schedule with the demands of the voter.[18] Unfortunately, that is the kind of decision which should be a standard operating procedure arrived at by staff and approved by council.

Note that the council-staff conflict described above is a reaction to the complaint of a voter who is external to the council staff relationship. This phenomenon illustrates the reactive nature of local government. Rarely do councillors or staff have time to reflect. Rather, the culture of a local government values expeditious action which ensures a sufficiently calm public, a frugal budget, and re-election. This generalization begins to breakdown once the community grows in size, becoming suburban or urban. Fortunately, the urban case goes beyond our current interest since volunteer emergency services interact with local governments which are rural (townships or counties), small towns, or suburbs.

Although local governments spring from that same rural community as the traditional rural volunteer fire departments, universal suffrage makes those local governments relatively more representative of their communities. Since local governments hire employees, affirmative action or employment equity policies must be heeded. Since council meetings are open, often observed by citizens and broadcast by the press, the values of a wider society are more prevalent.

As such, a value conflict is likely to arise between a local government and a traditional rural volunteer fire department. Although external forces may motivate the local government, it will seem to be an irresistible force. Conversely, the traditional rural volunteer fire depart-

---

[18]For example, dentists usually leave the lunch hour free to deal with dental emergencies. Usually, the relieved patient is signed up as a regular client (ensuring future revenue for the dentist). The dentist wins, the emergency patient wins, and the regular clients do not lose by being bumped from an appointment.

ment will be the immovable object. It is precisely this scenario which must be avoided, otherwise the volunteers will lose their motivation to volunteer. The local government may win the battle but it will be a costly victory.

CHANGING VOLUNTEER EMERGENCY ORGANIZATIONS: THE TYPOLOGY

What we have described so far is the traditional rural volunteer fire department and the typical suburban fire/rescue service. The description of the classic department is consistent with about 28,000 of the 32,000 volunteer emergency organizations in the United States and Canada (Penwell, 1993). However, this description requires further qualification because even though it applies to the vast majority of fire departments, this traditional type is a shrinking category.

Now, let us consider three methods of classification to develop a typology[19] of volunteer and quasi volunteer emergency organizations (VEO). One obvious distinction will be whether the VEO is volunteer or if it includes a combination of volunteer and career personnel. Thus, we have two categories: volunteer and combination. Another obvious distinction is whether the department is an independent organization or is dependent on local government. Thus, we have two more categories: independent or dependent. The third distinction is the domain of activity, or the purpose of the VEO. Is it exclusively a fire service, exclusively a rescue emergency medical service (EMS), or is it a mix of fire and EMS? This provides three categories: exclusively fire, a mix of fire and EMS, and exclusively EMS.

Logically, we can combine each of these categories to describe the volunteer emergency organizations which interest us. For each organization we can ask three questions:

1. Is it volunteer or combination?
2. Is it independent or connected?
3. Is its domain of activity fire, mixed, or EMS?

For example, as a simple step we can imagine four types of departments arising from the first two questions:

---

[19]A typology is a method of classifying any phenomenon, whether it be animals, plants, stars, or whatever. Classification brings order to complexity and helps to facilitate an understanding of change from one type to another. For example, in biology, Linnaeus' classification of plants and animals done in the late 18th century helped Darwin to develop a theory of evolution in the 19th century. In this chapter, we first use a typology to classify different types of volunteer emergency organizations. Then we begin to examine how VEOs change from one type to another.

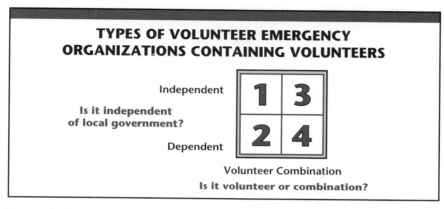

FIGURE 2.4

Type 1 is independent of local government and a volunteer service.

Type 2 is dependent on local government and a volunteer service.

Type 3 is independent of local government and a combination service.

Type 4 is dependent on local government and a combination service.

We can take advantage of a 15th century Renaissance technique of perspective to add the third question we asked above, namely: Is the volunteer emergency organization exclusively a fire service, a mixture of EMS and fire, or exclusively Rescue/EMS?

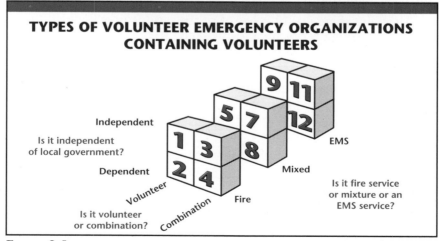

FIGURE 2.5

35

Note: Those types that are not visible on the figure are Type 6, that is volunteer, dependent, and mixed, and Type 10, that is volunteer, dependent, and EMS.

Type 1   is independent, volunteer, and essentially a fire service. (The Southbank Volunteer Fire Department is a good example.)

Type 2   is dependent, volunteer, and essentially a fire service.

Type 3   is independent, combination, and essentially a fire service.

Type 4   is dependent, combination, and essentially a fire service.

Type 5   is independent, volunteer, and a mix of fire and EMS services.

Type 6   is dependent, volunteer, and a mix of services.

Type 7   is independent, combination, and a mix of services.

Type 8   is dependent, combination, and a mix of services. (The Northbank Fire/Rescue Department is a good example.)

Type 9   is independent, volunteer, and essentially an emergency medical service.

Type 10 is dependent, volunteer, and essentially an emergency medical service.

Type 11 is independent, combination, and essentially an emergency medical service.

Type 12 is dependent, combination, and essentially an emergency medical service.

Although there are 12 types of organizations possible, we do not suggest that all 12 types are equally likely. For example, we are as yet aware of only a few combination departments which exclusively deliver EMS. (Indeed, one is introduced in Chapter Nine.)

The utility of the typology is that it helps us to understand the forces of change which impinge on that traditional rural volunteer fire department we described at the beginning of this chapter (the "redneck social club"). These forces are:

1. diversification of service as the fire threat declines and the population ages, (i.e., moving toward inclusion of EMS as part of the domain of the organization);

2. rural to suburban (as urban areas grow, those rural areas on the fringe are experiencing suburbanization);

3. increasing standards of department performance;

4. reduced government expenditure;

5. increased threat of litigation.

The reader will note that these same forces were introduced as "dragons" in Chapter One. Let us consider the impact of these forces on the classic, independent volunteer fire department (Type 1). We will start with relatively simple changes and introduce more and more complexities as we progress.

The change from rural to suburban merely involves changes on the front face of the cube of the typology. The classic Type 1 organization experiences a gradual increase in call volume as the rural area suburbanizes. Moreover, daytime response to fire calls declines because many volunteers are now commuters who often work in a central city. The department decides to hire drivers and perhaps even a day shift of career firefighters to address this gap in response. (It has now become Type 3.) Such a decision produces more demand for funds to pay these career personnel. The local government may be willing to provide these funds only if the department is willing to surrender some autonomy. Meanwhile, internal conflict is likely as the career personnel unionize. The result is similar to what has been already described, namely, pressure to be dependent upon local government funding, which will regularize the personnel issue (Type 3 becomes Type 4). We can illustrate the process as follows:

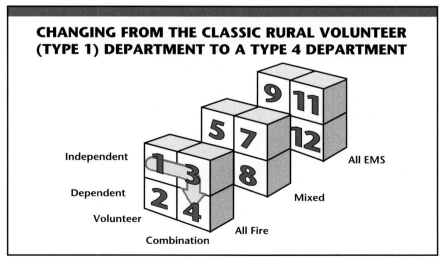

CHANGING FROM THE CLASSIC RURAL VOLUNTEER (TYPE 1) DEPARTMENT TO A TYPE 4 DEPARTMENT

FIGURE 2.6

The transition from an independent volunteer (Type 1) to an independent combination fire department (Type 3) is a common one. However, the transition from Type 3 to Type 4 requiring the surrender of independence is less likely, although the reasons we have presented are plausible. The reason that this transition is less likely is because other forces resist this change. First of all, VEOs resist loss of autonomy (power). It is axiomatic that organizations seek to maximize autonomy just as an organism strives to survive. A lot of conflict will attend a transition from Type 3 to Type 4. Perhaps even more important is the local government's desire to conserve money. It may have to accept the autonomy of the VEO and even the resulting legal risks. Thus, the local government's response to a request for increased funding may very well be: "Hire firefighters if you want to, but don't ask us for money. Raise it yourself."

In this chapter we are not so concerned about which path through the cube is most likely. Predictions of change from one type to another are presented in Chapter Ten. Rather, we wish to illustrate literally the processes and the forces which direct and deflect the path of change.

Let us consider another change on the front face of the cube. Within the local government council a "takeover" of the VEO may be motivated by a need to protect local government from litigation. Since sovereign immunity is in jeopardy (see Chapter Four) then local governments will want to control activities to reduce litigation lest they are left to pay the bill: "...if you are liable for your child's actions you will control your child." This change is the result of a "scandal" in the traditional rural volunteer fire department (Type 1). By "scandal" we mean such dramatic events as a treasurer embezzling department funds, a lawsuit arising from discriminatory harassment, gross negligence at a fire scene, or an excessive party at a fund-raiser. These "scandals" are magnified in the rural environment. Rapidly, it may lead to pressures on local government to control the fire department. A typical refrain might be: "If the local government pays our tax dollars to the XYZ volunteer fire department, it ought to control how that money is spent."

The result may be hiring a chief and transferring title on the assets of the department... resulting in a fight. In this scenario, the Type 1 volunteer fire department becomes Type 2. Several years ago, a local government would have spent more money hiring career firefighters, converting a Type 2 into a Type 4 department. This would "bribe" some potential opposition within the department by promising a chance at a firefighting job. Now, the typical local government will lack the resources to do this. The result may well be severe conflict which resolves itself as an election issue — both within the department and within the local government.

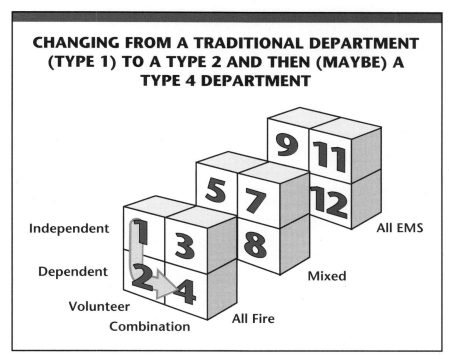

CHANGING FROM A TRADITIONAL DEPARTMENT (TYPE 1) TO A TYPE 2 AND THEN (MAYBE) A TYPE 4 DEPARTMENT

FIGURE 2.7

Now let us introduce the complication of diversifying the fire service by adding EMS. The classic independent, all volunteer, exclusive fire service (Type 1) accepts as volunteers career firefighters who live in the community but work in an urban complex or city. These career firefighters volunteer their time in the local area. They introduce an expertise on EMS delivery. (They had to learn EMS to keep their career jobs as firefighter/EMTs in the central city.) As these particular volunteers gain influence, the traditional rural volunteer fire department chooses to develop an EMS capability. A resource vehicle is purchased, contact with hospital emergency medical directors is made and training begins. Using our typology, the department has changed from Type 1 to Type 5.

This change produces unintended consequences. First of all, the call volume increases steadily as the department is connected into a 9-1-1 dispatch system. The call volume produces a strain on the existing volunteer resources so that more volunteers are needed. Indeed, some volunteers may quit saying they joined to fight fires, not to transport sick people. These strains, coupled with the change in their role, make the recruitment of women more likely. However, this change may very well engender more conflict because the classic "redneck social club" does not disappear overnight. As we will see in Chapter Four, the result may be a sexual harassment lawsuit. More likely, it will be tension which changes the club atmosphere of the organization. The ladies auxiliary (many of whom are wives of the volunteers) may complain about the introduction of female volunteers. Finally, the conflict reaches local government once any faction recognizes that the local government is a potential ally in the struggle. Inevitably, there will be demands that the Type 5 organization be held more accountable. **If** the local government gives in to these wishes, then the Type 5 organization loses its independence and becomes a Type 6 organization, that is a volunteer organization delivering a mix of fire and EMS dependent on local government. The change is as follows:

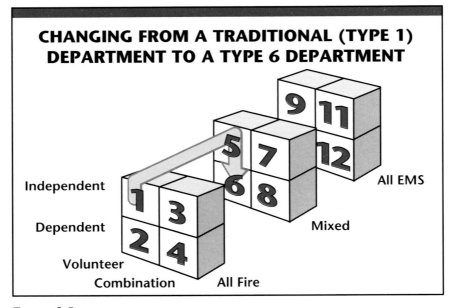

CHANGING FROM A TRADITIONAL (TYPE 1) DEPARTMENT TO A TYPE 6 DEPARTMENT

FIGURE 2.8

As a variation, the Type 5 organization, overwhelmed by calls, yet resisting diversifying its recruitment, decides that it needs to hire some EMTs to handle peak call volumes. Thus, it becomes an independent combination department offering a mixed service (Type 7). **If** this Type 7 department can meet the increased demand for funding, then it will remain Type 7. In all likelihood, an increased share of that funding will be asked from the local government. This change, coupled with possible labor relations problems as the career EMTs unionize and negotiate a first contract, are likely to involve the local government even more. Perhaps inevitably, (but perhaps not), the formerly independent organization becomes formally dependant upon local government as both politicians and the public demand increased accountability. (That is, it becomes Type 8). This change is illustrated as follows:

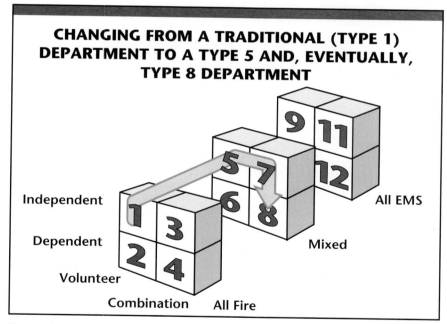

CHANGING FROM A TRADITIONAL (TYPE 1) DEPARTMENT TO A TYPE 5 AND, EVENTUALLY, TYPE 8 DEPARTMENT

FIGURE 2.9

CONCLUDING COMMENTS

We started this chapter by introducing the organizational culture of the classic rural volunteer fire department. We saw this culture as a means to attract young and middle-aged white male volunteers that gained from their strengths and suffered from their weaknesses. We also introduced the culture of the suburban fire/rescue service, a culture that was more modern, more closely allied with the dominant cultures found in big government and big business. The final introduction was a description of the culture of local government.

Given the issues we presented in Chapter One, we introduced a typology of fire and rescue services containing volunteers. This typology arose from asking three questions: 1. Is it independent of local government?; 2. Is it a volunteer or combination department?; and 3. Does it offer a fire service, an emergency medical service, or a mixture of both? Once the typology was created, we discovered that it was dynamic, which allowed us to explore changes from one type of organization to another. Although we did not fully explore the forces of change, we did begin to recognize how these forces affect and are affected by the relationship between the volunteer emergency organization and local government.

The key to an understanding of any inter-organizational relationship is power. Who has power over whom? Why? What can the less powerful do about it? These are the questions that we will examine in the next chapter.

THE HERO AND THE VILLAIN FIGHT

TROUBLE IN BLUCHERVILLE

Felix Onderdonck, councillor for District 7 in Blucherville, was worried. He had just left the Blucherville Ratepayers Association meeting. Its chair, Marge Schultz, had just criticized Felix for considering to raise the tax area rate 2½¢ just to pay for another fire department pumper. Felix had promised Chief Jensen too much when he agreed to increase the tax area rate to pay for the pumper. Felix was shocked when Chief Jensen said $175,000 was to be the likely purchase price. He had remembered when Jensen said the last pumper they bought cost $75,000 so he thought the price would be less then $100,000. Chief Jensen reminded Felix that the last pumper was purchased in 1980, some 12 years ago. Felix had forgotten about inflation.

Now, however, Felix knew he could not raise taxes that high, not in an election year. Marge Schultz and the Ratepayers were just too angry with him. He would just have to go back on his word with Jensen. He was certain that Chief Jensen and the Blucherville Volunteer Fire Department would understand.

Chief Jensen was furious. When Felix Onderdonck approached him and told him the result of the meeting with the Ratepayers, Jensen was not surprised. On one hand, he recognized that most citizens think that pumpers are just necessary toys for the Blucherville Volunteer Fire Department. On the other hand, "a deal is a deal"; he never expected Felix Onderdonck to break his word. In response, Jensen said that the pumper was already ordered. In the past, the word of an elected official was enough to start the ordering process, so Jensen reasoned that he was merely following past practice. Chief Jensen ended his response by hinting that it was an election year and that the membership of the Blucherville Volunteer Fire Department might question whether to continue the vigorous support they had given Felix Onderdonck at the last election. With that remark hanging in the air, Felix Onderdonck responded by saying he would see what he could do.

Two weeks later, Felix Onderdonck phoned Chief Jensen with the happy news that a federal grant program was accessed to pay for the lion's share of the pumper purchase. Chief Jensen only mildly thanked Felix. Indeed, shortly thereafter, Felix felt the frosty reception at the summer barbecue fund-raiser held by the Blucherville Volunteer Fire Department.

The frosty reception in summer was nothing compared with the mid-September gale when, to Felix's surprise, Marge Schultz, Chair of the Blucherville Ratepayers Association, announced her intent to run against Onderdonck in the October election. Even worse, Felix Onderdonck noticed that some of Marge Schultz's supporters were also key officers in the Blucherville Volunteer Fire Department.

The election was held and the result was posted on the chalkboard by the Admaston County Clerk. (Blucherville was part of Admaston County.)

COUNCILLOR: DISTRICT 7	
Candidate	Votes
Felix Onderdonck	387
Marge Schultz	415
Herman Zwicker	12

FIGURE 3.1

Three years later, Felix Onderdonck finally raised the subject of the 1992 election with Chief Jensen. (He was still chief, going into his fourteenth term.) Of course, both Onderdonck and Jensen had met many times since the election but both refrained from talking about the election. Now, however, Felix asked why the fire department had switched allegiance even though the money for that pumper was obtained by him? Jensen responded by saying:

Felix, we just didn't know we could trust you anymore. We knew that Marge Schultz would be even harder to convince about future funding needs, but we figured we could trust her. Besides, our strategy was to send a message to any local politician that this is what our fire department will do if a politician breaks his -- or her -- word.

POWER AND ITS SOURCES

This chapter is about the uncertainties that arise from multiple sources of power. Just as nation states have engaged in contests because their sources of power resided within the state — factories, raw materials, armies, and navies — so volunteer fire departments and local governments have their own sources of power — volunteer labor, legitimacy arising from election, taxation, fund-raising, and authority derived from a state or provincial government. These sources are distributed so that neither the local government nor the volunteer fire department has a monopoly on these sources of power. Often, although fortunately not always, the interests of local government and the volunteer fire departments clash. The resolution of these conflicting interests can find both parties believing that they must exercise power over the other party, believing that such an exercise of power will lead to victory. The result is inter-organizational conflict.[1] The management of this conflict is the goal of this book. First, however, we wish to explore how this conflict arises. We will consider the issues in the abstract and then apply them to local governments and volunteer fire departments.

Inter-organizational power is best understood by appreciating intra-organizational power.[2] In industrial societies, most of us are social-

---

[1]Inter-organizational conflict: conflict between or among organizations.

[2]Intra-organizational power: power **within** an organization. Inter-organizational power: power **between** or **among** organizations.

ized to the notion of hierarchical power. In public organizations, power may be granted to democratically elected leaders. However, this power is quickly delegated to a hierarchy of officials who exercise the power of their offices only constrained by broad policy. Typically, power descends throughout the hierarchy from high rank to low. Those in low rank aspire to high rank so as to acquire privilege, power, and responsibility. Those in high rank will often select for promotion from those in lower rank, thus ensuring their power over these subordinates. Orders are obeyed lest the route to promotion be too slow. Orders are obeyed because it is the right or legitimate thing to do. Orders are obeyed because those giving the orders have successfully communicated a vision of how the organization will be effective. Such, at least, is the orthodox view of intra-organizational power in our society encapsulated in such slogans as "rank has its privileges" or, more emphatically, "shit rolls down hill."[3] We propose an alternative view which suggests that power is rarely concentrated at the top of the hierarchy. Power is found in whomever controls the crucial contingency facing the organization.

For example, in a volunteer fire department there is usually a shortage of volunteers. This shortage is a crucial contingency facing the organization, the volunteer fire department. Other crucial contingencies tend to be money, especially when times are tough for most organizations. This view was first presented by Crozier (1964) in his famous study of a French tobacco manufacturer. To his surprise, he discovered that the mechanics repairing the machinery had the most power within the manufacturing plant. This particular plant was lagging in production of cigarettes. It was during the 1950s, long before connection was made between smoking and illness. Thus, this plant could easily sell whatever it produced. Profits were, therefore, proportional to production. Nevertheless, this particular plant was old. The cigarette-making machines frequently broke down, idling the entire plant. The machines were difficult to replace as this was post-war Europe. Thus, the mechanics' motivation and skill were major factors determining the magnitude of production and profit. Crozier was able to explain the inordinate power of mechanics. Equally significant, he argued that whoever controlled what was a crucial contingency of the organization had intra-organizational power.

---

[3]A frequent phrase in the fire service to describe the power of chief officers over junior officers and firefighters.

Does this mean that senior management in the cigarette plant was powerless? Let us consider some possible strategies it might have employed. It might have recruited more mechanics. The new mechanics could compete with the old ones to do the repair work. Perhaps fearing that the new and old mechanics would become friends and collectively maintain power, management might engage an outside company of mechanics to repair the machines. This is typically known as "contracting out" a service. If this were to work, or even if the current mechanics believed it might work, (that is to say management presents contracting out as a credible threat), then management would gain power over these mechanics. The mechanics, fearful that their privileges would be cut, would be more likely to comply with management directives.

In fact, this strategy was not realistic because the specific understanding the current mechanics had of the cigarette-making machines could only be acquired with years of experience that came from repairing those machines. It is as if each machine had acquired a personality. Repairing a defect was not merely a motor task. Rather, repair required diagnosis of the underlying problem using thought processes not very different from what a physician would use. Thus, a contracted service of rookie mechanics would not be able to do the job.

A second strategy management might have used could have been to offer the mechanics rewards that would require compliance. Extra pay, fringe benefits, honors, and titles might all be bestowed so as to create loyalty. Pensions might be used to bind the mechanics to the workplace lest they seek jobs elsewhere. These rewards could be offered for compliance in repairing the machinery. Unfortunately, management was not competent enough to recognize the wisdom of this strategy.

Rather, management threatened to punish the mechanics by raising the possibility that they might be fired. This led to a strike of all of the workers in the union, not just the mechanics. When the strike was settled, the mechanics returned to work with even greater power. Using punishment is similar to the "Trouble in Blucherville" case, the introductory story at the beginning of this chapter.

What lessons can we learn from this episode? First, the mechanics had power because they offered a unique service that was crucial for the success of the cigarette manufacturing plant. Second, management could not seek that service elsewhere without great cost. Third, management could have offered rewards to the mechanics so as to increase management power. This strategy would have empowered management but, instead, they chose the cheaper, third strategy, namely to punish the mechanics. This did not work.

We can generalize Crozier's story about the cigarette manufacturing plant. Let us imagine two persons unimaginatively called A and B. Then, according to the theory outlined by Blau (1964), the definition of **power** is:

A has power over B, if A can affect B's interests.

The definition of **interests** is:

B's interests might include profits, salary, prestige, love, fame, interesting work, and promotion.

Consequently:

Given that A has power over B, what can B do about it? That is, what are B's strategies?

Blau's Strategies

1. B can have its interests met elsewhere (perhaps from C or D or E);
2. B can offer to meet A's interests;
3. B can threaten to punish or actually punish A either legally or not;
4. B can decide that its own interests are unimportant (salary, promotion, etc.).

The first three strategies correspond to the alternatives that confronted management of the cigarette manufacturing plant. The fourth strategy (the so-called Eastern Way) is very uncommon in private sector management. Private sector managers are driven to seek profits at least large enough to ensure their own jobs and, perhaps to seek even larger profits, to ensure promotion or career advancement. Thus, to imagine that the management of the cigarette manufacturing plant does not care about the maintenance of production so as to ensure sufficient profit is very unlikely. Nevertheless, as we shall see below, this strategy is an important one for our purposes.

APPLICATION TO VOLUNTEER EMERGENCY ORGANIZATIONS

Now let us return to Blucherville and apply Blau's strategies to Chief Jensen (B) and Councillor Onderdonck (A):

Onderdonck has **power** over Jensen because Onderdonck can affect whether Jensen gets a pumper.

We know Jensen has an **interest** in getting a new pumper. Perhaps the new pumper is consistent with Jensen's vision of an up-to-date fire department in Blucherville.

What can Jensen do?

Strategies

1. Jensen can find another councillor to buy the pumper (Marge Schultz);

2. Jensen can re-elect Felix Onderdonck. (Felix has an interest in being re-elected);

3. Jensen can threaten to punish Onderdonck. (Remember the hint about withdrawing electoral support.) Or, actually punish Onderdonck by withdrawing support (as the department actually did do);

4. Jensen can decide that he does not want a pumper. Since Jensen has no interest in a pumper, Onderdonck has no power over Jensen.

Although the application of Blau's strategies seems reasonable there are, nevertheless, some differences we should identify. The first difference is that, whereas Blau developed the arguments for individuals, we have applied it to a private sector organization, namely Crozier's (1964) cigarette manufacturing plant and Blucherville. This does not seem to be a major problem, but we should be aware of it. The second difference is that so far the application of the definition, types, and strategies of power has been with intra-organizational relationships, (that is employees, whether workers, mechanics, or managers **within** an organization). We, however, are interested in the relationship **between** organizations (specifically volunteer emergency organizations and local governments). This second difference is very important as we shall see below. Finally, a third difference is that our illustrative example is a private sector organization. Yet, our interest is in the public sector, local government, and the volunteer sector, namely the volunteer emergency organization. This third difference is important, as we will see below.

Are the sources of power and the strategies for dealing with powerlessness the same between (or among) organizations as within organizations? The answer is perhaps "yes," except that the emphasis changes. Once inter-organizational relations are considered, then market forces assume greater importance. Relationships between organizations are governed by market forces, more than by contractual obligations. Moreover, the uncertainty of the power relationship increases because there is no legitimation of that power relationship. Does a volunteer emergency organization (for example, Jensen's) have more power over the corresponding local government (for example, Onderdonck's), or does the local government have more power over the volunteer emergency organization in question? Without any further information we cannot reach a conclusion. At first glance, the very least we can argue is that hierarchical relations must be considered within any organization.

Perhaps more important is the third difference noted above, namely the fact that a local government is in the public sector and that the volunteer emergency organization is in the volunteer sector. What increases uncertainty in the power relationship are that the goals (motives) of the organizations in these two sectors are less clear than the profit goal found in the private sector.

When the goals of a potential opponent are unclear, then any strategy relevant to the relationship becomes more uncertain. One reason that local governments establish a paid chief is because the paid chief may fear being fired. This gives local government some control over the chief, but it does not necessarily give the chief control over the department.

THE INTER-ORGANIZATIONAL NETWORK

So far, we have been examining the relationship between the volunteer emergency organization and local government in isolation from other types of organizations, for example, fire service organizations, hospital emergency medical directors, training schools, and the various agencies that interact with local government. Similarly, we have considered the volunteer emergency organization and the local government as monolithic organizations having a single set of interests. In this section, we will explore the fact that both the volunteer emergency organization and the local government are often fraught with conflicting interests. Furthermore, the origins of these conflicting interests often arise from the relationships with other organizations. Moreover, one consequence of conflicting interests within a volunteer emergency organization is typically harmful for the volunteer emergency organization/local government relationship.

We will first examine the broader network of organizations and institutions that affect both the volunteer emergency organization and local government. We will then examine the stress these relationships induce within the volunteer emergency organization. Finally, we will examine the effect of these stresses on the volunteer emergency organization/local government relationship.

Figure 3.2 outlines the network of relationships that impinge upon a volunteer emergency organization. The figure is by no means exhaustive. Rather, it describes the more central relationships a volunteer emergency organization must consider. Moreover, recognize that the figure ignores a far denser network of relations than local government has with such organizations as the state/province, various associations, boards, and commissions. Let us briefly consider each of the organizational relationships in turn.

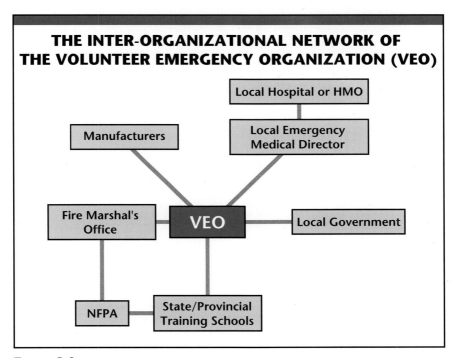

FIGURE 3.2

National Fire Protection Association

The National Fire Protection Association (NFPA), located in Quincy, Massachusetts, is a non-profit organization established by the insurance industry in 1896. This organization convenes interested (and often conflicting) parties to establish standards of performance related to equipment, training, and fire department performance. These standards are adopted by some states but, in the absence of formal adoption, they are voluntary. The increasing threat of litigation makes these standards still ever more important. Despite the prevalence of these standards in both the United States and Canada, few fire departments or volunteer emergency organizations fully comply with each standard.

Manufacturers

The equipment and apparatus manufacturers court each volunteer emergency organization because the volunteer emergency organizations are a major market for their products. Although a volunteer emergency organization is typically much smaller than a fully career urban fire department, much of the profit margin is obtained by manufacturing customized apparatus for each volunteer emergency organization. The mechanical appreciation of the key decision makers within a volunteer emergency organization is quite high. Thus, manufacturers appeal to these values. Stories are told about "free trips" and "drunken fire chiefs signing contracts." Even if these stories are myths, their telling strikes a responsive chord within the fire service community. Salespersons representing the manufacturers will visit rural departments as if they were walking into the purchasing department of a major city. Finally, recognize that intense competition exists among the manufacturers themselves. Despite the complaints made by many within the fire service about "profit gouging," bankruptcy is a very real possibility facing some apparatus manufacturers.

Fire Marshal's Office

The fire marshal's office (FMO) of the state/province often wishes to play a major role as a resource for the volunteer emergency organization.[4] Often, the FMO is called upon to investigate suspicious fires since that expertise cannot be maintained at the local level.[5] Many FMOs wish to enhance fire officer and firefighter training within the volunteer emergency organizations. Indeed, some FMOs conduct or facilitate volunteer firefighter training. Others assist the volunteer fire department in the purchase of apparatus. Unfortunately, the fiscal pressures facing some state and provincial governments severely constrain what these FMOs can do. Appropriately, nearly all FMOs do concen-

---

[4]The Fire Marshal's Office is often called a Fire Commissioner in some jurisdictions.

[5]In most rural areas, the number of fires of suspicious origin would be too infrequent to provide adequate skill maintenance for a fire investigator.

trate on fire prevention and encourage volunteer emergency organizations to diversify beyond fire suppression, expanding the VEOs' fire prevention function.

Training Schools

State/provincial training schools have assumed greater importance for volunteer emergency organizations in recent years as these schools have addressed "live burn" training. The advent of NFPA 1403 has regulated the practice of "live burns" for training within a volunteer emergency organization. As a consequence, more volunteer emergency organizations are using the training facilities of state and provincial schools, ensuring greater safety during training. This contact has facilitated the awareness of NFPA standards among the volunteer emergency organizations. Similarly, this contact has facilitated the diversification of volunteer emergency organizations including such programs as hazardous materials first responder training, vehicle extrication training, and risk management awareness. Unfortunately, as with FMOs, most state and provincial training schools face the same fiscal pressures facing FMOs in general. However, unlike the FMOs, many training schools can obtain substantial revenue from tuition fees.

Local Emergency Medical Director

This individual is usually an emergency physician, often the head of the hospital's emergency department. This person is responsible for both pre-hospital care and the initial in-hospital care of patients. Since the physician is legally accountable for patient care, but is unable to be at an automobile accident on a rural highway, the physician delegates pre-hospital care to the volunteer emergency organization. Thus, the volunteers have two masters: the chief of the VEO will direct its volunteers on administrative matters; the local emergency medical director will direct the volunteers on emergency medical matters. The overlap between emergency medical matters and administrative matters can sometimes be a problem. The differences in occupational prestige, income, and education can inhibit the cooperation needed between the chief and the emergency medical director.

Local Hospital Or Health Maintenance Organization

The local emergency medical director is either an employee or has admitting privileges at either type of organization. Since patients from the emergency department may be referred to other departments in the hospital (e.g., orthopaedics, surgery, internal medicine, etc.) these departments have an interest in the work of the emergency departments. Moreover, pre-hospital care serves as a major form of intake which may translate into revenue, particularly for a Health Maintenance Organization (HMO). These interests are likely to have an impact on the volunteer emergency organization. We will elaborate on these matters in Chapter Nine.

THE CONSEQUENCES OF THIS INTER-ORGANIZATIONAL NETWORK

Each relationship listed above pressures the volunteer emergency organization to improve the quality of its service. Some of the relationships pressure volunteer emergency organizations to increase the variety of their services as well. In either instance, the volunteer emergency organization faces the pressure of increasing the time commitments of its members and the expenditures of the volunteer emergency organization. Without any more careful examination, it should be evident that these pressures to spend money will be resisted by local government given its fiscal constraints.

However, we should not assume that these pressures affect the members of the volunteer emergency organization all in the same way. Within the volunteer emergency organization, some coalition of persons will seek more training. Another coalition will seek more apparatus. Another coalition will seek a broader mandate for the volunteer emergency organization to include some of the following functions: fire prevention, vehicle extrication, hazardous materials awareness and operations level training, rescue capability, emergency medical service to BLS, and emergency medical service to ALS.[6] Another coalition will want to institute a risk management program before considering to expand the mandate. Although many members of these coalitions will be in basic agreement with some, or even all of the other coalitions, the conflict can arise over the allocation of funds, or fund-raising time, to meet these objectives.

More fundamentally, arrayed against some of these coalitions will be a coalition which resists change. Nearly every change presented above requires expert knowledge that is a source of power often independent of the legitimate hierarchy within the volunteer emergency organization. When the fire chief has the most experience in fire suppression to be the incident commander, then introduction of new domains of activ-

---

[6]BLS: Basic Life Support; ALS: Advanced Life Support.

ity is a threat to his or her authority. Even when the chief is seeking change, others within the department will resist these changes. To illustrate this point, we can see how these external relationships affect the political agenda and conflict within a volunteer emergency organization. What we must now examine are the processes that expose and/or manage this conflict.

Most volunteer fire departments are combinations of democratic and hierarchical decision making. Typically, democratic values are subservient to hierarchal ones on the fireground. Fire suppression requires the rapid response that only hierarchical decision making can provide. In the firehall, however, the luxury of time and the absence of centralized resources requires more democratic procedures. Decisions on policy, rules, procedures, budgets, and fund-raising are almost always submitted to a vote. Even day-to-day expenditures, made by the volunteer fire chief, may have an upper limit.[7]

Most important of all is the officer election process. In most departments, even the fire chief is elected (and thus beholden to the membership rather than the CAO of the local governing body). Often, of course, the elections are contested. Thus, politicking is inevitable. Any volunteer emergency organization that engages in elections must be able to heal the divisions that arise from this process. Emotions are likely to run high because the results of the election will be well known within the small community. Indeed, personal reputation, highly valued in a small community, may be tested by this election process.

The monthly meeting can be the opportunity for the defeated candidate to "show up" the fire chief.[8] Given the investment of time made by these senior personnel (perhaps as much as 20-25 hours per week gratis), conflict over any decision, even the trivial ones, can be quite high. The effective volunteer emergency organization will learn to manage this conflict because cohesion remains a requirement to carry out the activities of the department.

---

[7]Occasionally, volunteer fire chiefs are caught between the "deal" offered by a salesperson and the requirement to defer significant purchases to the decisions of a monthly meeting of the membership. Salespeople often sell, at low price, demonstration equipment at conventions rather than return with the equipment. Usually, the fire chief has to take possession of the equipment on the spot, leaving the chief caught between saving money and exceeding his or her authority.

[8]Often, however, a defeated candidate for chief **may** become deputy chief, or training officer, or company captain. If the department is too divided, then the winning coalition of votes for chief may also produce a "slate" of officers as if a party is running for office.

One method to manage this **internal** conflict is to encourage **external** conflict. Conflict with local government over the degree of autonomy of the volunteer emergency organization, or the level of financial support provided by local government, may be just the medicine required to induce cohesion within the department. Thus, we can see that internal conflict, present in a volunteer emergency organization that alternates between hierarchical and democratic decision making, increases the likelihood of external conflict between the volunteer emergency organization and any other organization. The local government is handy for this purpose, although it may not be the only target of a volunteer emergency organization. In fact, however, we really do not know Chief Jensen's motives. Even if we asked, we might not get a straight answer. Nevertheless, the chief of any fire department is a key individual; thus, we need to explore the motivation to be chief and the motivation of a chief.

THE MOTIVATION TO BE CHIEF AND THE MOTIVATION OF A CHIEF

The reader might wonder why the managers of volunteer emergency organizations, volunteer fire chiefs, and volunteer senior officers, willingly devote so much time (20-25 hours per week) without significant remuneration. One answer often provided is akin to "its a tough job but somebody has to do it." The motivation develops in volunteer firefighters who seek election to be officers. One explanation is that because so much time is devoted, the task has to be satisfying. Social psychologists discover the human tendency toward cognitive consistency — that is a consistency between our thoughts and actions (Heider, 1958; Festinger, 1957). If we believe that something is worth doing (thought), then we invest a lot of time to see it done (action). Conversely, if we invest a lot of time in something (action), then it must be worth doing (thought). Since so much time is invested in a chief officer position, then it must be enjoyable and useful. If we fail to achieve cognitive consistency, then we suffer from cognitive dissonance. For example, if a chief works hard at what the chief perceives as useless, cognitive dissonance arises.[9] The chief can reduce the suffering by changing his or her opinion of the work (it is now useful), or he or she can stop working. Any threat to the maintenance or the development

---

[9]Developing a vision of how the volunteer emergency organization should operate, and working toward that vision, produces cognitive consistency in the chief.

of that vision can induce cognitive dissonance. As a result, volunteer chiefs have strong commitment to their work, a commitment that sometimes accepts little compromise. Under these conditions, if different coalitions have different visions, then conflict can be extreme. In effect, the personal financial stakes may be very low, but the psychological stakes are very high.

Let us return to Blucherville to illustrate the point. Going beyond the story, we can imagine that one coalition within the department wants a new pumper. Another coalition thinks money should be spent on fire prevention programs. Another coalition thinks the money should be spent on expanding the floor space of the hall so more revenue can be earned at bingo. Faced with these contending coalitions, Chief Jensen might be wise to "pick a fight" with Councillor Onderdonck. It unites his department, particularly during the campaign to elect Marge Schultz.

Perkins and Poole (1995) have illustrated this process. In their discussion of the Village Volunteer Fire Department, they present one former chief and his supporters who have rejected the new vision (a professional one) that had threatened their older vision (a community oriented vision). Indeed, a quotation from this former chief is instructive:

> *Do you see those cement blocks? I can name the people in the community who donated them for us to build this firehouse. A lot of others remember too. We started out with used equipment, no money but a lot of hard work. We have built this department into a good one...I don't go for all this mutual aid. (Part of the current chief's vision.)*

When the former chief's vision was supplanted by a newer, less local vision (such as mutual aid), then he suffered cognitive dissonance. All his hard work was now directed to something he did not see as worthwhile. The way he resolved the dissonance was to reduce his involvement in the Village Volunteer Fire Department.

Thus, if a vision is effectively threatened, then in order to maintain consistency and avoid dissonance, the chief officer can abandon the vision and withdraw much of the commitment and much of the volunteer time. This effect often manifests itself at election time. At this time, different coalitions may vie for office, altering involvement depending on the outcome. Clearly, the process can induce a significant amount of stress.

The dramatic swings in commitment of a few individuals can lead to instability in external relations, just as political instability within a nation can have major effects on international relations. Since these changes can be sudden, let us consider the psychological processes which make them possible. Consider the "career" path of the volunteer fire chief. Some ten to twenty years ago, he (over 99% of volunteer chiefs are male) was recruited by a respected uncle (or other relative or friend).

He joined for the apparent camaraderie and the prestige of the position expressed by his peer group of 19-year-old male friends. Perhaps he thought this prestige would increase his attractiveness to the opposite gender. After an initiation ceremony, he began to learn the trade of firefighting. This training included the excitement of unusual challenges, replaced by the confidence arising from the mastery of skills. As experience increased, our would-be chief faced the boredom of repetitive training and fund-raising; however, this was punctuated by the excitement of some fire calls, including the first significant working fire. Loyalty to the group was reinforced by these peak experiences. Even in the absence of significant calls, the social occasions which encouraged reminiscing about past working fires or rescue calls also reinforced group loyalty.

This loyalty induced interests within the would-be chief that became progressively more similar to the interests of the dominant coalition of officers. A senior officer might approach our now 25-year-old future volunteer chief with the suggestion to stand in nomination for election as a lieutenant responsible for a company of firefighters and responsible as incident commander at minor incidents.[10] Agreeing to do so, his group loyalty would be repaid by election to the office. Now he would be concerned with such phenomena as company morale, training, and committee work delegated by the current chief. His original motives for joining would progressively be fulfilled or disappear. Meanwhile, he would begin to take on the same interests as the volunteer emergency organization. In effect, he would be socialized by the volunteer emergency organization to take on the needs of the volunteer emergency organization.

As the would-be chief assumes chief officer status, the volunteer workload increases. Not only is he involved in five hours of prepara-

---

[10]On one hand, he might be officer on a first-due pumper making decisions that would knock down a kitchen fire, saving a house. If, on the other hand, he arrived at a fire in a print shop in a strip mall, his command would probably be superseded by the fire chief once the chief arrived.

tion and training each week, he is also devoting three hours to fundraising, two hours for fire prevention in the local mall, three hours to administrative duties, such as submitting grant applications, meetings with fellow officers, and equipment specification writing. And, of course, two hours are spent responding to calls. These 15 hours per week are the equivalent of working two days a week, full time (about 750 hours per year).

As a chief, our fully committed person has a vision of the volunteer emergency organization. In effect, it is a dream that helps to motivate him to volunteer so much time. Despite this vision, the crucial contingencies that determine whether the vision can be realized are beyond his control. These crucial contingencies may be:

1. a shortage of volunteers (recruitment);
2. a shortage of motivated, responsible, and skilled volunteers (leadership and training);
3. a restricted mandate;
4. a shortage of monies.

Of these contingencies, the last two are largely under the control of local government, particularly the CAO and council. Consequently, we should now introduce the key hero or villain who is the counterpart of the chief of the volunteer emergency organization. That hero or villain is the local government's Chief Administrative Officer.

THE CHIEF ADMINISTRATIVE OFFICER OF THE LOCAL GOVERNMENT

In order to understand the power relationship between the volunteer emergency organization and local government, let us explore a typical profile of a CAO. Unlike the fire chief, the motivation of a CAO in a local government is more calculating. Usually, CAOs began their careers with professional training as lawyers, accountants, or engineers because many CAOs are promoted from senior positions of the legal, finance, or public works departments. From experience, if not training, CAOs must be excellent negotiators. The reason is that the crucial contingency facing local governments are relations with the state or provincial government. Unlike a fire chief, a CAO is not usually committed to a vision of how the organization should be. This is for two reasons. First, unlike the volunteer fire chief, the CAO is compensated for labor and, thus, does not require a vision to enhance motivation. In a less cynical vein, the CAO can ill afford a vision when the multifaceted nature of government is the task. Government cannot chose "what business it is in." The electorate and local government legislation, enacted by state or provincial government, defines what local governments must do and, to some measure, what they cannot do. Councils change, priorities change, and coalitions change. Thus, no CAO can afford to be too strongly committed to a particular vision, or even agenda, of action. Conversely, CAOs may be passionate about processes either of policy making or administration taught by education. Aside from professional training, most CAOs receive some administrative training through attendance at workshops, registration in correspondence courses, or even a diploma or masters degree in public administration.[11]

THE UNEASY RELATIONSHIP

As a consequence of their different backgrounds, the fire chief will typically have strong interest in furthering a vision of the volunteer fire department. The CAO will have a weak interest in such a vision. Nevertheless, the CAO will control the fire chief's interests. Thus, by definition, the CAO has power over the fire chief.

Knowing this, we can now return to the strategies for dealing with powerlessness discussed at the beginning of this chapter and consider the fire chief's options. Offering the CAO and local government something it values is perhaps the most common strategy. "Selling the Vision" to the local government is, after all, a means to alter the local government's interests to match the vision. Unfortunately, most local governments want money or votes, not a level of service which exceeds its perceived requirements. Granted, a higher insurance rating (indicating a poor capacity to suppress fires) usually does increase homeowners' insurance premiums. However, the public is not conscious of this and rarely complains to the local government. On the other hand, that same public complains about many other issues, (such as taxes, potholes, and garbage collection). Offering to provide other services in addition to fire suppression is only likely to interest a local government if it is already responsible for those other services. In some states, (e.g., Illinois), the fire service has taken on EMS because the

---

[11]Aside from university education, various professional organizations offer administrative training to appointed officials in local government. Notable among these are the International City Management Association, the Carl Vinson Institute at the University of Georgia (Athens), Local Government Studies at the University of Alberta (Edmonton), and Henson College at Dalhousie University (Halifax).

state, by statute, has required local governments or fire districts to be responsible for EMS and required the fire departments (including volunteer ones) to deliver more than a fire service. Under these circumstances, the volunteer emergency organization can redress its power imbalance with the local government. The cost, however, is to change masters. Now, the volunteer emergency organization must address the dictates of an emergency medical director. The volunteer emergency organization has thrown off the yoke of legitimate and bureaucratic power found in the local government, only to replace it with the yoke of expert and bureaucratic power found in the emergency medical director.

The second strategy open to the fire chief and the volunteer emergency organization is to obtain money elsewhere — "Paying Your Own Way." In effect, resources will arise from fund-raising. In most departments, this has meant bingos, dances, fairs, lotteries, bake sales, and suppers. In many ways, these are valuable community events in their own right. Ironically, they help to fulfill the vague local government's mandate of its recreation department. Nevertheless, few volunteer emergency organizations consciously sell this recreational value to the local government. Clearly, the degree of success of this strategy depends on how well fund-raising can replace a line item in the local government's budget. First, fund-raising has its own expenses (prizes, food, hall rental, and band rental). Second, and less obvious, fund-raising of this nature requires a greater investment of volunteer labor. Usually, the volunteer firefighters are asked to fund-raise themselves. The response, "I joined the department to fight fires not call bingo numbers," is a common one. Thus, volunteer emergency organizations must be sensitive to avoid volunteer burnout during fund-raising. Some volunteer emergency organizations engage in fund-raising from other agencies of government, donations, insurance companies, and large corporations (usually present in the area). This strategy avoids some of the problems raised above. Unfortunately, few volunteer emergency organizations have "grantsmanship" skills contained within their membership.

The third strategy is to threaten to punish, or actually punish, the local government by actively campaigning against the council at the next election. The introductory story about the political trouble in Blucherville is an illustration of the use of this strategy. Similarly, **threats** to quit or go on strike, such as we saw in Queen County in Chapter One, is another illustration of "Punish the Government." In Canada, this is an infrequent but growing phenomenon. But in the Northeastern and Midwestern United States, there are a number of examples of the successful use of this strategy. Whereas the volunteer emergency organization may be "better off" having successfully used such a strategy, it is not necessarily clear that the community is "better off" as a whole. Granted, EMS and fire protection may well be at a higher standard, but some other community service might suffer in the competitive game known as the budget process.

Blau's fourth and final strategy, the reader will recall, is the most enigmatic. The fire chief and volunteer emergency organization can learn to live without fulfilment of the vision. Rationally, this is easy to understand if the pain arising from powerlessness is greater than the gain of fulfilling that passionate interest. Typically, the adoption of this strategy is rarely deliberate and unlikely to be found in the minutes of any meeting. The adoption of this strategy coincides with a period of great anguish for the chief. The easiest way to describe this is a precis of Aesop's fable of the "sour grapes." A fox eagerly spied a bunch of grapes hanging from a tall vine. After the considerable effort of jumping to grasp the grapes, fatigue sets in and subsequent jumps are lower and lower. The fox stops, then walks away, consoling itself with the fact that the grapes were probably sour anyway.

If the fire chief and the senior officers of the volunteer emergency organization undergo this sour grapes phenomenon (another form of cognitive dissonance reduction), then they lose interest in the vision for the volunteer emergency organization. (Recall Perkins and Poole's description of the Village Volunteer Fire Department, 1995.) The result is that the CAO and the local government lose power over the volunteer emergency organization. The likelihood of this strategy (unconscious though it may be) is greater than many realize because it is relatively covert. Unfortunately, the outcome may be the vicious volunteer emergency organization (see below). If so, the volunteer emergency organization and the local government may well both lose.

VICIOUS AND VIRTUOUS VOLUNTEER EMERGENCY ORGANIZATIONS

How a volunteer emergency organization will relate to local government depends partly on its type. Two ideal types of volunteer emergency organizations are presented here. Each type is relatively stable, enmeshed in a vicious or a virtuous circle of effects. We propose that volunteer emergency organizations can change from one type to the other, but that significantly greater energy (motivation, time, resources, political pressure, and legal pressure) is necessary to do this. Because each type is stabilized by vicious and virtuous circles of effects, we will call them the vicious volunteer emergency organization and the virtuous volunteer emergency organization, respectively. In the next few pages, we will describe the vicious volunteer emergency organization, the virtuous volunteer emergency organization, and then consider what determines which type is more likely. Finally, we will investigate the forces that can only, with difficulty, transform the volunteer emergency organization from one type to the other.

The Vicious Volunteer Emergency Organization

The vicious volunteer emergency organization is characterized by a narrow approach, its dominant management coalition lacking in vision. Such volunteer emergency organizations typically engage only in fire suppression as a domain of activity, often performing that function very poorly. Usually, these departments will be found in zero growth or declining rural districts. Usually, the number of alarms (and working fires) is sufficiently low that the public does not require more of this type of volunteer emergency organization. The local image of the department is as a white, middle-aged, male social club. The department recruits only by word of mouth. Members, therefore, recruit friends and relatives. Because the image is poor, only friends and relatives will consider joining. Because commitment is low, training (only for suppression) is easy and lazy. The department may not have a training officer because that would require excessive demands of the membership. The chief officers believe that the membership must be treated "with kid gloves," otherwise they might resign or become angry with management. Because many volunteers do not show up in response to alarms, more volunteers are needed. However, a shortage of volunteers always exists. The chief officers selected by the membership at election are popular because successful candidates believe (rightly!) that they need to be popular to be elected. Training is poor and isolation from the progressive elements of the fire service is necessary, lest these elements be too threatening. Often, fires will be extinguished only because the fire runs out of fuel. Exterior attack will be common, and perhaps appropriate, given insufficient training.[12] Since planning for water supply and training for water transport will not likely have

[12]Exterior Attack: fire fighting by applying water to a fire from the outside of the building.

occurred, the best we can hope is that exposures will be sufficiently protected and the fire will extinguish itself from lack of fuel before the water in the pumpers' tanks is drained.[13] In summary, we see the following pattern:

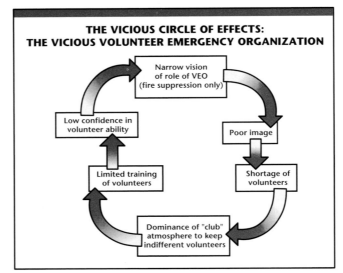

FIGURE 3.3

The Virtuous Volunteer Emergency Organization

We can contrast this vicious volunteer emergency organization with the virtuous volunteer emergency organization. The virtuous volunteer emergency organization has a vision of the future. That vision arises from a need for related local services such as the provision of EMS. The volunteer emergency organization occupies a domain sufficiently broad to be of service but sufficiently narrow so as not to duplicate existing services. At a practical level, that vision includes fire prevention and public education as major goals (but also as major activities). That vision leads to a fund-raising strategy and a recruiting strategy. Partly because the training curriculum will be broader, but mostly because standards for volunteer performance will be greater, more time will be devoted to training. In all likelihood, the volunteer emergency organization will have insufficient expertise to train the volunteers fully

[13]Exposures: adjacent structures that may catch fire unless they are cooled by the application of water.

to a standard.[14] Consequently, some of the training will be conducted by state/provincial training schools.

This organizational linkage opens the volunteer emergency organization to new ideas and methods. The virtuous volunteer emergency organization tends to evaluate its own personnel based on the mastery of the tasks the volunteer emergency organization must perform. To a greater extent, skill mastery will inform the voting preferences at election time. Politicking will still take place, but the politicking will be informed by issues affecting the department more than the popularity of the candidates. The volunteer emergency organization will have a positive image within the community, enhancing fund-raising and recruitment. At a practical level, we should expect a waiting list to join the department. This feature will allow management to endorse standards of training and performance among the volunteers. (In other words, the chief can say, "If you don't want to work then leave.") Finally, we should expect that volunteers will respond to a very high percentage of alarms when they are on call.[15] We should expect the following:

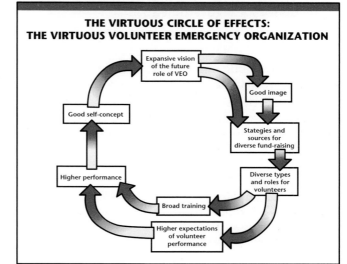

THE VIRTUOUS CIRCLE OF EFFECTS: THE VIRTUOUS VOLUNTEER EMERGENCY ORGANIZATION

- Expansive vision of the future role of VEO
- Good image
- Stategies and sources for diverse fund-raising
- Diverse types and roles for volunteers
- Higher expectations of volunteer performance
- Broad training
- Higher performance
- Good self-concept

FIGURE 3.4

---

[14]The vicious volunteer emergency organization has even less expertise, but the vicious volunteer emergency organization is partly unaware of this deficiency and partly defensive against the threat of external expertise.

[15]A volunteer emergency organization with a large number of alarms may divide responsibility for responding by time (one week on call; next week off call, etc.).

How Vicious And Virtuous VEOs Relate To Local Government

Local government faces more problems with a vicious volunteer emergency organization rather than a virtuous volunteer emergency organization. However, even a virtuous volunteer emergency organization will make demands on a local government that are increasingly difficult to meet. The virtuous volunteer emergency organization will tend to expand its mandate requiring more resources. Although its own fund-raising may be very effective, internally generated expectation of performance will always exceed the available money supply. As a result, local government will always be seen as the constraining factor. Nevertheless, this is a happy problem for local government.

Conversely, a vicious volunteer emergency organization is a literal liability for local government. Most important, a vicious volunteer emergency organization delivers inadequate service, happily masked by adherence to the building code and to the fire code, and by a general lack of public expectation on how volunteers ought to perform. However, the vicious volunteer emergency organization creates other problems for local government:

1. Its poor public image leads to poor fund-raising that increases the demands it makes on local government[16];

2. Its poor public image leads to poor recruiting, resulting in a "redneck social club." This image makes subsequent recruiting of non-whites and females difficult. It leaves the volunteer emergency organization open to charges of discrimination and then, subsequently, when correction is beginning, leads to charges of sexual or discriminatory harassment. This is a possible legal liability for local government. It is certainly a political liability for local government (see Chapter Four); and

3. The substandard behavior within the vicious volunteer emergency organization may result in a lawsuit. The local government may be sued as well as the vicious volunteer emergency organization. Even if the local government is **not** sued, a successful suit against the vicious volunteer emergency organization will probably lead to a greater request for funds by the volunteer emergency organization in the future.

---

[16]Sometimes the chief of a vicious volunteer emergency organization will not make demands because "nothing is needed." Inevitably, a fire committee (including a councillor) will recognize the existing problems and recommend that money from local government be used to solve these problems.

How Vicious And Virtuous VEOs Change

Both the vicious volunteer emergency organization and the virtuous volunteer emergency organization remain stable over several years. Logically, however, we should expect that a vicious volunteer emergency organization will eventually be a social club, an emergency service in name only. Alternatively, it might disband when the discrepancy between its avowed purpose and its actual purpose can no longer be ignored. In either instance, an effective emergency service is not being provided to the community. These two possibilities do arise, but neither is the prevailing trend. Volunteer fire departments, for example, have histories measured in scores of years and even centuries. How, therefore, can the vicious volunteer emergency organization last so long? The answer seems to be, it does not. That is, periodically the vicious volunteer emergency organization is converted into a virtuous volunteer emergency organization. Sometimes its just a question of waiting for that unpredictable major fire.

Equivalently, we should expect that a virtuous volunteer emergency organization will "take over the world" infinitely expanding either the range of its services or the geographic coverage of its services. Clearly, this does not happen. Consequently, we must recognize that a virtuous volunteer emergency organization can only expand within limits. Similarly, however, we should also recognize that a virtuous volunteer emergency organization can become a vicious volunteer emergency organization.

How does a virtuous volunteer emergency organization become a vicious one? One way is through the change in attitude of the fire chief. We have already seen that when a fire chief's goals are frustrated by local government, then one response is the "sour grapes" phenomenon. That is, in order to avoid cognitive dissonance, a chief expends less volunteer effort. This leads to a limited role for the volunteer fire department. Taking on new activities is just too much frustrating work. The membership observes this change, but is unlikely to correct it. For one thing, someone else must be willing to stand for nomination as chief and be willing to put up with the frustrations already evident in the relationship with local government.

Another danger is the consequence of overexpansion. As volunteer fire departments, hitherto financially independent, take on more services, particularly EMS, we can expect costs to rise. If fund-raising does not rise as rapidly, then greater dependence on an inherently fickle local government is inevitable. If this happens, then the "sour grapes" phenomenon will soon be activated in the fire chief. Alternatively, if independent fund-raising increases, then the volunteer emergency organization must guard against burnout among the volunteer members. This burnout will lead to recruiting problems within a year or two. This, in turn, will start the vicious circle.

One way to resist the consequences of a greater fund-raising burden is to recruit fund-raisers as volunteers. Currently, many "ladies' auxiliaries" perform this role; however, more efficient fund-raising methods are possible as well. What is required is the conscious recognition that those volunteering are providing a range of skills and aptitudes not otherwise available. The aptitude to fight fires may well be necessary to be a firefighter, but many volunteer activities can support the firefighter role. This issue is elaborated upon in Chapter Six, The Recruitment Dragon.

Fortunately, there remains a number of processes that can convert a vicious volunteer emergency organization into a virtuous one. Unfortunately, almost all are **external** to the volunteer emergency organization imposing shocks on the organization that requires a response. Often out of necessity, the local government will take a partner role in this change. However, it can only do so if the membership is willing. The typical shocks tend to be:

1. Large fires with loss of life and/or major property loss;
2. The addition of rescue and emergency medical service;
3. A major lawsuit arising from negligence within the volunteer emergency organization. (This need not be a result of action at a large fire; it might be a personnel issue such as sexual or discriminatory harassment.); and
4. Consolidation of the local governments resulting in consolidation of two or more fire departments.

For each of these external shocks, we might wonder whether the cure is worse than the original disease. In any case, even if it is worth it, the volunteer emergency organization has no control over that shock in the first place. The only controllable factor that transforms a vicious volunteer emergency organization into a virtuous one is patient, sustained, courageous, and selfless leadership. Unfortunately, given these qualifying adjectives describing the type of leadership needed, the task is not an easy one. Such a set of leaders can appeal to the autonomy desired by the membership by stating that the persistence of behaviors which characterize a vicious volunteer emergency organization is far more likely to lead to the "shocks" described above.

The problem of the vicious volunteer emergency organization is illustrated by Hampden-Turner (1990). Every organization must resolve the dilemma of adaptation and integration. Most organizations must adapt to a changing environment, but at the same time integrate the members to the organization itself. Extreme adaptation can sacrifice the cohesion necessary among its members. Conversely, extreme integration of its members can sacrifice the ability of the organization to adapt to a changing environment. Until now the volunteer fire department's environment has been placid. Now, however, turbulence has been introduced, requiring both the volunteer fire department and the local government to develop a culture that resolves the dilemma between adaptation and integration.

Hampden-Turner (1990) illustrates the failure to resolve this dilemma with the following diagram of a vicious circle:

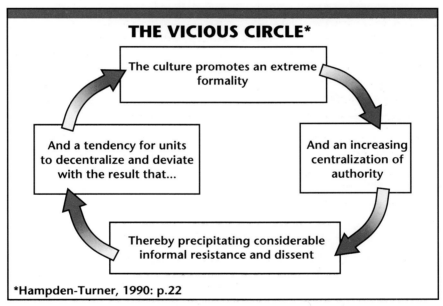

FIGURE 3.5

In effect, this culture will result in the collapse of the organization as it disintegrates. However, increasing control and accountability (synonyms for centralization of authority) only engender more resistance and deviance. If this is the problem in **one** organization, imagine the difficulties which arise when **two** organizations must work together:

two organizations such as a local government and a volunteer fire department. The following diagram is a modification of Hampden-Turner's Vicious Circle:

FIGURE 3.6

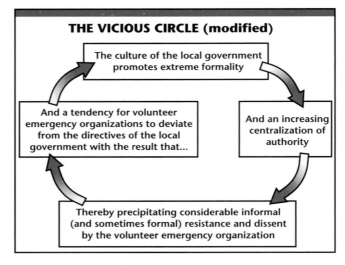

THE VICIOUS CIRCLE (modified)

The culture of the local government promotes extreme formality

And an increasing centralization of authority

Thereby precipitating considerable informal (and sometimes formal) resistance and dissent by the volunteer emergency organization

And a tendency for volunteer emergency organizations to deviate from the directives of the local government with the result that...

Fortunately, Hampden-Turner (1990) presents a virtuous circle as well. Effective informal processes are recognized formally and rewarded. This provides an incentive to provide a good service, as can be seen in the figure below (Hampden-Turner, 1990: p.23):

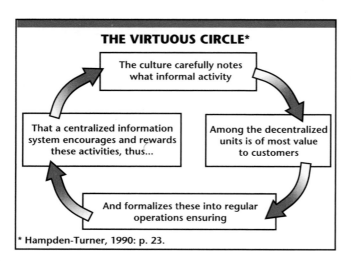

THE VIRTUOUS CIRCLE*

The culture carefully notes what informal activity

Among the decentralized units is of most value to customers

And formalizes these into regular operations ensuring

That a centralized information system encourages and rewards these activities, thus...

* Hampden-Turner, 1990: p. 23.

FIGURE 3.7

We can modify this virtuous circle to our advantage when considering the relations between the local government and the volunteer fire department. Thus:

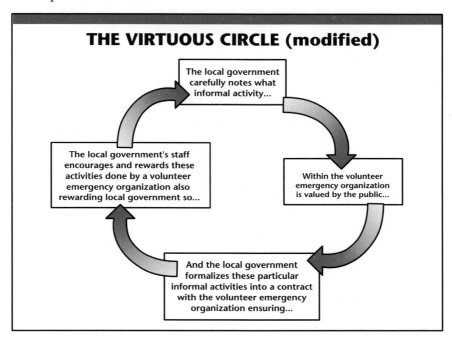

THE VIRTUOUS CIRCLE (modified)

The local government carefully notes what informal activity...

Within the volunteer emergency organization is valued by the public...

And the local government formalizes these particular informal activities into a contract with the volunteer emergency organization ensuring...

The local government's staff encourages and rewards these activities done by a volunteer emergency organization also rewarding local government so...

FIGURE 3.8

SUMMARY

This chapter has covered a number of interrelated issues. Fortunately, most of these issues relate to power. We say one organization, A, has power over another organization, B, if organization A can affect the interest of organization B. Thus, a local government has power over the VEO if it can affect the VEO's interests. When an organization like a VEO is relatively powerless to a local government then it can respond with any one, or a combination of the four strategies:

Strategy 1   The VEO can offer local government what it wants (such as volunteers to campaign for the local politicians at election time);

Strategy 2   The VEO can have its interests met elsewhere (for example, the VEO can fund-raise so as not to be dependent on a grant from local government);

Strategy 3   The VEO can threaten (bluff) to punish or actually punish the local government (for example, go on strike, damage equipment, support a rival politician);

Strategy 4   The VEO can decide it is no longer interested in money at all (as Rhett Butler said to Scarlet O'Hara in *Gone With The Wind*: "Frankly, my dear, I don't give a damn!").

We then examined the inter-organizational network that affects the VEO. Parts of that network included the fire marshal's office, the state/provincial training school, and the local emergency medical director's office, to name a few organizations. Essentially, these organizations encourage VEOs to improve the quantity and quality of their services, thus increasing the VEO's interests for money to make the improvements, and thus increasing the VEO dependence on local government to obtain a larger grant. Moreover, increasing standards of care tended to increase the risk of litigation placing both the VEO and the local government in jeopardy.

Complicating the analysis is the fact that VEOs are not monolithic organizations having one and only one set of interests. Rather, VEOs often contain competing coalitions that can often be suppressed by "picking a fight" with another organization...such as the local government. A further complication is the motivation of the chief. Often when a chief's goals (vision) are frustrated, the psychological pressure to avoid cognitive dissonance leads the chief to abandon the vision. This process is akin to Strategy 4 described above.

The chapter proceeded to analyze the Chief Administrative Officer of the local government who tends to be disinterested in the issues, thus increasing, necessarily, the ability to bargain. This personality type, or role, tends to place the local government at an advantage and the VEO at a disadvantage.

Finally, we examined two kinds of VEOs in a different way than we considered in the typology introduced in Chapter Two (and will continue in Chapter Ten). We introduced the vicious VEO and the virtuous VEO. This classification was useful for its own sake but it also informed us about how the power relationship with local government influences whether a VEO is vicious or virtuous. Similarly, knowing whether a VEO is vicious or virtuous also helped to tell us something about the power relationship. We ended the chapter by adapting Hampden-Turner's (1990) vicious and virtuous circles to the VEO/local government relationship.

Unfortunately, local government, whether heroes or villains, and volunteer emergency organizations, whether heroes or villains, are not isolated from the other issues (the dragons) around them. We shall consider each of these dragons, starting with the legal dragon.

LEGAL DRAGONS: TORTS, IMMUNITY, NEGLIGENCE, AND CIVIL RIGHTS

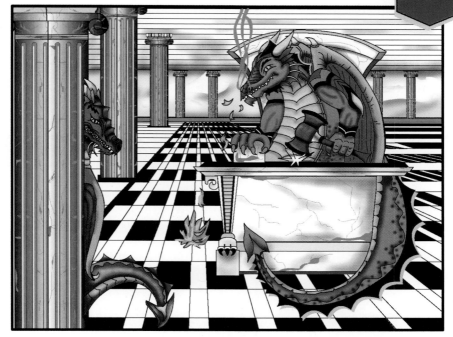

INTRODUCTION

Our intention in this chapter is to outline several legal issues relating to immunity, negligence, and civil rights as they relate to volunteer fire departments, and to some extent to volunteer EMS squads. All the issues surrounding negligence, immunity, and civil rights have practical implications for leadership of volunteer organizations, relations with government, and joint risk management efforts. We see this chapter as setting the stage for the other chapters. The legal position of volunteer organizations must be appreciated in order to give a backdrop to other problems they have to face.

Litigation for negligence seems to be the greatest external risk faced by volunteer fire and EMS organizations. Civil rights action by **members** appear to represent the greatest internal risks for litigation. We should note that volunteer EMS squads, which are not under the umbrella of a fire department, often have a different kind of legal protection (Good Samaritan laws) that is considerably less ambiguous than that for fire departments (sovereign immunity).

Canadian and U.S. legal systems are both derived in significant ways from Britain, but the trends affecting law move at different rates. For example, as will be elaborated upon below, sovereign immunity from civil litigation is being eroded in both countries. On one hand, a recent Supreme Court of Canada decision has almost entirely eliminated the sovereign immunity defense. In the United States, on the other hand, such a defense is still possible. (For these reasons we will present U. S. and Canadian legal issues separately.)

LITIGATION, VOLUNTEERS, AND LOCAL GOVERNMENT IN THE UNITED STATES

The reason government has a large presence in the legal life of volunteer fire departments is simple: **Volunteer fire departments in and of themselves have no immunity from tort damages, except by way of a local government**. As we will see below, for volunteer fire departments to share in any protection, courts have to research and conclude that a department is in fact a governmental agency. There are cases where perfectly legitimate volunteer fire departments have been excluded from this precious immunity. To make matters worse, the whole legal concept of governmental immunity is being rapidly eroded by the courts.

The area of constitutional law related to civil liberties represents another set of problems to which no immunity can apply. Freedom from sexual and racial discrimination, the liberty of free speech, due process, and other big legal questions affect volunteer fire departments and EMS squads in today's legal environment.

Leaders must be vigilant in steering their departments away from litigation, if for no other reason than the outcomes are too uncertain — even for an agency as honorable as a volunteer fire department. On the subject of leadership, we should say that in many legal struggles litigation almost invariably **forces** difficult changes, particularly those involving civil liberties of members or potential members. A much preferable strategy is if a voluntary and relatively peaceful imposition of change by good leadership occurs **before** litigation. The old saying, "Pay a little now or a lot later," is appropriate.

KEY PRACTICAL QUESTIONS

What is the legal environment of volunteer fire department/government relations? Specifically, what are torts, negligence, and governmental immunity? What is a volunteer department from the standpoint of sharing governmental immunity? Does the law suggest the best way for a government to formally relate to its volunteer departments so as to protect itself from liability? What are the constitutional issues of which both fire and EMS organizations must be aware? What are some practical, down to earth strategies leaders in government and emergency services can implement to guard against litigation? These are the main questions this chapter will address. In so doing, several actual cases will be discussed. For the reader who wishes to do further research, we encourage him or her to read the cases cited in those we discuss below.

Volunteer fire departments and their local government counterparts are caught up in legal relationships that are ambiguous. Much of the ambiguity centers around two concepts: sovereign or governmental immunity, and the complex idea of whether or not a volunteer department (or EMS squad) is a "state actor." We will consider the question of immunity first.

SOVEREIGN IMMUNITY FROM TORTS

The idea of any kind of immunity always implies there is something from which one wishes to be immune. In the part of the legal world we are considering, issues of immunity are called torts. Prosser and Keeton, widely cited authorities on tort law, stated:

> A tort is not the same thing as a crime...A crime is an offense against the public at large, for which the state, as a representative of the public, will bring proceedings in the form of a criminal prosecution....The civil action for a tort, on the other hand, is commenced and maintained by the injured person, and its primary purpose is to compensate for the damage suffered, at the expense of the wrongdoer. (Keeton, 1984: p.7)

Black's Law Dictionary (6th Edition) includes the definition of a tort as a legal wrong stemming from "a violation of a duty imposed by general law or otherwise." Different from crimes, torts include such things as trespassing, intentional interference with another person (assault, battery, false imprisonment, and infliction of mental distress), defamation (libel and slander), and negligence. Negligence is of special interest. We recognize that members of volunteer organizations are sometimes caught up in criminal litigation (arson is an all too familiar example) but we will limit our discussion here to torts.

In the world of litigation for damages resulting from "tortious behavior," there are several forms of immunities. People who are legally insane are immune from having to pay damages for their misconduct.

Infants and children are usually considered to be immune from having to pay for their otherwise tortious behavior. There is also the presence of laws that extend what is commonly called the "Good Samaritan" immunity to those who attempt to render medical aid outside of a legal duty to do so. (See, *Tatum v. Gigliott*, 583 A.2d. 1062, Maryland, 1991.)[1] Sovereign immunity is the particular immunity that is important in understanding litigation involving volunteer fire departments.

Generally speaking, sovereign immunity comes from the historical notion that "the King can do no wrong." Historically, it has been considered illogical for a governmental power (once a sovereign king or queen, but now, in our society, a government of elected officials) to open itself for damages. This is because the government granted the power to conduct litigation in the first place. Furthermore, local government is legally an arm of the state or province and thus has enjoyed, to varying degrees, the protection of sovereign immunity that is now generally limited to when government officials' (not its employees') discretionary conduct resulted in citizens' beliefs that they were victims of wrongdoing.

Immunity from torts, granted through the old concept of sovereign immunity, is being greatly limited throughout the United States and Canada (Keeton, 1984). However, courts have been willing to extend governmental immunity to volunteer fire departments. This immunity from tort litigation, in which local governments can "cloak" themselves, is sometimes "imported" to a volunteer fire department when it is sued for damages resulting from an alleged negligence in performing some duty. This extension of immunity to a volunteer fire department is by no means automatic. Court decisions vary within and between states.

Sometimes a department may be immunized, but individuals may not. The Maryland case of *Macy v. Heverin* (408 A.2d 1067) is an example. In this case an ambulance out on a "spin dry" drive after being washed (so as to check if electrical systems were damaged from washing) collided with a tractor-trailer truck. The department was immune, but the driver was liable for property damages. In an adjacent state, when the driver of a fire truck failed to stop at a railroad crossing and was hit by an Amtrack train, the Supreme Court of Virginia in *National Railroad Passenger Corporation v. Catlett Volunteer Fire Department* (404 S.E.2d 216 VA, 1991) stated:

---

[1] The full case references are usually provided in the text rather than in the bibliography.

(1) volunteer fire company had an implied contract which rendered it immune from suit for damages caused by the negligent operation of a fire truck on route to the scene of a fire, and (2) firefighter who drove the fire truck across railroad tracks without stopping was entitled to invoke the defense of sovereign immunity and was liable only for gross negligence.

As a side note, *National Railroad Passenger Corporation v. Catlett Volunteer Fire Department* was the basis for one of the questions on a recent Virginia Bar Association exam, perhaps foreshadowing increased litigation involving volunteer fire departments.

The problems that cause uncertainty in this "cloaking" have to do with the eroded nature of this form of immunity and with the fact that volunteer fire departments are unusual legal creatures in their varied relationship with government.

COORDINATION AND CONTROL BY GOVERNMENT: A THORNY ISSUE

Is a volunteer fire department an arm of government and thus entitled to immunity? To answer this question, the courts usually ask about the coordination and control exercised by the local government. How much of this coordination and control does it take to prove that the volunteer organization deserves to share in governmental immunity?

The theme of ambiguity in the legal situation of volunteer fire departments can be illustrated by contrasting the case above that involves the Catlett Volunteer Fire Department, with that of another volunteer department in a different state. The present case is one where the insurance company sued the fire department for damages resulting from its failure to completely extinguish a fire that later rekindled and burned down a warehouse. The Court of Special Appeals of Maryland in *Utica Mutual Insurance Company v. Gaithersburg-Washington Grove Fire Department, Inc.* (455 A.2d 987, Md. 1983) stated after a review of how the department was formally related to its local government:

> *...[T]he evidence tended to refute any governmental entity relationship. The [department] owns its own property, buildings, and equipment, pays its own non-volunteer employees and enacts its own rules and regulations...We do not mean to imply that a volunteer fire company may never be a governmental agency...We simply hold that the evidence presented at this trial was insufficient to establish the [department] as a governmental agency...*

As we have said, a court's extension of governmental immunity to a fire department is not automatic. Usually involved is a considerable amount of research to establish that this immunity applies. While all of us know, in a social and operational sense, exactly what volunteer fire departments are, it is rarely clear in court that these organizations deserve immunity **without question** from their alleged tortious behavior. The amount of coordination and control by a local government — albeit distasteful for many volunteer departments — is a pivotal point in decisions about immunity. Unfortunately, there is no standard by which to determine how much is enough.

Just because these organizations are honorable, heroic, public servants, they are not necessarily deserving of any kind of immunity. Furthermore, since there is some legal question about whether or not firefighting is the sole responsibility of any government, there can be no guaranteed importation of government immunity to these organizations even if they have a high degree of governmental regulation. Additionally, given the variety of ways volunteer fire departments are constituted and their various relations with local government — the varying configurations of "coordination and control" by government — the argument that they are sort of an "arm of government" must be supported by facts unique to each situation. And, underpinning all of these questions is the fact that modern courts find unsavory the whole idea of governmental immunity. In addition, many volunteer fire departments wish for no governmental involvement whatsoever in their affairs. The reality is that a volunteer fire department's relationship with government can be complicated.

The general rule in court seems to be that each claim for immunity by a volunteer department has to be considered on **a case-by-case basis**. It does appear that the courts in the United States recognize the importance of volunteer fire and EMS services to their communities and are **currently** unwilling, on a wholesale basis, to take away the defense provided by governmental immunity.

It appears to us, however, that time is not on the side of the volunteer fire service when it comes to immunity from torts. The rate at which governmental immunity is being curtailed and even abandoned, can only spell increased risks for damages to be paid by volunteer fire departments.

A Note About Negligence And Standards

It has been our experience that many members of volunteer fire departments, including leaders, believe that the unintentional sins of their organizations will be forgiven by the public they serve. However, some sins are bigger than others. Take the tort of negligence. This is an attractive tort for an aggrieved property owner.

Negligence generally has these preconditions:

1. A duty, or obligation recognized by the law, requiring the person to conform to a certain standard of conduct for the protection of others against unreasonable risks.

2. A failure on the person's part to conform to the standard required. (Keeton, 1984: p. 164.)

There are at least two issues here that directly affect volunteer fire and EMS organizations. First, negligence has various gradations. Gross negligence (or extreme negligence) is one tort from which it is almost impossible to be immune. Even Good Samaritan laws offer no insurance against this tort. *Black's Law Dictionary (6th Edition)* includes this definition:

> *The intentional failure to perform a manifest duty is reckless disregard of the consequences as affecting the life or property of another....Ordinary and gross negligence differ in degree of inattention....Gross negligence consists of conscious and voluntary act or omission that is likely to result in grave injury when in the face of clear and present danger of which the alleged tortfeasor is aware (p. 1489).*

No one really knows what actually constitutes gross negligence until it is decided by a court.

The second issue, "standards of conduct," invariably mean training standards. Into this come federal and state standards (mandated or advisory, depending on the state) and departmental standards. The seemingly sporting contest[2] about training standards for volunteers being waged at the national level is of no small importance when we consider the life in court of such a set (or sets) of training standards. Ultimately, any effects will be felt at the local level.

Departmental standards will be the ones held up for the closest scrutiny by lawyers for a plaintiff. They may be judged against prevailing standards of surrounding departments, state standards, and/or na-

---

[2] This "sporting contest" will be elaborated upon in the next chapter. For examples of standard-setting bodies at the national level consider the National Fire Protection Association (NFPA), Occupational Safety and Health Administration (OSHA), and Insurance Services Organization (ISO). We could also mention the U.S. Department of Justice with its Fair Labor Standards Act (FLSA).

tional ones in order to determine if the "level of compliance" falls so far below that a lawsuit alleging gross negligence is appropriate. We can only say, woe be it to the department that has ignored the need for written and enforceable "reasonable" training standards based on some external criteria for its officers and members. In many volunteer departments, this compliance with a set of standards is no small task.

This problem of negligence and training standards never will be completely solved by a chief, but it cannot be ignored. It presents one of the thorniest issues for good leadership. In a sense, the good chief has to operate his or her department as if he or she expected to be in court tomorrow to win. Regretfully, there is no magic formula for how to do this.

DOES THE LAW SUGGEST A WAY FOR LOCAL GOVERNMENT TO PROTECT ITSELF?

Of interest to any governmental body is how to protect itself from litigation. At the local level, concern for lowering risks of lawsuits is a concern (which is often misplaced) in how relationships are negotiated with volunteer fire and EMS organizations. There seems to be two general models for this relationship. One of these was evidenced in the case of the EMS squad presented in Chapter One. It was symbolized by the "the ten-foot pole rule." The opposite is a model based on a government actively serving the needs of its volunteer system, and thus having considerable formal involvement in the departments.

In several of our interviews with local government officials, there was concern about maintaining the least legally risky relationship with the volunteer organizations in individual jurisdictions.

One county administrator, along with his chairman of the board, told us they had all this "figured out." They proudly pointed to a relatively recently created "County Firefighters' Association" to which money was granted and no further questions asked. This organization that existed above the level of individual departments was made up of elected representatives from each of the seven volunteer departments in the county. This county-wide association was believed by the county government to act as a buffer for lawsuits aimed at the volunteer departments. Conversations like these prompted us to consider the question of whether less formal involvement was **legally** (not politically) the less risky option.

Is Ignorance Legal Bliss?

The "ten-foot pole rule" suggests that it is in the interest of government to be as ignorant as possible as to the workings of its volunteer fire departments and EMS squads. This typically translates into a yearly grant of money by the county or city with basically no contract for services or accounting, training, or performance strings attached. Such a model relies on the honor system. It is often surrounded by the sentiments of government officials such as: "The volunteers do so much for us we can't ask them what they do with the money"; "What would we do without them?"; "We don't want to make them mad or they might quit."

While such sentiments of debt and gratitude are genuinely held, another clear reason for not wanting to know much about the volunteer organizations is fear. By having anything more than a simple financial interest in these organizations, it is believed that somehow the local government will become legally non-liable for the volunteer departments. Thus, the "ten-foot pole" rule serves several purposes.

This relationship, based on intentional ignorance, is just fine with fire departments that are not in much need. However, this kind of relationship is problematic when there is a need to prove the applicability of governmental immunity in suits involving tort litigation. Outside of a specific legal threat it still can place hardships on departments when there is a need for funding or other kinds of support, such as help with recruitment or vehicle maintenance. One could argue that failure to provide resources (and thus some coordination and control) might have the intended consequence of increasing the departments' risks of negligence suits.

The opposite model is represented by some of the more progressive local governments. In this scenario, the local government embraces the whole idea of volunteer fire and EMS organizations. It would attempt to offer a wide variety of its resources to the "volunteer system." The government would also make clear public policy statements about its support of the volunteer system that could easily include contracts for services with departments.

From our reading of the court cases, the intentional ignorance model is based on myth and wishful thinking when it comes to insulation from liability risks. The court cases suggest that it is, at least, very difficult and, at most, impossible to predict exactly how the formal relations (or lack of them) between government and its volunteer organizations would result in the issue of protection for government from liability for a tort suit brought against a volunteer department. It seems that a government is in a much better position than its volunteer fire departments in protecting itself with sovereign immunity.

We cautiously suggest that local governments in the United States seem to be fairly well protected from blunders by their fire departments. Fire departments are often non-profit corporations, community based with a charitable nature, yet providing a highly valued service to areas which could not pay for a career service (Perkins, 1987b; 1990). The legal cases tend to indicate that the courts — except where there have been blatant civil rights violations in the form of a conspiracy to discriminate against members or clients — seem to recognize the social and economic value of these groups to a community.

How a government relates to its local departments (contracts, financial grants, fire tax levies, accountability, pension plans, workman's compensation insurance on volunteers, and vehicle maintenance) appears to be difficult to predict as it relates to who will get sued, the extension of governmental immunity, and the success of the legal action. The concept of coordination and control a government's relation to its volunteer departments has acted as an indicator of whether or not immunity could be extended to volunteer departments. It seems to us that, since government has traditionally enjoyed varying amounts of immunity for its own torts, it need not be overly fearful about volunteer fire departments. Volunteer fire departments are the more vulnerable of the two entities. The legal (and community service) interests of fire departments may be best served by having a more "hands on" rather than "hands off" relationship with government in the form of written agreements and other visible signs of governmental coordination and control.

We turn now to the main external threat of litigation for volunteer fire departments: civil rights suits brought by members. Volunteer EMS squads are considered in this vein. Volunteer EMS agencies have generally not been able to share in governmental immunity mainly due to the lack of historical relationships with government. The issue of civil rights and liberties makes no distinction between volunteer fire organizations and volunteer EMS groups.

CIVIL LIBERTIES OF MEMBERS

Oddly enough, members of volunteer fire departments and EMS squads, and those who seek to join them, can create some of the toughest legal problems. The traditional image, and the experience of many veterans in the fire and EMS service, is of a relatively harmonious working group dedicated to the public good and enjoying close, clublike relationships that so many of these groups have. There are strong sentiments that are involved in the consensus of decision making in a highly valued democratic context. The idea that internal conflict could be such that the courts have to get involved to resolve it is disturbing to consider.

Before we turn to several cases where internal conflict resulted in litigation, it should be noted that volunteer fire departments, in particular, have existed for decades as primarily white male associations that drew on local residents for membership. As mentioned above, there has always been a fraternal, clublike nature to much of the activities of the department. This is not to say that there has not been internal conflict in the past. The point is that the clublike nature of these groups may now limit many departments in understanding changing public expectations and interests of new recruits, and in adapting to legal challenges that face all modern organizations.

The kind of conflict that has led to litigation in the cases below is different from factional disputes by coalitions about control of the organization. It is conflict that typically arises out of a member's belief that his or her constitutional rights were violated by some action of the leadership of the department or squad. For the most part, after several appeals, the outcomes of these cases generally favored the specific department in question; but in several cases, the courts made rulings which could affect future legal action. To be caught up in this kind of litigation at all is a terrible, long-lasting blow to the morale and public image of the organization. And of course, both these issues affect retention and recruitment. Furthermore, such litigation invites close scrutiny by the media and the government.

One final issue before we present the cases is that good leadership can lower the risks of litigation in some instances. In others, as we will see, plaintiffs cannot be deterred from taking legal action. In such cases, a leader is challenged on two fronts at once — bracing the organization for litigation and demonstrating "grace under pressure" for the members who will be acutely observant of the leader.

The cases that follow consist of excerpted portions of long, complex arguments. The reader has been spared the tedious legal notations and citations of other background cases. However, since they are matters of public record, names, departmental identities, dates, and facts have not been altered.

THE HAAVISTOLA CASE

The case excerpted below is about a member of a volunteer fire department who sued for monetary damages and an injunction ordering reinstatement in the fire department because she was placed on indefinite suspension from the fire department due to her gender (sexual discrimation). An "injunction" is a "court order prohibiting someone from doing some specified act or commanding someone to undo some wrong or injury" (*Black's Law Dictionary,* 1990). She also argued that she was deprived, without due process of law, of her opportunity to continue her EMT training. Furthermore, she argued that the fire department made false and stigmatizing statements related to her being "fired."

Paula Haavistola v. Community Fire Company of Rising Sun, Inc. (812 F.Supp. 1379, D. Maryland, 1993)

This suit stems from an occurrence on March 24, 1990, in which the plaintiff, Paula Haavistola, ("Haavistola") alleges that she was sexually assaulted by Kenneth Truitt ("Truitt"). At the time of the alleged assault, both Ms. Haavistola and Mr. Truitt were volunteers at the Community Fire Company of Rising Sun, Inc. ("The Fire Company"). The Fire Company is a Maryland corporation providing firefighting, emergency medical/paramedic, and EMS services to the Rising Sun, Maryland community and elsewhere... Haavistola's service as a volunteer ambulance aide with the Fire Company began in March, 1989...

Plaintiff Haavistola alleges that the assault occurred in the ambulance bay at The Fire Company's station, immediately after Haavistola and Truitt had returned from responding to an emergency call... Shortly thereafter, Haavistola reported the alleged assault to Assistant Fire Chief Carl Rickenboch, who advised her to present her complaint to the Fire Company's Board of Directors at their next monthly meeting, scheduled for March 26, 1990...

Haavistola did appear before the Board of Directors on March 26, 1990, and reported both the March 24th incident and prior allegedly unwanted touching by Mr. Truitt to the Directors present... In addition, she indicated her intention to file criminal charges against Truitt. After hearing her account, the Board asked Haavistola to confront Truitt at the meeting with the details of her allegation...Haavistola agreed to this request. She also agreed to leave the Board's meeting room while the Directors met with Truitt alone. After a short period (approximately five (5) minutes), Haavistola was called back in and confronted Truitt with her allegations, which he summarily denied. The Board, following brief deliberations outside the presence of either of the parties, suspended both Haavistola and Truitt indefinitely from membership in the Company, with such suspension to take effect immediately. At that time, the Board conducted no further investigation.

The Haavistola case presents some immediately recognizable problems which all fire departments and EMS squads could confront. On the basis of the published court case only, it would appear that on hindsight this case might have been avoidable if the leaders had handled Ms. Haavistola's complaint in a less summary manner. Such a quick dismissal, without any serious, formal investigation of any complaint, would tend to invite retaliation. Luckily, the Community of Rising Sun Fire Company essentially won the case on appeal based on the rulings by the court that (1) the fire company was not an employer in a legal sense and (2) it was not considered to be a state actor. It strikes us that The Fire Company had a bit of luck. As we discussed earlier, volunteer emergency organizations are considered on a case-by-case basis when in court whether it is in reference to torts or in this case civil rights issues. To us, the court could have just as easily found that the fire company was a state actor, as it did in another case (*Janusaitis v. Middlebury Volunteer Fire Department*) discussed below.

The important point is that a volunteer in a fire department, when dismissed in an environment of what could be construed to be gender discrimination, has recourse to nothing less than the United States Constitution, particularly the Amendments. Relative to being an employer, The Civil Rights Act of 1964 (and 1991) forbids, on the basis of race, color, religion, sex, and national origin, the failure, refusal, or discharge of any individual. Furthermore, it is unlawful for an employer to discriminate against any employees because they opposed any illegal employment practice or "made a charge, testified, assisted, or participated in any manner in an investigation..." about unlawful employment practices (42 U.S.C. Section 2000e-3). (For a discussion of how to manage a sexual harassment issue, see Bingham's 1995 article in *Fire Engineering*.)

In regards to the "state actor," Section 1983 commands the court to inquire:

(1.) whether this conduct was committed by a person acting under color of state law; and (2.) whether this conduct deprived a person of rights, privileges or immunities secured by the Constitution or laws of the United States. (Cited from Flagg Bros., Inc v. Brooks, 436 U.S. 149.)

In the present case, the court spent considerable time examining whether or not the Community Fire Company acted "under the color of state law." Ultimately, they ruled in the negative. The court stated, more on public policy grounds than legal ones:

> This court is of the opinion that neither the Town of Rising Sun nor the State of Maryland is so involved in the provision of firefighting services in the community here to make the Fire Company liable under [section] 1983. Public policy demands that this Court recognize the realities of small community fire department operation. Such companies play a vital role in the communities which they serve and, when possible, their continued existence should be encouraged. The law should not treat such volunteer organizations as mini-municipalities — forced to make decisions as are required of such local governments, but without the benefit of legal counsel, training, or the public treasury to satisfy judgments. Rather, public policy should foster the volunteer spirit and promote greater levels of service to these fire companies. It would be imprudent for this Court to require this Fire Company — comprised of volunteers — to function as the State does. To the extent that the case law is read to support such a result, it is rejected by this Court. Placing such a burden upon voluntary community associations might well force them to abandon their core mission: to provide quality, cost-effective fire protection to the rural communities of Maryland. This Court cannot countenance such a result.

The reader might notice the apparent tension between government immunity from torts and the concept of state actor. In the best of all possible worlds, a department would want to be considered an arm of the state in tort litigation for the immunity question, but as far away as possible when it comes to civil rights litigation.

THE JANUSAITIS CASE

Robert Janusaitis v. Middlebury Volunteer Fire Department el al. (607 F.2d 17 1979)

In April 1977, the appellant submitted a report containing numerous criticisms of the management of the Department to the Executive Committee, a small body of non-officers. The report included charges that morale was low, that training and discipline were inadequate, that accounting procedures deviated from generally accepted accounting principles, and that his past recommendations on these subjects had been ignored.

In July, apparently dissatisfied with the reaction of the Executive Committee, the appellant drafted a letter to the Internal Revenue Service. The text was as follows:

Dear Mr. Alexander:

I hereby relinquish myself from all liability both financially and crimminally [sic] from any action against the Middlebury Volunteer Fire Department, concerning their accounting procedures.

I have notified the department that they are violating the Internal Revenue Code and generally accepted accounting principles.

I can document all my findings.

The appellant handed a copy of the letter to the Chief and to the Chairman of the Executive Committee, and threatened to mail the original to the IRS if accounting practices were not changed promptly. Though a committee was appointed on July 11 to investigate the tax exempt status and accounting policies of the Department, both the Executive Committee and the Chief were annoyed by the threat and determined that some disciplinary action was warranted. The Chief initially executed an informal suspension and then, after the Executive Committee formally recommended a 30-day suspension, suspended the appellant pursuant to Rule 13 of the by-laws, which provides for the discipline of any member engaging in "unbecoming conduct detrimental to the welfare or good name of the Department." At the time of the suspension, the appellant admitted that he was aware of the Department's policy that complaints should first be brought in house, and conceded that his conduct was in error.

On September 4, several days after returning to active duty, the appellant nevertheless wrote a letter to the Chief charging that his suspension was politically motivated and that the actions of the officers and Executive Committee with regard to the suspension were malicious, reckless, imprudent, illogical, immoral, unethical, and in violation of the appellant's rights "as a citizen of the United States..." The appellant demanded "an immediate apology." In addition, the appellant consulted a law firm, which wrote to the Executive Committee requesting that the suspension be expunged and suggesting that otherwise litigation would follow.

On October 24, the appellant delivered a letter to the First Selectman of the Town. The cover page stated, "Attached is a copy of a letter which will be sent to the news media within seven (7) days." The attached letter, addressed to the editor of a Waterbury paper with copies to two other local papers and a radio-TV station, suggested that the First Selectman lacked "respect for the law," that the Department and the First Selectman were trying to "cover up," and that the appellant, "with deep regret," was planning to sue the Department for "violating [his] rights as a citizen of this country." When the Selectman showed him the letter one week later, the Chief stated, "[T]his is it — he's got to go." The Chief promised the Selectman, however, that he would discuss the letter with no one until after the coming election, less than one week away.

The final episode in the events preceding the dismissal concerns a newspaper story, published on November 5, entitled "Fireman Tells Story After Reinstatement." The story, printed after several conversations between the appellant and a reporter, stated the appellant's complaint with regard to the failure of MVFD to have its own federal income tax number as a nonprofit organization, indicated that the appellant intended to bring the matter to the attention of the Internal Revenue Service if the violations were not corrected, and reported that the appellant was considering suing the MVFD on the grounds that the 30-day suspension involved a denial of due process.

On November 6, the Chief summoned the appellant to appear before a meeting of the officers on November 9 "to discuss [the appellant's] recent conduct in statements made and documented in public which may constitute conduct detrimental to the good of the Department." At the conclusion of the meeting the appellant was dismissed from the Department. In a subsequent letter detailing the grounds for dismissal, the Chief pointed to dereliction of duties, the threat posed by the IRS letter, the threat of legal action if the suspension were not rescinded, misinformation given to the public in the newspaper article with regard to the grounds for the suspension, the threat to the First Selectman, and contribution to the decline of morale as well as participation in "activities detrimental to the Good Welfare of the Department."

Mr. Janusaitis sued the Middlebury fire chief and all members of its executive committee arguing that his dismissal violated civil guarantees of free speech and due process. He sought an injunction ordering his reinstatement.

The legal arguments in this case again center around whether the fire department was a state actor (which it was found to be), exactly what speech of the plaintiff should be protected, and the question of the constitutionality of the by-law about "activities detrimental to the Good Welfare of the Department."

This case, like a good play, has a number of subplots unfolding around Mr. Janusaitis. One doubts that he could have been deterred from litigation. Nevertheless, here we have a member, greatly concerned about the financial record keeping of the department, who "made trouble" for the department to such a degree that a departmental by-law was invoked to remove him from service. How this conflict in the department could have been handled to forestall litigation is open to speculation. What is important is the court's ruling.

The U.S. Court of Appeals found the fire department to be a state actor. It stated:

> We hold that the Department's dismissal of the appellant from the MVFD constituted state action and that his conduct involved speech, but that balancing the appellant's abrasive and personally motivated conduct against the particular need for close and harmonious relations among the members of a volunteer fire force, the dismissal did not violate the appellant's First Amendment rights. We hold, moreover, that Rule 13 of the Department's by-laws, under which the appellant was dismissed, is neither unconstitutionally vague nor overbroad as applied.

Janusaitis directly says that the dismissal of a volunteer by a fire department because of what he or she said in criticizing the department's procedures could open up the possibility of successful legal action of a plaintiff. This is the implication of the finding that the department was a state actor. Both this case and *Haavistola* suggest, as with the idea of extension of governmental immunity for torts, that a court can only decide on a case-by-case basis in regards to particular lawsuits. There is no general ruling that can be applied to protect departments from being found to be state actors in civil rights cases. As we have said, they are legally unusual creatures with an ambiguous relationship to local government that does not allow for any generalized decision beyond each specific case.

The practical issue is how to best handle disgruntled volunteers who publicly criticize the department's operations. To summarily throw these people out without consideration of due process would be tempting. A department cannot do this without great risk. However, Middlebury's use of its own by-laws to support its hearings and decisions was a smart course of action.

THE EGGLESTON CASE

Mr. Eggleston of Virginia sued the Prince Edward County Volunteer Rescue Squad, Incorporated, and individual members for both compensatory damages and "injunctive relief" (his reinstatement and a cessation of discriminatory action by the squad). The details of this case will make it clear as to why he did this.

Carl U. Eggleston v. Prince Edward Volunteer Rescue Squad, Inc., et al (569 F.Supp. 1344, 1983)

The following material facts are undisputed. Defendant Prince Edward Volunteer Rescue Squad, Inc., located in Prince Edward County, Virginia, is a private non-profit corporation whose purpose is to provide emergency medical transportation and services to the community without charge. Prior to 12 May 1982, plaintiff Carl U. Eggleston, a black man, had held positions in defendant Rescue Squad as officer, executive committee member, and general member.

On 14 January 1982, John Thompson, a white member of the Rescue Squad, used the term "niggers" in the presence of plaintiff and other members of the Rescue Squad. Plaintiff sought some official action [by the] defendant Rescue Squad against Thompson for his racially derogatory remark. On 14 April 1982, plaintiff moved the Executive Committee and then, at the Committee's direction, moved the general membership to suspend Thompson from the Rescue Squad for six months. Plaintiff's motion failed for lack of a second. On 11 May 1982, plaintiff appeared before the Prince Edward County Board of Supervisors, advised the Board of Thompson's remark and of the membership's inaction, and requested that the County withhold any donation to the Squad pending disciplinary action against Thompson.

The following day, 12 May 1982, at the Rescue Squad's general membership meeting, a motion was made by defendant Baldwin, seconded by defendant Davis, and adopted by a sixteen to two vote of the general membership to dismiss plaintiff from the Rescue Squad. The amended complaint alleges that all individual defendants participated in the decision to dismiss plaintiff and implies the vote to dismiss plaintiff was split along racial lines, there being only two voting black members present.

According to the amended complaint, plaintiff was expelled from the Rescue Squad because he appeared before the Board of Supervisors, because he did not keep his grievance "within the Squad," and because he is black and was protecting the rights and dignity of black people. Defendants assert that plaintiff was dismissed for the "good of the organization" pursuant to the Rescue Squad's constitution and by-laws.

(Concluding Statements by the Court)
Though this unfortunate incident might best have been dealt with in the locality without recourse to a federal court, there is no gainsaying the serious implications of the conduct of the several participants on the life of the community. In a small community, particularly one with the historical-legal legacy of Prince Edward County, the actions and reactions of a Rescue Squad command widespread attention. A tone is set by what is done and not done. Quite often high profile examples of right and wrong have more impact than the legal significance of such concepts as State action or contractual base or legally cognizable conspiracy. In other words, if these parties can now transcend the serious differences that arose between them and set an example of racial reconciliation, no victory in a lawsuit could equal the benefit to the community.

Like the other cases, this one has a number of complex legal arguments. In essence, the court found the squad not to be a state actor, and found no conspiracy to remove Mr. Eggleston because of his race. To say the EMS squad won very much in this case is to ignore the damage this kind of litigation causes regardless of the outcome. It occurs to us that *Eggleston* clearly appears to be a case that could have been avoided.

THE HYLAND CASE

Lanric Hyland v. Roy L Wonder (972 F.2d 1129, 9th Cir. 1992)
Lanric Hyland worked for a lengthy period of time as a vol-

unteer for the San Francisco Juvenile Probation Department. In February 1989, Hyland prepared a memorandum to the judges supervising the San Francisco Juvenile Hall that detailed numerous problems at the Hall and the failings of its director. Hyland's supervisor terminated Hyland's volunteer status and privileges immediately upon learning of the memorandum's existence. Hyland filed suit alleging that his termination constituted impermissible retaliation for protected speech in violation of the First and Fourteenth Amendments to the federal Constitution...

In May 1987, Hyland commenced work as an assistant to Dennis Sweeney, the Chief Probation Officer of the JPD. From October to December 1987, Hyland was paid for his work by the Youth Guidance Center Improvement Committee. From January through June 1988, Hyland received compensation as a non-civil service employee of the City and County of San Francisco. At all remaining times, Hyland served in the JPD as a volunteer.

In June 1988, Stephen La Plante became the Director of Juvenile Hall. Sweeney had actively promoted La Plante for this position. Conditions at Juvenile Hall deteriorated rapidly under La Plante's supervision. The first nine months of La Plante's tenure saw twenty-seven escapes from Juvenile Hall. Assaults on the staff also increased. Meanwhile, the California Youth Authority threatened to sue the JPD if conditions did not improve. La Plante's allegedly unsatisfactory service as Director was a frequent topic of communication between Hyland and Sweeney in late 1988. In January 1989, Hyland assisted Sweeney in the preparation of a highly critical evaluation of La Plante.

In February 1989, frustrated by the lack of change at Juvenile Hall, Hyland drafted a memorandum to Judge Daniel Hanlon, the presiding judge of the Superior Court in San Francisco; Judge Roy Wonder, supervising judge of the Juvenile Court; and Judge Daniel Weinstein, the former supervising judge of the Juvenile Court. The eight-page memorandum documented in detail La Plante's alleged mistakes, failures, and overall incompetence in administering Juvenile Hall. Drawing upon information gleaned from his work experiences, Hyland described the precipitous decline in staff morale, accountability, and leadership at Juvenile Hall. Hyland also cited problems with the living conditions at Juvenile Hall and the treatment of minors detained there. Hyland concluded that La Plante should be terminated immediately "for the good of the youth and Staff at Juvenile Hall."

Before circulating the memorandum to the judges, Hyland shared it with Sweeney. Immediately upon receiving it, Sweeney allegedly told Hyland: "You have no right to do this. Your relationship with the Juvenile Court is finished. I want your keys [to the Youth Guidance Center] and I'm going to issue a memorandum stating you are not to be allowed into Juvenile Hall ever again."

On February 27, 1989, Hyland delivered his memorandum to the judges and provided copies to the Juvenile Justice Commission and the California Youth Authority.

Obviously, this case does not involve a volunteer fire department or EMS squad. It is about dismissal of a **volunteer** generally. What makes it important is that it is a recent appeals case that underscores the risk any agency now takes when it "fires" a volunteer who has been publicly critical.

Mr. Hyland's case raises a new issue. Along with a concern for the Fourteenth Amendment's concern for due process, the First Amendment now enters into the picture. Mr. Hyland's claim for redress under the Fourteenth Amendment was not supported, but the question of his volunteer status was left open to question.

Basically, the appeals court set a legal precedent that volunteer status cannot be denied on the basis of constitutionally protected speech. However, the appeals court "remanded" (sent back) to the lower court the question about Mr. Hyland's abrasive conduct and "whether the defendant's (the probation department) need to maintain an efficient and effective workplace justified Hyland's dismissal."

The question of state actor was obviously not at issue in this case. But the court was very clear about the potential legal implications of taking away a volunteer status as a punishment for free speech. The court stated:

The injury to position or privilege necessary to activate the First Amendment thus need not rise to the level of lost employment. Retaliatory actions with less momentous consequences, such as loss of a volunteer position, are equally egregious in the eyes of the Constitution because a person is being punished for engaging in protected speech. (*Hyland v. Wonder*)

This case came to our attention while we were reading information about EMS. It was discussed in *EMS Insider* (October 1992) as representing a legal threat to the many EMS agencies that utilize volunteers and volunteer EMS corporations. We see implications for all volunteer organizations.

CONCLUSION OF U.S. SECTION

We began this chapter with the myth that because an organization is volunteer it is believed by many to be immune from litigation. The idea of negligence as a basis for tort action was considered in the context of immunity extended by a local governmental immunity. We tried to make these points: governmental immunity is being curtailed; it is the only immunity from torts to which a volunteer fire department could "cloak itself"; the legal definition of a volunteer department is ambiguous thus making it necessary for courts to consider each claim on a case-by-case basis; the legal cases are inconsistent in extending governmental immunity; and, the law provides no firm guidelines for how a local government should best form relations with its departments. Standards of training become increasingly important in this legal environment.

We then considered a typical internal legal threat to both fire departments and EMS squads. This threat was posed by volunteers themselves who believed that they had been denied constitutional rights such as free speech, due process, and/or suffered sexual or racial discrimination. As with governmental immunity from torts, the concept of "state actor" showed a need for a case-by-case examination of each squad or fire department. We suggested that, in some of these cases, litigation could have been avoided by the department taking a different approach to the unhappy volunteer. Our final case — not related to fire departments or EMS organizations — drove home the point that the status of being a volunteer can have serious legal implications if it is denied on the basis of anything protected by the Constitution. If nothing else, all these cases suggest the importance of leaders to be familiar with the Amendments to the Constitution and relevant civil rights legislation.

CANADIAN TRENDS ON SOVEREIGN IMMUNITY

As in the United States, much of Canada's legal system derives from British common law. That is, a system where legal judgments are informed by precedents established in cases rather than statutes enacted by a government. Nevertheless, changes in society and changes in various legal principles alter judgments and are the grounds to deviate from precedent. For the next few pages we will outline the basis for the erosion of sovereign immunity in Canada. In doing so, we rely heavily on *Fire Loss Litigation in Canada* (Hewitt, 1995).

ISSUES AFFECTING LITIGATION BEFORE 1980

Up until the 1980s, the behavior of most local governments and volunteer emergency organizations was protected from litigation by the principle of sovereign immunity. Nevertheless, when this principle was challenged, an important distinction was made between whether a local government had a **duty** to perform a service or had **power** to perform a service. Usually, the key phrase in any legislation was the distinction between "shall," implying a duty, and "may," implying a power. For example, imagine if a fire chief of a community were to fail to protect evidence at a fire scene resulting in a failure to link a manufacturer with a faulty stove and a building loss. As a result, the building owner's insurance company is unable to sue for damages (i.e., the owner's claim) from the manufacturer. Consequently, the insurance company sues the fire chief. The insurance company argues that the fire chief had a duty of care to protect evidence in his or her capacity as the local assistant to the fire marshal of the province. The insurance company quotes that the provincial fire prevention act requires that the fire chief **shall** preserve evidence on the origin of a fire. As such, the insurance company argues that the fire chief breached a duty of care by failing to preserve that evidence. The insurance company sues the fire chief and the province (not the local government) since the chief was acting in his or her provincial role as local assistant to the fire marshal. Under these conditions, assuming the facts of the case are proven in support of the insurance company, the lawsuit would likely be awarded in favor of the plaintiff, the insurance company.

Conversely, let us consider a case where the legislation guiding behavior is permissive. An owner calls the local government's fire department reporting a fire in his house. Through a series of errors the fire department does not arrive until 15 minutes after the owner's call. As a result, the house is destroyed and the insurance company, considering the fire department negligent, sues the local government for damages. The local government responds in court that it had no duty to provide fire protection to its residents. Rather, the local government argues that any local government **may** establish a fire protection force. Since the local government did not have a **duty** of care, despite its admitted negligent acts, then the local government maintains its sovereign immunity. The judge agrees with the local government.

Until the 1980s, such a defense by a local government would likely have been successful in Canada; however, several events over the last twenty years or so have led to a change in the prevailing legal opinion. Now, a local government would not likely be granted sovereign immunity. Let us explore these changes.

The first change has its origins in Britain in a case decided in the House of Lords in 1977, *Anns v. the Borough of Merton* (Hewitt, 1995). The reader might wonder why a British case should affect Canadian law. Whereas Canadian courts are not required to follow British legal decision, there is, nevertheless, a tendency to respect such decisions. In the 1960s, the London Borough of Merton oversaw the construction of a block of apartment buildings. Despite plans that specified a deeper foundation, the actual foundation was too shallow. Moreover, the Borough's surveyor approved the apartment building despite the shallow foundation. Over the next few years, cracks appeared and floors tilted. The current owner sought damages from the Borough of Merton. As might be expected, the Borough of Merton argued that the statute to inspect was discretionary and thus the Borough had the **power** to inspect, not a **duty** to inspect. The court, however, held the Borough as liable, arguing that the distinction between a power to inspect and a duty to inspect was unimportant. Rather, the court maintained that so long as the Borough, acting as a "reasonable man," could contemplate doing harm by allowing an improper foundation, then it is liable for damages.

The second change was the Constitution Act of 1982 in Canada. At this time, the Canadian Government and the ten provinces finally agreed on how they would amend the constitution of Canada described in that Act and the British North America Act, which formed Canada in 1867. Included in the Constitution Act is a Charter of Rights and Freedoms analogous to the Bill of Rights in the American Constitution. This promulgation of the Act suddenly increased the interpretive powers of the Supreme Court of Canada. Any existing legislation could be challenged for its consistency with the charter. As a result, the Supreme Court of Canada assumed a more aggressive role.

In the early 1980s, the Supreme Court of Canada ruled that local governments were indeed liable using the same reasoning as the House of Lords in its ruling on *Anns v. London Borough of Merton*. However, the most significant ruling of the Supreme Court of Canada was in *Laurentide Motel v. Ville de (City of) Beauport* (Hewitt, 1995) in Quebec.

In 1982, a motel guest in the Laurentide Motel in Beauport Quebec carelessly started a fire in his motel room. The alarm was sounded and the Ville de Beauport's Fire Department responded. The firefighters had difficulty "hooking up" to the fire hydrant and, just as the fire was nearly extinguished using water from the pumper's tank, the water supply was exhausted. This would not normally be a problem except that, owing to the bitter cold, the hydrant was frozen. The fire rekindled and was not extinguished until an entire wing of the motel was destroyed. The ensuing litigation was adjudicated and appealed until it reached the Supreme Court of Canada in 1989. As expected, the Ville de Beauport argued that since it has a power to suppress fires, not a duty, it therefore did not breach a duty during its fire suppression because of its failure to inspect the hydrant in question. The Supreme Court, however, used the precedent of *Anns v. London Borough of Merton* in its reasoning. The Supreme Court found for the plaintiff, Laurentide Motel, and ordered the Ville de Beauport to pay over $1.5 million in damages.

As Hewitt (1995) reports, only a year later in 1990, the British House of Lords, reversing itself on its earlier decision in *Anns*, declined to pursue the expansion of public authority liability that had originated with the *Anns* case. This led to speculation that the Supreme Court of Canada might do so as well. In 1991, it had an opportunity to do so but chose not to. As Hewitt puts it, "the vestiges of *Anns* are here to stay" (Hewitt, 1995: pp. 5-21).

The Policy Loophole

At this point, it is clear that in Canada a local government's use of sovereign immunity as a defense for the negligent actions of its employees is likely to fail. Indeed, lawyers say that local governments can be vicariously liable because they have the right to direct their employees. In effect, a council ought to foresee how the actions it directs through its employees will impinge on its citizens. Does this mean then that all communities must have working fire hydrants? After all, if the Ville de Beauport can be sued for having a frozen fire hydrant why cannot thousands of Canadian local governments be sued for not having fire hydrants at all?

The Canadian legal system has addressed these questions by differentiating decisions that are a matter of policy from decisions which are operational. Those decisions, which are matters of policy, include such issues as the level of service, the type of service, the annual budget, by-laws, minutes of council meetings, and master plans. These are the typical formats where policy is found. Councillors, the CAO, and local government department heads usually make such policy decisions. Those decisions, which are operational, are typically day-to-day dealings with response to alarms, training, dispatching, personnel issues, bookkeeping, inspections, and prevention programming. Typically, those decisions are found on tapes, logs, daily reports, incident reports, and grievance reports. Operational decisions are often made by fire chiefs, EMS squad captains, incident commanders, inspectors, trainers, and even EMTs, paramedics, or firefighters. While policy decisions are usually made by those occupying positions of authority in the municipality, it is important to note that the courts distinguish policy from operational decisions based on the nature of the decision itself, not simply on the status of the decision maker in the hierarchy.

Essentially the courts argue that policy issues, on one hand, are the concern of politicians, not judges. The courts reason that voters will hold politicians accountable for their own policy decisions. On the other hand, the court has a role in ensuring that operational decisions are held accountable to civil law. This line of reasoning suggests that local governments can divest themselves of any involvement in activities that are discretionary, thereby reducing the risk of liability. For example, a local government could disband its fire department because no provincial law requires that a fire department exist. In this fashion, it should not be held legally responsible since any subsequent fire protection would not be linked with the local government. This course of action might very well reduce the risk of liability, but most voters would regard such a policy decision as irresponsible, probably punishing the local politicians at the next election.

What is more realistic, however, is to define an acceptable level of service (say a certain magnitude of response within a certain response time for 95% of responses) and to develop a planning, budgeting, and staffing level accordingly. The other strategies, which manage the level of risk from liability, will be presented below.

Local Government's Liability Resulting From Volunteers' Actions

At this stage, we have determined that the local government can be sued for negligence arising from the operational decisions and subsequent behavior of its employees. What arises if the fire department or EMS squad contains volunteers? What arises if the volunteer emergency organization is indeed an entirely separate organization operating under a contract with, or receiving a grant from, the local government?

Part of the answer to these questions is Hewitt's response:

While a person is responsible for his own acts or omissions by reason of the principle of personal or direct liability, a third party might also be responsible for that person's transgressions through the principle of vicarious or indirect liability. Vicarious liability is simply the liability of one party for the actionable conduct of another. It arises in several types of relationships...

In Canada, most volunteer fire departments are created and controlled by the municipalities they protect and as such, the municipality will be vicariously liable for the negligence of its firefighters. (Hewitt, 1995: pp.6-27)

However, as Hewitt points out, this is not always the case. Some Canadian volunteer departments are separately incorporated and do not operate under the direction or control of the municipalities they serve. In such situations, the municipality is unlikely to be held liable for the negligent acts or omissions of its firefighters. As we have already seen, sovereign immunity appears to be dying, albeit a slow death, in both Canada and the United States. The cases that were examined in the United States included a number of volunteer fire departments claiming sovereign immunity despite their often negligent actions. Judging from the ambiguous outcome of the decision of many courts, it seems that the linkage between the volunteer organization and the local government was sometimes tenuous. Similarly in Canada, while few cases have addressed the relationship between local government and its volunteer fire departments, the relationship between the two is often ill-defined.

Can a local government control a volunteer emergency organization operating within its boundaries as an independent contractor? While technically the answer is "yes," it may be difficult to change existing relationships. A local government could choose to end its contract when it expires or abolishes its grant unless a volunteer emergency organization were to comply with its wishes. Doing so, however, might be "political suicide." Thus, it may well be that local governments are caught in a difficult situation.

The local government can no longer claim sovereign immunity as an absolute defense in all situations. Thus, it can be held liable. Local government often does not choose to control or provide direction to the volunteer emergency organizations within its boundaries; yet these volunteer emergency organizations may, by their actions, make the local government liable. This outcome is more and more likely as:

1. Standards for EMS and fire service behavior rise (Hewitt, 1995).

2. The standard of the "reasonable man" rises as training and education improve (Hewitt, 1995).

3. Insurance companies are more likely to sue so as to reduce their own expenses (Hewitt, 1995).

4. The local government (backed by the province) has a "deeper pocket" than a volunteer emergency organization. That is, there is little point in suing for damages from those organizations that are poor or have limited liability coverage.[3]

5. Economic forces in Canada may be another factor motivating the increase in lawsuits against the fire service. Sometimes, the impetus comes from the legal community which is experiencing a downturn in some of the more lucrative types of litigation that were available a decade ago. Also, many insurance companies are looking for ways to recover payments they make as a consequence of fire losses.

THE RESURRECTION OF COMMON SENSE

Countering these tendencies is an extremely recent decision made by the Supreme Court of Newfoundland (*Hammond and Hammond v. the Town of Wabana and Winston Kitchen et al.*, Orsborn, 1995). On February 16, 1988 at 7:45 p.m., the Wabana Volunteer Fire Department (Fire Chief Winston Kitchen) responded to a call where smoke was detected at the Wabana Bargain Centre. Despite attempts to knock down the fire, the fire spread from the fully involved Wabana Bargain Centre to the plaintiffs' adjacent buildings by 11:00 p.m. The plaintiffs, Benedict and Eileen Hammond, contended that better judgment on the part of Fire Chief Winston Kitchen would have prevented any damage to their property. In particular, the Hammonds argued that Chief Kitchen failed to engage in aggressive interior attack, failed to ventilate the Wabana Bargain Centre, and failed to call for mutual aid until it was too late.

Clearly, damages to the plaintiffs had occurred. Moreover, the Town of Wabana (perhaps mindful of the outcome of *Laurentides v. Beauport*) was willing to accept vicarious liability for the actions of the Wabana Volunteer Fire Department. Thus, a duty of care was established. What was at issue was: Had Chief Kitchen violated the standard of care by his actions or inactions as identified by the Hammonds?

---

[3]Deep Pocket: In other words, a lot of money! Since plaintiffs and their lawyers seek financial compensation, then it makes sense to name respondents who have the money to pay the compensation.

In answering this question, Judge Orsborn (1995) argued that the level of the standard of care must take into account the resources the community of Wabana had. Quoting from the judgment is useful here:

A volunteer fire department provides an ongoing source of assurance for residents of the community. It is an assurance that goes very much to an individual's basic needs — security and safety of the person. The law should not act as a deterrent to those who, for no benefit or compensation, are prepared to put themselves at risk to help in providing this assurance. Nor, without compelling reason, should the law establish for such an activity a standard of conduct which departs from the legitimate expectations of the community. A standard of "due care" or "the ordinary volunteer firefighter" is too high. While one may well be prepared to be judged by comparison to the reasonable person when driving one's car down the road, the flexibility, and, indeed, uncertainty of the standard may dissuade an individual from volunteering his or her time, without compensation, to undertake an inherently risky activity for the benefit of others. An additional degree of protection is warranted; the law should facilitate the desire to help the residents of one's community, even though reflecting the overall community interest in maintaining the service may, in individual cases, preclude the recovery of compensation for deficient service. On the other hand, the standard should not be so low as to excuse conduct which, because of inattention to basic principles, actively worsens the situation and adds to the damage.

Taking into the account the inherently risky nature of the activity, the interests of society as a whole in encouraging and supporting voluntary efforts directed to the preservation of life and safety, and the legitimate expectations of a community serviced by a volunteer fire department, my conclusion is as follows: the standard expected of a volunteer fire department and its members is that, with the resources available to them, they will do their best to put the fire out. A *bona fide* decision or action will not be open to question unless it causes the worsening of the fire and is a substantial departure from the basic principles of firefighting.

...Although they were not successful, their efforts did nothing to make the situation worse. Their conduct did not fall short of the standard required of volunteer firefighters by the law. (Orsborn, 1995: pp. 81-83)

Orsborn concluded that there was no evidence to support a violation of the standard of care. However, just as clearly, the judge argues that that standard of care must be lower where the lack of resources prevent adherence to a higher standard. Otherwise there would exist a disincentive to volunteer which would leave the community in a more precarious position. While this case is encouraging for rural volunteer departments and the local governments they serve, it is not a decision that is binding on any court in Canada, even the court in which it was decided. If this case is upheld on appeal, or if it is followed in other Canadian courts, it might have some interesting implications. For example, if, as in the case appears to suggest, the standard of care is a function of the resources of the community, then most rural volunteer fire departments are "off the hook." This could be a relief for rural local governments in Canada. However, volunteers are also found in suburban communities where, following this decision, the standard of care will be higher. The legal position of volunteer fire departments and the local governments they serve is still unfolding in Canada and only time will provide clearer answers to these issues.

THE EFFECT OF LIABILITY ON THE VEO/LOCAL GOVERNMENT RELATIONSHIP

In the next section we will elaborate upon strategies that volunteer emergency organizations and local governments might employ to reduce the risk of a lawsuit as well as any damages which might ensue from an unfavorable judgment. At this stage, let us consider how the status quo can induce inter-organizational conflict. Recall that A has power over B to the extent that A affects B's interests. Local government B has an interest in not being sued; yet volunteer emergency organization A can affect B whether or not B is sued. Thus, the volunteer emergency organization has power over the local government now that sovereign immunity is no longer a defense in Canada. The reader will recall that when an organization is dependent on another organization it can alter the relationship. For instance, a local government could contract out the volunteer emergency service to another provider. It could offer an inducement to lower the risk of liability (such as money for the development of a risk management program). It could decide that it no longer needs the service, (for example, it let the barns burn), or it could punish the volunteer emergency organization unless it "gets its act together" and establishes a risk management program. Of these four alternatives, only the second one — offering an inducement — will reduce conflict. The other three are likely to increase conflict. Facing fiscal pressures, local governments are unlikely to be able to afford to "bribe" the volunteer emergency organization. Thus, conflict is even more likely.

PRACTICAL STRATEGIES TO CONSIDER IN BOTH COUNTRIES

Questions A Local Government Might Ask

Q. *How does the local government avoid being sued as a consequence of a volunteer emergency organization's actions or inactions?*

A. The local government encourages a risk management program in concert with the volunteer emergency organizations. The local government also sets policies in consultation with volunteer emergency organizations, addressing the type and extent of service it can afford.

Q. *What do we do if the local government is sued?*

A. An American county or city can likely appeal to the sovereign immunity defense; however, that defense is being eroded. Moreover, whereas such a defense might work in a court of law, it will not likely work in the "court of public opinion." That "court" might render its judgment on election day. On the one hand, a Canadian local government does not have the luxury of sovereign immunity. On the other hand, Canadian litigation is less frequent, and awards to plaintiffs tend to be lower. Once again, the "court of public opinion" may be harsher still.

Questions A Volunteer Emergency Organization Might Ask

Q. *How does the volunteer emergency organization avoid being sued as a consequence of members' actions or inactions?*

A. The volunteer fire department or rescue squad develops a risk management program in concert with other such organizations and the local government (see below).

Q. *What do we do if the volunteer emergency organization is sued?*

A. Litigation, although serious, nevertheless remains improbable. While there are nearly 100 cases pending in Canada, we remember there are over 5000 fire departments. Thus, only 2% (100/5000) of the departments at any one time face a possible lawsuit. In turn, most of these will settle out of court. For these reasons, the **perceived** probability is greater in the volunteer department than is perceived by the local government. Moreover, the local government is far more likely to believe that the volunteer organization is using "scare tactics" in order to ensure a larger grant or contract.

It is for this reason that any risk management program must be jointly conducted by both parties. After all, this method allows government personnel and volunteers to appreciate the operational risks to the government. If a particular risk is too large and too costly to correct, the local government can address an adjusted level of service as a policy question. Once volunteer organizations recognize this option then "scare tactics" will be just as likely to backfire.

Risk Management

Risk management is primarily a program to prevent being sued. It is a process of identifying risks, assigning priorities to risk planning so as to reduce the risk, implementing the plan and monitoring the plan, and modifying it or implementing it as necessary. The amount of effort in establishing a risk management program is considerable. Fortunately, with a few exceptions, most of that effort is the labor of the local government and the volunteer emergency organization. Moreover, the consequence is to increase safety within the volunteer emergency organization, a consequence desired by all. However, it is misleading to assume that all safety measures correspond to risk management. For example, an affirmative action program (employment equity in Canada) may not increase safety; nevertheless, the improper application of such a program may lead to a lawsuit.

The first step is to identify those risks which face a volunteer emergency organization. Typically, these risks relate to any one of personnel issues, including operations, safety, and training. Useful sources include: OSHA legislation, health and safety acts and regulations, industry standards such as NFPA 1500, NFPA 1403, and training standards. Invariably, discussions with the local government solicitor are useful. Learning from discussion will occur on both sides.

Once identification is completed (at least on the first iteration) many risk management committees consider the list daunting. Consequently, assigning priorities to risk are necessary, given the dwindling resources such as time and money.

How is this done? Essentially, each risk is ranked in terms of severity and probability of occurrence. The local government solicitor should be able to provide some research on awards in lawsuits (usually in the $50,000 to $5 million range). The probability of occurrence can be estimated from both the nature of the lawsuits **and** the distribution claims made by the insurance company. The Insurance Bureau of Canada may be useful here, as well as the Insurance Advisory Organization (IAO) or Insurance Services Office (ISO). In the absence of reliable external information, an average estimate made by the committee is a reasonable approach. Assigning priorities for action partly depends upon the combination of severity and probability of occurrence. For example, an automobile accident is far more probable than litigation on a hazardous materals incident. However, the consequence of faulty response to the hazardous materials incident is far greater. Clearly, risks which are more probable **and** severe in consequence should achieve highest attention. However, two other factors have to be considered as well. The next factor to consider is cost, both in terms of actual expenditures (consultants, repairs, and training cost) and the amount of time required. Recognizing the limit to volunteer time is no easy task. Finally, the risk management committee should consider what other volunteer emergency organizations are doing as well. For example, if most departments in the fire service are complying with a higher standard for apparatus driver qualifications, then failure to mimic other departments could be disastrous should a road accident occur. The plaintiff's lawyer will undoubtedly point out this deficiency in preparation for a trial.

Once priorities have been assigned based on the four criteria mentioned above, the appropriate corrective measures (repairs, training, equipment purchase, and SOPs) can be developed. Once this is done, monitoring is necessary. Indeed, recertification may be required (such as CPR). The committee's work may reduce, perhaps two years after its inception. Nevertheless, monitoring legal trends and the risk management programs implemented elsewhere will be necessary.

If a risk is probable, severe, and costly to address, then both the volunteer organization and the local government (be it county, town, or city) must seek a different kind of solution. This solution requires council to define the limits on the kind of protection it can afford. For example, a small community might not be able to provide protection to a large factory. If it cannot, the by-laws of the local government can exclude it. Conversely, that same local government might require that the factory's management establish an industrial fire brigade of its own workers. Also, the local government's by-law could require that the level of service provided by the factory fire brigade comply with NFPA 600 (standards on industrial fire brigades).

In effect, local government council is setting policy which defines the limits of what it can do. Clearly, these limits must be set in consultation with the various volunteer emergency organizations within its political boundaries. These operational standards would be much greater if, to use our example, the volunteer fire department had to protect the factory as well.

This great load of work, often unfamiliar to many officers in volunteer emergency organizations, may be very daunting. Therefore, let us consider ways to make the work more palatable.

NFPA 1500 is the code phrase for the *Standard on Fire Department Occupational Safety and Health* (1992h). In particular, the 1992 edition included a comprehensive checklist as an appendix to the document. In all, there are 16 pages of items in the worksheet at the end of the standard, referenced in accordance with the standard. In response to each item, the department can identify the degree of compliance and the expected compliance date. And it is possible to estimate the cost of compliance.

One of the earlier publications is still a very useful one. The Justice Institute of British Columbia (1988) has succinctly presented the theory on the application of risk management to the fire service. Aside from presenting some of the criteria to prioritize risks that we presented above, this book presents a series of issues (questions) to be considered by officers within a fire department, legal council for any local government, chief administrative officers, and insurance agents underwriting local government risks. Finally, the Justice Institute presents a series of steps (16 in all) that can be taken immediately in any fire department. It is a very brief, two-page presentation appropriate to post on a bulletin board for all members to read.

Most readable is *The Volunteer Chief's Guide to Avoiding the Hot Seat* (Davis, 1994). This publication assigns priorities to the items identified by NFPA 1500. It recognizes the labor shortage confronting most volunteer departments, proposing three categories of fire scene volunteers. (These three categories will be addressed in Chapter 5.)

THE STANDARDS DRAGONS

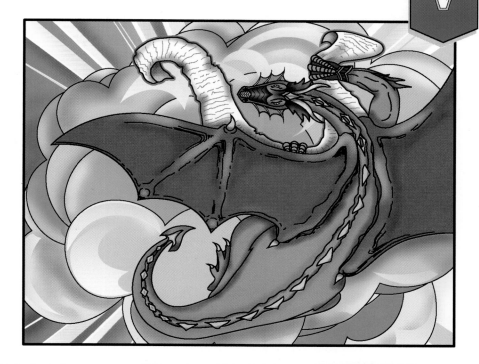

V

A FICTITIOUS BUT PLAUSIBLE CONVERSATION

We overhear a telephone conversation between Training Officer Rural of the Tradition Volunteer Fire Department and Deputy Fire Marshal Urban from the mythical state/province of Manippi. (The reason for selecting these names for persons and places will become evident in the next section.)

Rural: Hello Urban, I just called to see whether I could use an abandoned structure and burn it to train our volunteer firefighters in Tradition. I heard somewhere that there might be a problem. It might violate standards.

Urban: Well, *NFPA 1403* (1992g)[1] significantly restricts the conducting of live burns for training purposes. There have been too many deaths during live fire training in the last several years. It was for the reason of safety that NFPA 1403 was developed. We strongly discour-

---

[1]This is *NFPA 1403: Live Fire Training Evolutions* (1992g); see bibliography for full reference.

age you from conducting your own live burns for training purposes. We recommend you use the Manippi Fire Academy to train your volunteers.

Rural: But that's a six-hour drive from Tradition to the fire academy. It will also cost our department a lot of money to pay the tuition for the course. You may want safe training, but what about unsafe working fires? The best way I can prepare these volunteers is to give them the training, even if it is in a substandard building, that, nevertheless, will teach them what to do in a structural fire.

Urban: I understand your position, Rural, but you have to understand ours. We can't recommend that you violate NFPA standards. If anything at the live burn goes wrong, you probably will be sued along with your department and the village.

Rural: But you leave me with no affordable alternative.

Urban: Why don't you get your chief to convince the town to raise taxes to increase your budget to pay for the appropriate training of your volunteers. Otherwise, you could reshuffle your financial priorities.

Rural: Our budget is bare bones already. If we reshuffled our budget, we would not be able to buy the bunker gear we need, and we'd remain in violation of NFPA 1500 (1992h)[2] on departmental safety.

Urban: Don't you see we're trying to help you? We want you to convince your village that the Tradition Volunteer Fire Department must comply with nationally (even internationally) recognized standards. Otherwise, a lawsuit may be just around the corner.

Rural: I understand that, but I have to convince our department. We're not called Tradition for nothing. A lot of my fellow volunteers just see these standards as a scam to be forced to purchase new apparatus and equipment from big city manufacturers. Everybody knows it's those big city people who sit on NFPA standard committees. They may want safety, but only if it lines their wallets.

---

[2]This is *NFPA 1500: Fire Department Occupational Safety and Health Program* (1992h); see bibliography for full reference.

Urban: No, I can't agree with that. You have to understand that standards have to fit about 32,000 fire departments in the U.S. alone. What applies to Tradition also applies to Metropolis.

Rural: That's one of our problems. Those big city boys develop the rules, and you guys in the fire marshal's office adopt them. We'd be better off in Tradition if fire service standards never existed.

RURAL RESENTMENT

Most training officers in the traditional rural volunteer department (Type 1)[3] can identify with Training Officer Rural in the fictitious conversation above. Many social scientists have observed and documented the resentment that many rural citizens feel about the domination of big city institutions that make decisions that affect their lives. Indeed, a quotation from a famous study of small town life is particularly illuminating:

> Governmental, business, religious and educational super bureaucracies far distant from the rural town formulate policies to which the rural world can respond only with resentment. (Vidich and Bensman, 1968: p. 323)

This attitude is a common one expressed against the decision makers who are always found elsewhere. The same attitudes often exist in cities as well, except that in cities the resentment is focused on **who** the decision makers are, not **where** the decision makers are. The small population of rural local governments permits easy access by anyone to the local decision maker. Unfortunately, it soon becomes evident that most local decision makers also have little power. Even the local decision makers, such as those found in local government, schools, or even local volunteer fire departments, recognize their powerlessness. The following quotation suggests the pervasiveness of powerlessness:

> Small communities have a sense of powerlessness in relation to national institutions and provincial bureaucracies. The proverbial "they" (referring to city institutions and corporations) may be blamed for almost every problem in a town or village. This attitude is not

---

[3]The reader will recall that a Type 1 volunteer emergency organization is independent from local government, fully volunteer, and only engaged in fire suppression as opposed to only engaging in rescue/EMS or mixing the two services. For a detailed discussion see Chapter Two.

*limited to the common citizen; it is shared equally by local power
wielders. (Hodge and Qadeer, 1983: p. 137)*

This resentment of the big city might forge a common bond between a volunteer fire department and a local government. As we saw
in Chapter Three, just as a fight with local government can unite the
coalitions within a volunteer fire department, so a fight with the distant fire marshal's office and, the even more distant, standards makers
can unite the volunteer fire department with local government.

However, as our fictitious conversation suggests, the alliances are
not so simple. Deputy Fire Marshal Urban was trying to form an alliance with the Tradition Fire Department to convince the local government in Tradition to spend its money to enhance their safety by meeting NFPA standards. On one hand, fire marshals' offices (FMO), after
all, have an interest in fire departments complying with standards, but
they do not have the full means to ensure that compliance. In some
states and provinces, the fire marshal's office will contribute significantly
to apparatus purchasing made by the local government or the volunteer fire department. This contribution gives them leverage (power)
over the local governments and the volunteer fire departments. Consequently, the fire marshal's office can ensure a greater degree of compliance with standards.[4] On the other hand, other FMOs do not have
the resources to make such contributions toward apparatus purchasing. These FMOs are far more likely to form alliances with volunteer
fire departments by "ganging up" on the respective local governments
to provide the funding to ensure increased compliance with standards.

Returning to our fictitious conversation for an illustration of this
point, Deputy Fire Marshal Urban was trying to enlist the support of
Training Officer Rural to persuade the village of Tradition to spend more
money on the Tradition Volunteer Fire Department. The question of
the legitimacy of standards complicates the attempt at an alliance. If
standards makers have an image of being in a conflict of interest (as
some rural volunteer firefighters often suggest), then convincing local
government to spend money to ensure compliance is more difficult.
Moreover, the recent presence of what appears to be a competing set of
standards developed by the Alliance for Fire and Emergency Management questions the appropriateness of some of the NFPA standards,

---

[4]For example, some FMOs that contribute to apparatus purchasing require that a certain
number, or proportion, of volunteers meet Firefighter Level I training outlined in *NFPA Standard
1001: Fire Fighter Professional Qualifications* (1992e); see bibliography for full reference.

particularly those standards relevant to volunteer fire departments. In order to understand the impact standard setting has on the attitudes of volunteers in traditional rural fire departments, we need to discuss the standards setting process.

THE SETTING OF STANDARDS

The principal standards setting body remains the National Fire Protection Association (NFPA). The NFPA is not an arm of government. Rather, its origins are in Boston from the insurance industry and the infant sprinkler industry in 1895 and 1896. Clearly, adherence to a higher standard of fire protection will reduce fire losses and, thus, reduce claims payable by fire insurers. As such, the insurance industry has an interest in the setting of high standards and the enforcement of these standards.

In all, NFPA has produced about 280 different sets of standards related to ensuring fire and electrical safety and other fire service subjects, such as apparatus specifications and training. Since these standards relate to many technical matters — for example, *NFPA 36: Solvent Extraction* (1992a); *NFPA 211: Chimneys, Fireplaces, Vents* (1992b); *NFPA 1901: Pumper Fire Apparatus* (1992j) — usually engineers and manufacturers dominate many committees. On technical matters where the tasks are analyzable and where measurement error is low, standard enforcement is more likely. For example, a fire chief purchasing a pumper may ask the manufacturer to provide a quote consistent with specifications derived from NFPA 1901. Accurately written specifications and signed contracts are usually sufficient to ensure compliance. Conversely, standards related to personnel or organizational performance tend to be more vague. Moreover, compliance also tends to be more vague as well.

Unfortunately, as we have seen when examining legal issues in Chapter Four, it is precisely these vague standards that are being addressed in case law. Thus, these cases provide the impetus for changing the standard. One result of case law was the initiation of the NFPA 1500 standard on the safety of firefighters and fire departments.

However, before we consider standard setting for NFPA 1500, let us consider the standards setting process in general. The following description relies heavily on *NFPA Standards and You* (NFPA, 1995b), graciously and expeditiously supplied to us by Steve Foley of the NFPA. The heart of the process is the technical committee. Technical committees work on a host of NFPA standards ranging from sprinklers to aerials to officer qualifications, to name merely three of about 280 subjects. Each technical committee is drawn from the following classifications:

users,
manufacturers,
enforcers,
testers/researchers,
experts,
insurers,
installers/maintainers,
consumers, and
labor (sometimes career, sometimes volunteer).

Although not all classifications are likely to be on any one committee, no more than one third of the committee members will come from any one classification. About every three to five years, the existing standard enters a revision cycle. This revision cycle is as follows:

1. The technical committee notifies the Standards Council of the intent to begin a revision cycle (week 1).

2. The NFPA publishes a request for proposals in various fire service trade publications, allowing about 23 weeks to submit proposals for revision.

3. The NFPA distributes the proposals received to the members of the technical committee. (Members of the technical committee may submit their own proposals as well.)

4. At about week 24, the technical committee meets and votes on each proposal to accept, accept in part/principle, reject, or hold for further study. The technical committee writes a report on proposals (ROP) that includes an explanation of any rejection or decision to hold for further study. The technical committee might meet more than once; indeed, the committee's response and report to proposals might take 26 weeks. One reason for this is that acceptance of any proposal requires an affirmative vote by at least two thirds of the committee members present.

5. For the next nine weeks (52-61) the ROP is distributed to all those who submitted proposals. During this time, the proposal writers can comment on the ROP.

6. From week 62 to week 92, the technical committee responds to the comments, developing the Report on Comments (ROC). The techni-

cal committee also prepares its final report for submission to the annual or fall meeting of the NFPA membership.

7. At these meetings the membership votes on the committee report. Those proposal writers whose proposals have **not** been accepted can raise the proposal on the floor of the meeting. A majority vote is sufficient to accept both the committee report and/or any proposal arising from the floor.

8. Following the meeting, the Standards Council of NFPA acts on the report of the technical committee, any proposals arising from the floor of the meeting, or any complaints arising from the process. Usually, the formal adoption of the revised standard occurs at this stage.[5]

The reader will see that any interested party is given ample opportunity for input into the committee. Moveover, given the consultative steps in the process and the varying interests within the technical committee, the room for debate, and sometimes controversy, is quite large.

For these reasons, we should not be surprised that many discussions within the technical committee result in compromises. This is particularly true when we recognize that the committee members often submit many of the proposals themselves, especially when we recall that a two thirds vote is necessary to accept any proposal. Indeed, technical committees are encouraged to seek a consensus where possible, which probably lies somewhere above a two thirds agreement but below unanimity.[6]

CONFLICT OVER CREW SIZE

Now let us consider the interests of one important committee addressing firefighter and fire department safety (*NFPA 1500: Fire Department Occupational Safety and Health Program*). This technical committee was recruited from the following sources:

[5]Appeals to the board of directors of NFPA can be made if the proposal writer, or anyone on the technical committee, questions the decision of the Standards Council. This is rare, although it did happen during the NFPA 1500 standards revision process.

[6]The NFPA definition of consensus is: "... in the judgement of the Standards Council of the NFPA, substantial agreement has been reached by materially affected interest categories. Substantial agreement means more than a simple majority, but not necessarily unanimity. Consensus requires that all views and objections be considered and that a concerted effort be made toward their resolution" (NFPA, 1995b: p. 7).

Metro fire chiefs

Protective clothing manufacturers

Underwriters Laboratories

International Association of Fire Fighters (IAFF)

Insurance industry

Combination departments

Volunteer departments

U.S. Fire Administration

NFPA

Satisfying all these interests by one standard is a virtually impossible task; thus, any standard represents a compromise so as to satisfy many competing interests. Ironically, the forces and processes are analogous to those facing the council of a local government.

We have already made reference to NFPA 1500 in the previous chapter. However, a brief description may be desirable, particularly for readers who are local government officials. The standard addresses the following areas:

1. Organizing for safety;

2. Training requirements for personnel;

3. Vehicle standards;

4. Protective clothing;

5. Emergency operations;

6. Fire station safety;

7. Medical and physical requirements; and

8. Member assistance programs.

NFPA 1500 refers to other standards, such as NFPA 472[7] on hazardous materials response or NFPA 1401[8] on training records. As such, the document is extremely comprehensive.

The development and publication of NFPA 1500 has engendered controversy among several groups within the fire service. These groups are:

---

[7]This is *NFPA 472: Hazardous Materials Responder Professional Competencies* (1992c); see bibliography for full reference.

[8]This is *NFPA 1401: Recommended Practice for Fire Service Training Reports and Records* (1989); see bibliography for full reference.

1. The urban fire chiefs essentially advocating the standard as is;

2. The volunteer fire chiefs, essentially advocating a different standard; and

3. The IAFF advocating the standard as long as it includes a requirement for at least four persons on each responding apparatus.

The IAFF has a mandate to maximize the compensation and benefits for its member firefighters. Faced with the possible downsizing of the large metropolitan fire departments resulting from fiscal constraint, the IAFF chose to resist this trend by addressing the safety violations that would arise from smaller companies (crews). Thus began the debate over crew size. During the development of NFPA 1500, the IAFF proposed that a four-person crew be the minimum standard for safety. This met resistance from other members of the committee, particularly urban fire chiefs operating in cities that already employ three- or fewer-person crews. The intrinsic merits of the issue as it relates to safety is difficult to argue. In general, more personnel is safer, but clearly a four-person crew is more costly than a three-person crew.[9]

Unfortunately, the intrinsic merits of the case were lost in the argument. In a rare occurrence, this NFPA standards committee was unable to develop a compromise. As a result, to the dismay of most, the IAFF resigned from the NFPA. However, the IAFF subsequently returned after much negotiation. Indeed, the Occupational Safety and Health Administration (OSHA) is regulating four-person crews at the moment

---

[9]Indeed, the International City Management Association (ICMA) has published various standards it deems appropriate for local governments. The ICMA fire standard states the following: "Fire manpower is sufficient to provide a minimum of *three* persons on each apparatus responding to a fire." However, in the standard's own commentary it states, wrongly, that "the NFPA standard calls for 4 men on each apparatus." In fact, NFPA 1500 only *recommends* in its appendix A-6-4.1, "a minimum acceptable fire company staffing level should be 4 members" (NFPA 1500, 1992h: p.40).

More to the point, however, is the fact that the ICMA will knowingly publish a standard below the level of NFPA 1500, undoubtedly conscious of the cost implications for local governments. In one sense, it can do so because the local governments often are the "authority having jurisdiction." The authority having jurisdiction is the governing body having legal responsibility for, and power over, the fire department's actions. Usually this is the local government; however, as we saw in the previous chapter, this is unclear when dealing with volunteer fire departments. Some states and provinces are redrafting legislation so as to make the fire marshal's office the "authority having jurisdiction." We doubt this will include exceeding the standards set out by NFPA.

[10]In the summer of 1995, the OSHA promulgated regulations requiring a four-person crew,

and it seems that the IAFF has won on a different battlefield.[10] Nevertheless, the NFPA 1500 standard spawned a second conflict as well.

CONFLICT OVER STANDARDS

To understand this second conflict we must study the reaction to the publication of NFPA 1500. The initial response to the publication of the standard varied. Byrne-Walsh and Wojcik (1990) interviewed 20 fire chiefs on their individual departments' responses toward the NFPA 1500 standard. As might be expected, all chiefs regarded the intent of the standard as admirable. It is, after all, hard to oppose safety. Moreover, some chiefs had already used "NFPA 1500 as a bargaining tool with their city councils — they used this nationally recognized standard to get needed equipment or staffing" (Byrne-Walsh and Wojcik, 1990: p. 44). Does this not remind you of the fictitious conversation that introduced this chapter?

Some chiefs of volunteer departments applauded the NFPA's concern for higher standards of all types. Nevertheless, the fire chiefs' responses were not uniformly positive. Many smaller career and volunteer departments had difficulty scheduling when complete compliance would be achieved owing to budgetary constraints. In many volunteer departments, the training requirements were believed to compromise the available time a volunteer had. This constraint led to criticisms that NFPA 1500 is a "big city" standard. In effect, if volunteers are going to invest more hours training, then the training should be relevant to their needs.

Essentially, this is the response made by the Alliance for Fire and Emergency Management (The Alliance). The Alliance maintains that "the 'one size fits all' fire service standards are not working and never will" (Davis, 1995: p. 62). Essentially, The Alliance argues that:

---

except when a smaller crew believes that victims are in the kind of danger requiring the need of firefighters to provide rescue, such as when a victim is in a burning house (Davis, 1995). This requirement may not be the victory the IAFF would want. It may be that this regulation will force local governments to recruit volunteers to provide the additional personnel rather than hire these additional personnel.

Conversely, the election of a Republican Congress in November of 1994 led to a proposed legislation that will prevent one government from passing regulations that require expenditure of another government. If this legislation is passed, then the OSHA regulation may be overturned. (To follow this debate, see Bruno's columns in *Firehouse*, Bruno, 1995a, 1995b, 1995c, and 1995d.) Once again, **one** way to comply with both this proposed legislation and the OSHA regulation is to use volunteers. This strategy is elaborated upon in Chapter Ten.

1. NFPA 1001(1992a) and NFPA 1500 did not address the impoverished reality of many volunteer fire departments;

2. NFPA 1582 (1995a) was a difficult medical standard to attain.

These arguments are similar to the reaction Byrne-Walsh and Wojcik (1990) found, as presented earlier. However, not all organizations containing volunteer firefighting criticized the NFPA. Indeed, the National Volunteer Fire Council has supported one, and only one standard, and that is the NFPA standard (Stittleburg, 1995). Nevertheless, in the summer of 1995, the Standards Cabinet of The Alliance passed the following alternative standards:

2001 Volunteer Fire Department Organization & Operation (1995f)

201 Performance Standard for Volunteer Fire Department Suppression Personnel (1995a)

502 Performance Standard for Incident Scene Safety Officer (1995b)

601 Performance Standard for Demonstrator (1995c)

602 Performance Standard for Educator (1995d)

603 Performance Standard for Trainer (1995e)

The Alliance standards employ much of the reasoning employed in the NFPA standards for industrial fire brigades (NFPA 600, 1992d). A major concern in the development of a volunteer firefighter standard was to analyze the tasks involved at various levels of firefighting and then train individuals to these levels. Thus, only those trained and competent would engage in the most challenging work: interior structural firefighting. The fire ground was divided into hot, warm, and cold zones in a fashion analogous to hazardous materials operations. The hot zone, the interior of the building on fire, could only be entered once exacting questions were addressed, including the competence of the entry team member. That entry team member should be trained to a standard at least equal to Firefighter Level I, as defined by NFPA 1001 (the Alliance for Fire and Emergency Management, 1995a; NFPA 1001, 1992e). The Alliance accepted a lower standard for those who engage only in exterior activities, including exterior attack (the warm zone). Finally, The Alliance defined the support member who neither enters the hot zone, nor engages in exterior attack, but provides essential support for fire suppression, such as air bottle changing or pump operation (the cold zone).

On one hand, dividing the role of firefighter into entry team member, exterior team member, and support member allows for the use of personnel who do not meet the standards specified in NFPA 1001. On the other hand, personnel who do engage in interior attack (the entry team members) are at least as competent as Firefighter I as defined by NFPA 1001. The Alliance Standard for Volunteer Fire Suppression Personnel also includes "menus" whereby volunteers may be required to demonstrate proficiency using certain equipment, if and only if the volunteers' department possesses that equipment. Similarly, The Alliance standard requires demonstrations of knowledge of the local community. For example, consider the following:

1. For Support Members:

    3-4.1.14 Identify and explain each of the service area-specific hazards within the service area that the department serves (Alliance, 1995a).

- or -

2. For Entry Team Members:

    6-4.11.5 If a standpipe system has been installed within the service area, explain how to ensure that an adequate water supply is available for the entry team to perform interior fire suppression operations (Alliance, 1995a).

This "menu" approach increases flexibility, but it lowers standardization. Many working with The Alliance argue that this is not as serious a loss for volunteers, unlike career firefighters who might wish to change jobs moving to different areas and different fire departments.

The Alliance standards and the NFPA standards reflect the interests of the different constituents of each organization. Those volunteers who support The Alliance want a menu of standards that can be readily adapted to their supposedly unique situations. For example, a volunteer fire department in D'Escousse, Nova Scotia, sees no need to develop skills in operating aerial apparatus (no buildings are higher than two stories). Conversely, that same department requires skill in fund-raising, volunteer recruiting, and water transport — skills not needed in large urban areas. To be fair, it can be argued that nothing prevents the rural volunteer from learning such administrative skills right now. Nevertheless, many rural volunteers feel that their needs are being ignored. The notion that the merits of any organization or person must be judged according to particular circumstances is known as **particularism**.[11] This view is prevalent in rural areas where people have a wealth of information on the characteristics of their neighbors. When judgment is made based on particular circumstances, then the application of one group of criteria set at a certain standard is impossible.

Conversely, the tendency to evaluate people and organizations by applying one standard of rules is more highly valued in urban areas. This notion is called **universalism**.[12] Indeed, many social scientists argue that, because most urban dwellers are strangers to each other, the resulting unfamiliarity reduces an understanding of others; consequently, rules must be relatively objectively applied to judge others. Thus, the desirability of a single standard would be high. As a consequence, we should expect any standard setting body that represents large urban fire departments to be sensitive to the need for one and only one standard. From our opening converstaion at the beginning of this chapter, this is why Training Officer Rural did not want standardization to happen.

Even the National Volunteer Fire Council's (NVFC) argument champions universalism (Stittleburg, 1995). Thus, volunteer firefighting organizations do not have a common viewpoint. The saying, "the fire doesn't know who is career and who is a volunteer" is a typical response to those who advocate a single standard. The NVFC is fearful that a separate volunteer standard will seem to be (whether it actually is) an inferior standard, devaluing the worth of volunteers.

Given the rural-urban differences presented above, what is the position of suburban career, volunteer, or combination departments? To date we have not found any consistent position; nevertheless, we speculate that the suburban area may act as a mediator between the particularistic rural positions and the universalistic urban positions.

---

[11]Talcott Parsons, a significant social theorist, devised several polar opposites to describe the values found in various societies. Among these is the dimension known as particularism/universalism. The specific definitions Parsons provides are as follows:

Particularism: Expectation of active achievements relative to and/or on behalf of the particular relational context in which an actor is involved (Parsons, 1951: p. 102).

[12]*Universalism*:   The expectation of active achievements in accord with universal standards and generalized rules relative to other actors (Parsons, 1951: p. 102).

Despite the convoluted writing style of Parsons, his theory has had considerable influence on an understanding of differences between rural and urban values in the United States and Canada.

Conceivably, the tension might have always existed in the fire service between rural volunteer departments and metropolitan career ones. However, it is the threat of litigation that makes this tension acute. In particular, as we have seen, it was the development in 1987 of NFPA 1500 that has created the conditions which ignited the two-stage conflict: first, between urban fire chiefs and the IAFF, and second, between the NFPA and The Alliance.

TRAINING

We can ask: Does it matter whether there are two standards for volunteer firefighters when a significant number of volunteer fire departments do not meet either of them? At one time, the answer was probably not. However, there remain several issues to consider now and in the future. Obviously, as litigation increases, volunteer fire departments will feel pressure to meet a standard of care. They will wonder: which standard must be met?

The state or provincial training schools induce the greatest level of the change within volunteer fire departments. These schools train volunteers directly and train the training officers of volunteer fire departments. They, in turn, train volunteers within their own and other communities. Much of the training provided by these schools is done on an outreach basis in the volunteers' communities. This training is typically done to reach the first level of NFPA 1001 (standard known as Firefighter Level I.[13] (This standard of training is also the minium requirement for firefighters as specified by NFPA 1500.)

Most state and provincial training schools are attempting to provide this training despite the state and provincial funding restrictions they face. Indeed, in the United States and part of Canada, there is considerable evidence that many schools have broadened their funding by receiving a levy from the insurance industry, such as a small percentage of all insurance premiums paid by policy holders that are used for the training of firefighters (Monigold, 1995). The rationale here is that just as the insurance industry benefits most from fire protection, so it should pay to train firefighters.

We can now ask: How do these issues inform us about the relationship between volunteer fire departments and local governments? Both changes in law and the interpretation of law drive standard setting.

---

[13]This is *NFPA 1001: Fire Fighter Professional Qualifications* (1992e); see bibliography for full reference.

Similarly, standard setting drives the decisions arising from case law. Obviously, the more exacting a standard is, the more likely a breach of care will occur. Thus, negligence is more likely. Equally as significant is that higher standards alter the curriculum and increase the need for training at state or provincial fire training schools. These changes increase the need for, and the content of, a risk management program within the volunteer fire department. These changes also affect how much money the fire department will ask of its local government and the exposure to liability that local government faces. We can observe these effects in Figure 5.1:

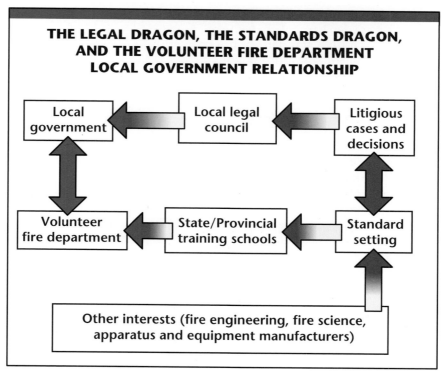

FIGURE 5.1

It is usually the local government that is the last to know and the first to pay. The operative word is **pay** because standard setting leads to increased risk of litigation and, therefore, increased expenditure to avoid this risk. Often, many local government officials feel that the money is "extorted" from them. It may be that each fire chief is saying:

"Give us money to protect the citizens of our community."

Unfortunately, the politician on council in local government often hears:

"Give us some money to protect us and you from litigation. If you don't give us the money to do this, then something bad might happen and we (both volunteer fire department and local government) will be sued."

To be fair, extortion implies the belief that failure to pay will result in increasing the probability that a bad thing will happen (as in a protection racket). Fortunately, no volunteer fire department wants a lawsuit and, also fortunately, local governments recognize this. In general, volunteer fire departments have not properly sold to local government the need for a high standard of fire protection. Recognizing this fact, let us consider the questions below.

QUESTIONS

Q. *Should local government be concerned about standards for the fire service?*

A. The answer is clearly, "yes!" The last chapter indicated a trend toward the erosion of sovereign immunity. Thus, a local government can be sued for the actions of the fire departments within its jurisdiction, even if little control over those fire departments is exercised. Any local government will have little influence on the standards setting process, but it can have influence on the fire departments within its boundaries. For example, if a local government has little relationship with these departments now, it can influence them to enhance risk management by underwriting a portion of the cost.

Q. *Should a local government believe the local volunteer fire chief when the threat of litigation is raised?*

A. The answer is unclear. First of all, despite the trends, the likelihood of a lawsuit is very low. It is rather the very negative consequences of lawsuit that forces prudent thought about the issue. It may be thought that the fire marshal's office and the local fire departments are in collusion to spend local government monies. However, even if this were true, both of these parties would be responding to a North American process of increasing fire service standards. Perhaps the wisest act is not only to pay heed to what the local chiefs are saying but also obtain advice from the fire marshal's office (or possibly a consultant). They can assist the local government and the local fire departments to develop a sound plan of risk management.

Q. *Given the uncertainty over what standard should be followed, should a local fire department care about meeting standards?*

The answer is definitely, "yes!" Many volunteer (and even career) departments do not fully comply with either standard now, even though those standards are **minimum** standards. Despite the differences, there are far greater similarities between both sets of standards. Consequently, any effort to comply will increase the safety of the volunteers and the community they protect. Moreover, any demonstration of a plan and implementation of standards will protect the fire department and the local government in a lawsuit.

Q. *Which is the better standard?*

A. We refuse to write a position on this issue. Not because we do not have opinions, but rather because our opinions do not count. In the final analysis, judges will make these decisions in courts. What we do hope is that both the NFPA and The Alliance can settle their differences because we are confident that such a settlement will be superior to the decisions of judges. According to a survey of readers of *Fire Engineering* (Manning, 1995a), volunteer and career personnel disagreed on whether separate standards should exist; nevertheless, both groups felt that both organizations should "work together to create new fire service standards." Interestingly, a majority of respondents from each sector (volunteer, career, and combination) agreed that standards should be "site specific." (Recall particularism.) The reader survey obtained about 345 responses and by its nature is in no way a scientific sample.[14] Nevertheless, the striking results suggest that both volunteer and career firefighters seek some form of reconciliation between the NFPA and The Alliance.

---

[14]The sample size is reasonable; however, the sample is not random. Readers of *Fire Engineering* are likely more progressive than the average volunteer firefighter. Moreover, those who took the time to respond may be more concerned about the issue.

THE RECRUITMENT DRAGON

VI

THE SAD BUT TRUE STORY OF TOMMY THE BAD RECRUIT

Tommy's father and uncles had been in the fire department for years. After moving back to the village from a large city, he decided to join the department. His reputation was well known. He was, as several firefighters put it, "one brick shy of a load." Thought to be somewhat mentally slow, and a devoted drinker with a spotty driving record, he did not present the kind of recruit even the small Village Volunteer Fire Department, Inc. (VVFD) would welcome enthusiastically.

The department had no standard recruitment procedure. Usually people came in through family and friendship connections in the department. The chief would often invite his friends into the department, and was usually successful. As an aside, the personal recruits of the chief often seemed to have the feeling they were especially valuable members who had inside knowledge of departmental politics. Other members were suspicious of their motives. Tommy was neither of these.

The by-laws stated that anyone interested in becoming a member had to attend three consecutive monthly meetings after having been sponsored by a current member. At the third meeting, a secret vote would be taken on the interested individual. A simple majority was enough to vote someone into the organization with full membership status. There was no probationary period.

Customarily, Tommy was asked to leave the building while the vote was taken. The first vote was a tie. There was no discussion of this since Tommy's father and two uncles were in attendance and voting. Then one person changed his or her vote (there were two female firefighters in the department — including the chief's wife who was the vice-president). Tommy was voted in. About six months went by with no incident.

The first problem was more embarrassing than serious. Deciding that his membership in one department had given him the authority to show up at fire calls of other departments, Tommy dutifully assisted another department at a brush fire. As a passenger in the brush truck en route back to their station, he apparently fell asleep with his foot on the siren switch. Reports were that it was difficult to wake him up, and that he smelled of alcohol. One can easily imagine the stories and jokes about this, all at the expense of the VVFD.

The second problem involved his unsolicited attendance at a rescue squad call. Of course he had had no EMS training. Squad members reported that he just showed up in his own car, identified himself as a member of the VVFD, and tried to assist. Upon leaving the scene, he decided to use his personal vehicle as a high-speed escort through the town limits and into the local hospital. Having called considerable attention to himself by his erratic driving, a town police officer (and member of another fire department) arrested him for reckless driving. Tommy's defense was that he was a member of the VVFD.

The fire chief put Tommy on what the chief called strict probation. There was nothing in the by-laws which defined this status. He could not drive any of the fire trucks nor was he to assist any other department. Eventually, he and his father resigned by leaving their turnout gear thrown down in the firehouse.

Almost every fire department has a horror story of recruitment and retention. Though this case is not really funny, it does have comic elements. The Village Volunteer Fire Department was lucky that tragedy did not result. The case was included to add a bit of levity to the serious discussion to follow. There are themes from this story that the reader will recognize in several sections below.

INTRODUCTION

Recruitment is generally seen as the sole province of the department and upon which no thoughtful government would ever tread. The inclusion of this chapter indicates that we see an increasing need for government to support recruitment efforts of departments; and for the latter to recognize the range of aid that many governments could supply — such as publicly promoting volunteer emergency services, providing pensions to volunteers, lending legal assistance in risk management, retention, and even screening would-be volunteers.

We can think of several reasons recruitment and local government are linked. First, because of the erosion of sovereign immunity (see Chapter Four), governments will have greater interest in healthy, low-risk volunteer fire departments. Second, the issue of standards for volunteers (see Chapter Five) even suggested local government could get into the business of adopting a set of standards for their fire departments, and therefore would have to be interested in recruitment. Third, and probably most importantly, because of the complexity of recruiting, volunteer departments are going to need government to help market themselves.

This chapter presents a frank discussion of recruitment, in a context of leadership, public image, and retention. Following this, a continuum will be suggested of potentially positive connection points between volunteer departments and local governments. This continuum is based on real models in the U.S. and Canada. Recruitment has become much more complex in recent years, as most of us are aware.

The reader may be relieved in that our effort here is not a rehash or review of the numerous articles and opinions on recruitment nor is it to present a catalog of tactics for actually attracting volunteers. Many very good magazine articles and manuals have appeared in recent years which do this, such as the practical, research-based report produced by the National Volunteer Fire Council (1993) in cooperation with the U.S. Fire Administration and Federal Emergency Management Agency. (See also Goldfeder, 1992.) Let us begin by making several remarks about recruitment in general and then turn to specific issues where we see potential for healthy government-volunteer relations.

All kinds of organizations face recruitment problems because people continually move in and out of them. Regardless of whether the organization is a business, a university, a church, or a fire department, recruitment is an open file. It is never completely solved and it requires frequent, if not constant, attention.

Volunteer fire and rescue organizations have a considerable advantage over many other kinds of organizations when it comes to recruitment, although many departments do not recognize the advantages they have. What other organizations can claim some excitement, personal rewards, and honor associated with being in a volunteer fire department? What other organizations have the kind of control over their operations that volunteer departments have? What other organizations have the legal protection for their volunteers that these have? Finally, what other organizations are so supported by their communities? In light of these questions, volunteer fire departments can approach recruitment with a level of confidence that is to be envied.

Having said all this, we acknowledge that there is much discussion of doom and gloom related to recruitment. This issue seems to be a lightning rod that channels much negativity about the volunteer fire service. Often, concern over recruitment dominates discussion about the volunteer service in such a way that other more troublesome issues like retention and leadership are left aside. Arguably, as Stittleburg (1994a) noted, retention and leadership are more important than recruitment in that they are the reasons recruitment is necessary in many situations. We make these assertions not to trivialize recruitment as a problem, but only to suggest that it can be a symptom of other problems less apparently ominous and more internal to departments. This point is strongly supported by our interviews with fire service leaders. Moreover, it is consistent with the vicious volunteer emergency organization we introduced at the end of Chapter Three.

We would like to organize the remainder of this section around several key questions that might allow some insight into the whole idea of recruitment. We start with the simple question about exactly what individuals are recruited to do.

What Do Volunteer Firefighters Really Do?

Fight fires, of course, is the stock answer to the question of what volunteers are recruited to do. We suggest, in contrast, that any recruitment effort that is based on the idea that volunteers are recruited just to fight fires is on shaky ground. In the typical volunteer fire department, with or without an EMS mission, members spend considerable time doing a whole host of other, interesting, and time-consuming activities. Fund-raising, maintaining the apparatus, painting the firehouse, mowing the grass, taking inventory and ordering personal protective equipment and supplies, attending training schools, planning drills, providing education programs for senior citizens and school children, preparing for parades and competitions, interacting with other fire departments, inspecting buildings, attending departmental meetings, keeping up with tables and chairs loaned out to families and community groups, and filling swimming pools are some activities that quickly come to mind. In most cases, actual firefighting is only a very small part of the job.

The point is not to show how demanding the job is, but to suggest that an individual is being recruited to work on a wide variety of tasks — all of which are important to the welfare of the department, many of which are important to the welfare of the community. We wonder how many departments seriously consider this in their approach to recruitment, and, furthermore, explain all this to a potential recruit. To us, accurately portraying the job as it really is might set the expectations correctly for new recruits and perhaps create less turnover.

What Do Retention And Leadership Have To Do With Recruitment?

In most cases, departments that have a good record of retaining members and strong leadership are unlikely to have a serious recruitment problem. Stittleburg (1994a: p. 20), summarizing a National Volunteer Fire Council (NVFC) (1993) study of recruitment and retention, wrote: "According to the report, good leadership is critical, and nearly all retention failures can be attributed, either directly or indirectly, to leadership shortcomings." We would temper this finding a bit because some members' exit from the department cannot be avoided due to their relocation, health, or other factors unrelated to leadership. However, as we note at length in Chapter Nine concerning EMS, internal politics and personnel dynamics left uncontrolled by leaders (or worse, intensified by unwitting leaders) is a serious problem for retention and actually threatens service provision.

What can a leader do wrong that would cause retention "failures?" Some leadership problems found in the NVFC study (1993) include leaders being dictatorial, their lack of empathy for emotions and personal problems of members, and their inability to communicate policies. From our research for this book and previous studies that support the NVFC findings, leadership problems in volunteer departments are really no different than those that can characterize any other organization. Here is a provocative list of leadership "failures," in no particular order, gleaned from our interviews and research:

1. *Lack of understanding of the organization, particularly the erroneous assumption that a volunteer organization is easy to lead or will "lead itself."* A related problem is the reluctance of a chief to assume fully the role of leader. A reluctant leader inspires no one. Leschak's (1995) article in *Firehouse* titled "Taking the Heat: Volunteer Fire Chiefs Confront a New Age" is an excellent overview of the complexities of leading the volunteer fire department. Goldfeder's (1994) article, "Redirecting Behavior," contributes to an understanding of obstacles faced by a volunteer chief in dealing with personnel problems.

2. *"Driving into the future looking in the rear-view mirror"* (a quote from an international fire service leader). This means a love affair with the past glory of the department while neglecting any planning for the future.

3. *Playing favorites with a few cronies.* This is an easy trap into which to fall because leaders naturally wish to surround and insulate themselves with those who agree with them. Such behavior leads to the formation of factions.

4. *Having secrets.* This relates to a leader's yearning for power based on withholding and selectively brokering information. This is one of many kinds of poor communications between the leader and membership.

5. *Not attending to the public image of the organization.* We have a section below about this problem. It is a sure way to instill the same attitude in the membership.

6. *Lack of community outreach.* Poor leaders see no need to spend time on this, yet building linkages to groups and organizations only helps the department. Public relations are a vital part of the life of a successful volunteer department.

7. *Poor screening of recruits in the first place.* This is one area where many leaders are woefully negligent. New recruits are not subject to the same informal screening that the older members were. We say more about this below, but only mention here that departments should have objective membership requirements.

8. *Lack of utilization of boards of directors.* In every department that is legally incorporated, there has to be a board of directors. This structure and the expertise of its members can easily be neglected by the chief anxious about sharing his or her power.

9. *Failure to demand training.* Training equals professionalism. Professionalism equals pride. Pride equals commitment. Being soft on training is to cheat members out of something that will enhance their loyalty to the department, not to mention their safety and effectiveness on the fireground. (See Buckman, 1995, on training volunteers.)

10. *Ignoring the need to develop positive relations with locally elected government officials and government administrators.* Like it or not, volunteer fire departments are like arms of government. Local government supplies funding and can give other forms of support. The leader has to establish a balance between the autonomy of his or her department and linkage to the political structure. Members need to see the leader as informed and politically astute, not just as a good firefighter.

Each and every one of these problems can cause dissatisfaction and quitting. Many times, members do not formally quit, they just stop contributing anything and become deadwood on the roster. Recruitment efforts are likely to fail in a context of bad leadership. The disgruntled ex-members will almost see to it themselves. The reader will recall that these same charateristics described the vicious volunteer emergency organization presented in Chapter Three.

Does The Typical Volunteer Department Know How To Recruit?

We would have to say "no" to this question. The reason we say this has to do with what we see as a "cultural lag" between the department and the community. To put this simply, many departments' recruitment history has been that individuals came to them through family and friendship networks. Joining the volunteer fire department was often an unstated expectation. Recruitment in this traditional manner was unintentional and not particularly bothersome, except in cases where there was fear of offending a set of members should a potential recruit fail to be accepted by vote. Individuals were known to the department well before they were sponsored for membership. The department could safely assume that new members would conform to rules and regulations through pressures by family and friends. The "club" survived quite well. Today there is considerable mobility of individuals and changing family occupational dynamics that have left the department with potential recruits, but not the same kind that once came to it. Informal, unintentional, and "clublike" recruitment methods are now, at least, only slightly effective and, at most, counterproductive in that they are perceived as exclusive of "non-traditional" individuals — anyone other than white male friends and family members of the old-timers.

In many cases, departments sing the song of doom and gloom over recruitment while relying on methods that do not fit the modern community environment. At the risk of sounding harsh, this may be the reason that recruitment is so often bemoaned. It is much easier to blame something seen as external and uncontrollable than to change the way one does business. As we have already seen, the vicious volunteer organization operates in this fashion, often blaming local government for its own deficiencies.

Does Public Image Affect Recruitment?

An unqualified "yes" is the answer to this question. By public image we mean everything seen and heard relating to the fire department. There is virtually no way for the public to know very much about the fire department except through its interpretation of what is seen and heard about it. The appearance of the building sends a message to the public. The looks of the apparatus says something about pride. The physical appearance of members, their demeanor, and their speech at the fire scene, fund-raisers, and, in general, interaction with the public send very strong signals.

The creation and maintenance of a positive public image and thus an attraction for recruits is done through conscious effort, not left to chance. Simply because a volunteer fire department is honorable, brave, and selfless is not enough to ensure a good image in the public mind.

Many firefighters and leaders resist the notion of working on a positive public image because they believe the demanding service they donate to their community free of charge should be immediately obvious to everyone. It may be obvious and deeply appreciated by those who know the firefighters. But as we mentioned above, it is those who may not know the firefighters as friends or family that now make up an important recruitment pool.

A Note About The Club Culture

The fact that volunteer fire departments tend to have a clublike nature is a point we need to bring up again. (We first introduced this in

Chapter Two.) This is a sensitive issue and we do not want to be misread here. Unquestionably, the close, fraternal nature of a department's culture is highly valuable. In fact, such a culture is to be expected of groups that confront great danger. But again, balancing this important feature with acceptance of members who happen not to be white males with deep community roots is critical to the survival of most volunteer fire departments.

A club culture that obstructs firefighting professionalism can fuel an all too familiar stereotype of volunteer firefighters. There is a popular myth of the volunteer firefighters as blue-collar, red-neck, beer-loving, siren jockeys. We know from Perkins' (1987a) national study of several thousand volunteer firefighters from departments in five states that this stereotype is not accurate. However, this stereotype persists, with now an even worse companion: volunteer firefighter as a latent firesetter. We see these stereotypes as one of the most serious challenges for leaders. The damage they do to the fire service generally, and to a department's ability to recruit quality firefighters specifically, is without parallel.

The club culture has its strengths and weaknesses. The strengths are its social functions and support of bonds among firefighters. It does add a special attractiveness to the volunteer fire department that other organizations can only mimic. Thus, in a limited way, it is a positive recruitment and retention device. Its weakness is that a club culture can easily become the goal of the fire department. When this happens, the real missions of professionalism and human service take on secondary importance.

A volunteer fire department that emphasizes the club over professionalism greatly risks undermining community support. This risk is serious because in any given community, a large percentage of people usually do not know their fire services are volunteer. This is especially true of new residents, many of whom may have migrated from large cities where they assumed (usually correctly) that fire service and EMS were paid. This belief tends to persist.

Are Women And Minority Members Less Committed?

The answer is "no." We are confident in this answer because of our interviews and observations of fire departments that have included "non-traditional" firefighters and have noticed no difference in commitment. Chiefs report that these new members fit in and adapt to the norms of the department just like the white males. Additionally, Perkins

(1987a) provided statistical evidence for the lack of a difference in commitment between white male and female and minority volunteer firefighters.

We have heard old-timers say that women and minority members and otherwise "non-traditional" folks just **do not** have what it takes to be firefighters. They **do not** work as hard; they **cannot** handle the physical stress. Women will cause trouble with the married male firefighters' wives, and they just want to prove they can get into the department. Blacks just want to have access to free water to wash their personal cars. Blacks, like women, want to prove they can get into the organization but do not want to contribute to the group. If women get a toehold in the department, then the next thing they will be doing is running it... All these sadly familiar ideas abound in many departments. At the same time, many of these departments claim recruitment is beyond their control.

There is probably no way to change the thinking of many, backward-looking members except for forward-looking leaders to recruit non-traditional members. Once in a fire department, these new members typically prove their commitment and value in such a way that many suspicious old-guard members change their minds. The old-guard can come to realize that no one gender, race, or category of people has a monopoly of good volunteer firefighters. Besides, the old guard dies...eventually.

Are The Motivations To Join Different Today?

To a degree, "yes." Some would quickly say "yes" emphatically, pointing to some mythical sort of general decline of a true spirit of volunteering and increasing self-interest. Perhaps, but the fact remains that recruits must be found and retained. We could speculate wildly about all this only to arrive at two basic facts. First, most of what we know about motivations for joining a volunteer fire department has come from people after they joined. Second, firefighting (and medical rescue) have become much more technical, requiring skills that have application in a number of paid jobs. Let us look at this last fact first.

One difference between veteran and new volunteers that seems to be real is that many recent volunteers join volunteer departments in order to gain skills that will enhance their "human capital" in the job market (Benoit, 1990). This is especially true of medical rescue volunteers who have aspirations to become nurses or physicians. On one hand, this does create a retention problem for departments in areas where these members have to leave to have a career. On the other hand, these members often make some of the best volunteers because they are motivated to learn and experience as much as possible. There is nothing wrong with a department highlighting the fact that joining could be beneficial to one's career.

We also know from Thompson's (1995) research that the person who volunteers to provide emergency medical service is different from the person who volunteers to fight fire. His study of separate volunteer fire departments and EMS squads revealed that the EMS people are more likely to be a balance of males and females, older, possessing somewhat greater formal education, and with fewer friends already in the organization. Thompson's study suggests that when a fire department "diversifies" by offering any level of EMS, a wider pool of recruits may be required. So far we have considered the objective attributes of potential volunteers. What happens when we inquire about motivations and attitudes?

We know about motives from survey research done on members of volunteer departments (Perkins, 1987a; Benoit and MacMillan, 1984; Thompson, 1995). The research revealed data suggestive of problems with the whole question of trying to figure out "true" motivations. People typically learn why they joined a fire department after the fact, because the organization taught them their motivations. This may sound silly at first reading, but it happens. We are not suggesting the individuals come to a department with their minds blank slates; and only that once the department gets hold of them, either formally or informally, they are socialized into a view of why they decided to join.

When given a choice such as "I wanted to serve my community," the vast majority of volunteers would most likely pick this reason as the prime motivation to join. We do not wish to sound cynical, but we doubt such a motivation is in the forefront of most people's minds before they join. Practical motivations probably work first. Getting to know people in the community, being a member of a close-knit group, experiencing comradeship, learning something new and building skills, doing something to relieve boredom, getting away from domestic chores...these motivations, we suggest, prompt people to join more so than abstract humanitarian or religious ethics. Once a member, other motivations are often discovered (taught) and become real.

So, "true" motives for doing almost anything are difficult to learn. Practical concerns should not be ignored as groundwork upon which to base recruitment efforts. The best motive of all might be highlighting practical advantages within the context of the ethics of community service.

STRATEGIC PLANNING FOR RECRUITMENT

Don't let the sun set on another day without consideration of where your department's manpower will come from and a strategy on how you will recruit, retain, and train new personnel. (Carlson, 1995c)

The forceful statement above is from a working document accompanying a presentation on recruitment often given by Gene Carlson of Fire Protection Publications at Oklahoma State University (1995c). Recruitment requires planning. The place to start is to examine the history of one's particular volunteer organization, eventually arriving at an assessment of the present situation. The goal is to lay some groundwork for figuring out what the organization is to become in, say, five to ten years into the future. Recall from Chapter Three that the virtuous volunteer organization has a vision. Organizations simply do not arrive in the present without a history. What is the age profile of the current membership? By what method did they arrive on the membership roster? How has the department handled retention? How many new members are needed? What skills and educational level would be ideal for new members? Again, **by what method** (as the famous organizational theorist William Demming would say) will these new recruits get into the department? Confronting all these questions is a way, figuratively speaking, to make the future come to you, rather than have the future recede from you. (See Marinucci, 1989, for practical guidelines in setting recruitment standards.)

Let us make several assumptions about a typical volunteer fire department as we continue our discussion of strategic recruitment planning. First, we will assume that its leadership is stable, intelligent, and committed to the department. Second, and related to the first assumption, we will assume that any retention problems are due to members relocating because of occupational changes or some other factor out of control of the department. The department itself is not driving members away. Third, we assume that the department is located in a community that has a reasonable local government that is supportive of volunteer services, if not by gracious funding, at least in principle.

Two Tempting Recruitment "Methods" To Avoid

Returning to the assessment of past and current recruitment practices, we would likely find that this typical department recruited members in the past by an informal but highly effective process called "word of mouth." Upon finding a need to recruit new members, and seeing that family and friendship networks were not working anymore, there might be the strong temptation to adopt either one of the two methods of recruitment that will likely fail.

The "Church Model" is one that simply does not work, but it is a model upon which volunteer departments can often find themselves relying. The heart of this almost non-method goes something like this: "Given enough time, people in the community will realize how valuable the department is and will feel led by some spirit (sacred or otherwise) to join." Furthermore, "perhaps even if we close our doors," says the vicious (versus the virtuous) department, "the community will finally notice we need help." Many churches use this recruitment method, hence its name. Of course, people cannot be counted on to realize the value of any group and very few will join an organization that expects them to join but does nothing by way of invitation. The results of this method can be a blaming of the public for not recognizing the nearly sacred character of the volunteer department. This method of confronting the future has a self-destructive element.

Adopting the "Sinking Ship Model" is another tempting method to approach recruitment. One can recognize departments that use this strategy by the presence of a mobile sign with a blinking light across the top and bright plastic letters spelling out "H-E-L-P — V-O-L-U-N-T-E-E-R-S N-E-E-D-E-D." The message really being received is that the department is like a sinking ship. Few want to come aboard.

There is one point that is common to both these methods. Assuming for a moment the unlikely fact that both would work, there would be no way to predict how many people might show up on the doorsteps of the fire department. Conceivably, the department could be faced with taking in more people than it really needed, or turning away some potentially good members, who would bring on a whole set of additional problems.

Positive Positioning And Protection Against Bad Recruits

What changes in the present recruitment situation of the typical department might be implemented to allow for positive strategic planning? Having avoided thinking like a dying church or sending an SOS, the department is now in a position to assess further some specific and practical steps in positioning for the future and protecting itself against bad recruits. Here are several key questions:

1. *Is there a role for youth in the department?* The "grow your own" idea is a good one. Providing a structure for youth involvement in auxiliary activities is both good management and good community service.

2. *Does the department involve the recruit's* **family***?* The highly successful Wayne Township Fire Department in the suburbs of Indianapolis, which is a fully volunteer system (with some paid administration), has as a standard practice to involve the families of its members in a conscious effort to increase retention. (Interview with Jack Winkler, 1994.)

3. *Are there any public relations or public education initiatives by the department in local high schools and with local businesses?* Such programs pave the route for the potential recruit to the department. (See Carlson, 1995a, on the advantages of forming partnerships with local industry.)

4. *Is there a waiting list?* A waiting list allows control over membership size, which is a necessity. It suggests an image of an organization solidly afloat. It also allows for time whereby the serious recruit can anticipate his or her role.

5. *Are the by-laws litigation waiting to happen?* Such a rule as a "three negative-vote blackball" is now an invitation for civil rights litigation. Such a mechanism, perhaps used to act as a screening device, is far too risky and unfair to have such rules like this.

6. *What objective screening is in place for people interested in becoming members?* There are some people who do not belong in a volunteer fire department period: alcohol abusers, reckless drivers, fire-starters, and individuals with criminal backgrounds such as would compromise the public image of the department. Other individuals do belong in the department, but just not in the capacity of firefighting. These people, due to their age or health, might be interested in some support role. Clearly, many citizens can volunteer for a fire prevention role, such as for home inspections or public fire safety education. Of course, fire prevention training would be necessary before assuming such a role.

7. *Is there use of a probationary period for membership?* In many departments known to us, the probationary period is something in an obscure part of the by-laws. Both the new member and the older ones are vaguely aware of its existence. We mention below the

importance of bringing a new member over the boundary the right way. A well-defined probationary period is a great method to make sure departmental policies are understood and followed. More than this, during a probationary period, a tone can be set for training expectations and fire-ground behavior. We might add that this is a time when the department can communicate its expectations of the public image it expects its members to portray (dress, speech, attitudes, and behavior in public).

8. *Is "mentoring" used?* This effective technique is when a new member — usually during his or her probationary period — is "assigned" to a veteran in an apprenticeshiplike relationship. Rather than building social linkages with only new members, a mentorship program will establish a reliable pipeline through which will flow the knowledge and experience of veterans to the rookies.

Allow us to follow-up on the screening idea. A screening process is very important for the obvious reason of sifting out undesirable people before they get into the organization. Unfortunately, even the most careful screening efforts are no guarantee for having good recruits.

Another function of screening is to set a context where expectations can be communicated both to and from the potential recruit. Screening is what sociologists call a boundary-maintaining mechanism that is important to all groups. **Bringing people over the boundary the proper way works toward retention.**

A volunteer fire department is a very attractive organization. Upon becoming a member, individuals usually have considerable freedom in the organization in such matters as handling money, using tools, and having access to incredibly expensive apparatus. Criminal enterprise could easily thrive in such an environment.

A criminal background and motor vehicle records check on every individual interested in becoming a member is a good idea. The department might wish to contact a local school that does this check on its employees to see what policies might be needed. The department sooner or later will be faced with an applicant with a criminal record. Some records would immediately disqualify an applicant (arson, theft,); some may not. Having these checks may seem a bit drastic, but they will pay off in the confidence they give the department and in their deterrent effect. Usually, such a screening method not only avoids embarrassment for the department, it also avoids embarrassment for the elected and appointed officials in the local government.

FIRING A VOLUNTEER

There is another point that has been mentioned that deserves more discussion. How does a department rid itself of a volunteer that has become a liability? We recognize that the typical volunteer department operates with a high degree of informality and cooperation. In the event that it has to expel a member, it should have **policies and procedures** in place to protect itself — both from litigation and accusations of unfairness by members.

Several of the legal cases in Chapter Four had expulsion of a volunteer as a central theme. *Hyland v. Wonder* made the point that a volunteer cannot be dismissed because of constitutionally protected speech. However, the appeals left it to the lower court to decide if Mr. Hyland's "end run" around his supervisor and his unauthorized use of confidential files constituted a threat to the welfare of the department. *Haavistola v. The Community of Rising Sun Volunteer Fire Department, Inc.* was even more illustrative. The board of directors summarily dismissed a male and female member after the female complained about sexual harassment. This charge seemed to be treated too lightly and without sufficient due process to satisfy the plaintiff.

There should be written, detailed procedures based on due process for expulsion of members. These procedures should be followed to the letter. Complaints such as Ms. Haavistola's should not be taken lightly and assumed to be the result of a trouble-maker, and thus ignored. Expulsions represent a high-risk time for litigation against the department. This is not to suggest that departments shrink from expelling members, but that they should be careful. When this has to occur, it is usually during a time that is highly emotionally charged. So attention to pre-established, agreed upon procedures is the watchword.

The best advice we can pass on from our interviews is that in a situation where expulsion seems the only choice, the leadership should seek legal council from their local government's attorney prior to initiating the separation.

A CONTINUUM MODEL OF RELATIONS WITH GOVERNMENT

A typical view of local government held by a volunteer department is that of necessary evil. Depending upon the political climate, the elected officials and the administrative staff are viewed with suspicion and worry over interference in the internal affairs of the department. In most cases, this fear is not well founded in reality. Traditionally, governments wanted as little to do with volunteer departments as possible. But the economic realities of funding, the public expectation of a professional fire service, and the increasing complexity of recruitment and retention set the stage for relationships with government that go beyond mere funding. One way to illustrate possibilities is to conceive of a continuum going from very little to extensive relations with government.

We are aided in our analysis here by the typology of volunteer emergency organizations outlined in Chapter Two. This typology included the all-volunteer fire (without EMS) department (Types 1 and 2); the combination (volunteer and paid) department (Types 3 and 4); the all-volunteer fire and EMS corporation (Types 5 and 6); and the volunteer and paid fire and EMS department (Types 7 and 8). If we consider these types of volunteer departments as going from the least complex to the most complex, we have a conceptual starting point to suggest how government might play various roles in regards to recruitment. What we offer below is only a general view. In the thousands of counties, towns, townships, and suburban cities, there are substantial variations in how government and volunteer departments interface to address recruitment.

Government As A Public Voice For Volunteers

The most nominal form of government support, in addition to a yearly grant of money with no strings attached, is a strong public position on the value of volunteer fire and rescue service. Sadly, many governments only consider their volunteer services during budget preparations. Sending a strong, official message to the public that government supports volunteer services, and that it expects citizens to do likewise, would seem to make recruitment efforts easier. It has been our research experience that even in areas where there have only been volunteer services many individuals are not aware that volunteers are responsible for emergency services as well as the accompanying property insurance premium reductions.

Government Acts As A Marketing Agent And A Pension Provider

Moving toward more local government support might be the point where not only does government make public declarations of support but where it actually helps in marketing the various departments. This might be in the form of fliers and signs, advertisements in phone books, and mailers with utility bills. Note, in this scenario, that the departments have total control over recruitment. Government only acts as a marketing agent.

Monetary rewards for length of service — or a pension plan — is another point of positive connection between government and its volunteer departments. We argue in Chapter Nine that such a plan is a concrete step in proving to departments that they are needed. Recruitment and retention, as well as individual performance and training, can be addressed with a monetary service award program sponsored by government.

A Volunteer Coordinator As Government Support

At the next point of the continuum, the situation changes noticeably. If the government is needed to do more to support recruitment, it may well have to hire a volunteer coordinator. This type of governmental staff person, assuming he or she is not encumbered by a host of other duties and is not in a token position, has a very important job. The assumption here is that this position has been created at the request of the volunteer organizations, not done unilaterally by government. Unilateral creation would be seen by volunteers as a threat.

The volunteer coordinator has the difficult task of providing concrete help to all the volunteer organizations in their recruitment efforts. This may mean acting as a recruiting agent. His or her office might also serve as a screening body that sends good applicants to various departments. This person has to be knowledgeable, not only of the history and culture of the departments, but also of legal issues associated with screening applicants. This form of close government-volunteer relations is often what volunteer departments think they need in principle, but actually often have difficulty accepting "outside" help in recruitment. This form of relations between volunteer departments and government is usually found where EMS is present in the missions of fire departments and especially where combination departments are required.

A Volunteer Coordinator With An Expanded Role

The volunteer coordinator in the next level of government-volunteer department relations has the role, not only to work at recruitment, but to do this in the context of helping retention efforts and in leadership development. This position is a natural extension of the previous one, since it has been established that recruitment is best understood in light of retention and leadership. To do this work, the volunteer coordinator needs not only to be full-time, but also needs a staff. Under such a design, fire training for volunteers (and paid personnel) might be a service of this individual's office. Loudoun County Fire and Rescue

Services in Virginia has a close variation of this scheme. One of its more effective endeavors is its county-wide Retention and Recruitment Committee made up of chiefs and EMS squad leaders and Fire and Rescue Services employees.

A Separate Government For Fire And Rescue

The last point on our continuum is the situation characterized by Montgomery County Fire and Rescue Commission. This commission is the government for fire and rescue. It has its own staff and a volunteer coordinator who reports directly to the commissioners themselves. A host of services are provided by the Commission which include all those mentioned above. (See Chapter Eight on combination departments.)

CONCLUSION

Recruitment is most effectively addressed in the context of leadership and retention. There are forces at work that are creating opportunities for volunteer departments and local governments to work together in strengthening volunteer services. The modern environment for most departments has changed faster than the recruitment methods. The club culture must be tempered with professionalism and acceptance of individuals who may not have shared in the same local culture as the old-timers.

At the same time, the fraternal nature of volunteer fire departments can serve as a conduit through which to communicate the longstanding, worthy history and traditions of the volunteer service. We noted in the outset of this chapter that we can see no volunteer organizations with more attractive assets than those of volunteer fire departments. We conclude with the same idea.

THE CONSOLIDATION DRAGON

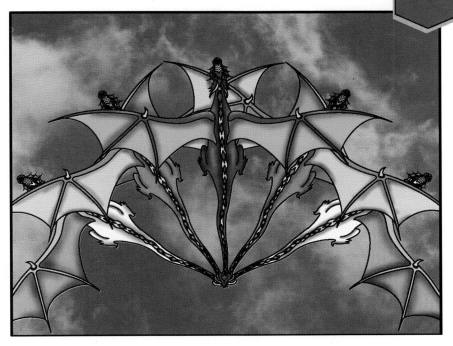

VII

To this point we have examined volunteer fire departments and local government by concentrating on issues evident to the fire service. The legal "dragon" can be seen by both the fire service and local government. The standards dragon is evident to the fire service only. The recruiting dragon is primarily visible to the fire service although some local governments are aware of the problem. In this chapter we consider an issue that is increasingly evident to local governments, but barely understood by the fire service, and least of all understood by volunteer fire departments. This issue is local government consolidation.[1] To demonstrate the invisibility of the "dragon" even further, local government consolidation is still a relatively rare phenomenon in the United States, thus, we rely primarily on the Canadian context to describe the phenomenon. Nevertheless, the same trends that cause

---

[1]A brief glossary is necessary here. Consolidation (or its synonym, amalgamation) is the combining of adjacent local governments resulting in one local government with one local council. Regionalization of services is the combining of local service departments (such as police, fire, and public works) from adjacent local governments. Regionalization of services retains separate political councils to oversee collectively these regionalized services.

local government consolidation are found in both countries. (Indeed, the last case we present is from Virginia.) We can use the Canadian experience as a proving ground for U.S. local government policy. In Chapter Nine, we will reverse the roles — the United States is Canada's proving ground when considering EMS delivery policy.

Historically, nearly all combination fire departments were formed as suburban communities grew beyond the capacity of a full volunteer force. Typically, serious volunteers would have been offered full-time jobs as firefighters. More recently, however, combination departments are forming, in a different way, as adjacent communities consolidate their fire departments to become one. Until recently, the result was the expansion of the urban fully career department.

This chapter will examine the antecedents of this new phenomenon. It will proceed by presenting several cases of the consolidation process and then speculate on the future trends.

ANTECEDENTS

The ideology of local government consolidation is fairly clear. Whether this ideology will correct the problems it seeks to address remains to be seen. The apparent reason for the combination of local governments is that economies of scale are found as local governments increase in size, at least until the consolidated community has a population of about half a million. Much of this combination faces considerable local resistance. After all, few councillors will willingly support their own extinction. Nevertheless, the events in various Canadian provinces over the last few years suggest that this consolidation will take place. Let us consider what these irresistible forces are that move an "immovable object."

The first force is legal authority. Local governments are, after all, "creatures of the province."[2] Not only must a local government comply with the appropriate laws passed by the legislature of the province (usually a local government's act, a town's act or village's act), but as well, all by-laws must be approved by the province before they have the force of law. Any province can, therefore, dissolve, combine, and annex any set of local governments it chooses to affect within the borders of the province. Clearly, any province has the ability to affect the future of any local government contained within it.

---

[2]In the United States, local governments are "creatures of the state."

Nevertheless, a province must have the will to combine local governments as well as a legal right. Such a right has existed since the 19th century; however, the will to exercise that right is more recent. To understand that will, a brief description of public finance at all three levels of government is necessary.

When Canada had "consolidated" itself in 1867, the principal powers of taxation resided with the federal government, the Government of Canada. This made sense because, except for about a dozen areas of activity which were the jurisdiction of the provinces, all residual powers were conferred on that federal government. Thus, the government with the most power and responsibility acquires the most resources by ways of taxation. During the first 50 years after Confederation, however, a number of legal decisions have tended to erode the power of the federal government, increasing the power and the responsibility of the provinces. Similarly, the role of government had changed. Provincial authority over human rights and social welfare grew with the advent of the welfare state arising during the Great Depression of the 1930s. Despite the increase in power and responsibility, provincial governments did not obtain a corresponding increase in taxation. Rather, the federal government collected taxes and dispersed much of it to the various provincial governments. In addition, equalization became a political, if not a legal, necessity. That is, the federal government gave additional funds to poorer provinces so that various programs, such as health, education, and welfare, could meet a national standard of delivery.

During the 1960s, much of the growth in various government programs was funded by an expanding economy. Some of the growth of government in the early '70s was funded by economic growth and inflation. Any shortfall of funds resulting from a decline in revenue (a weak economy) or by an increase in expenditures was met by printing more money. This increase in the money supply increased inflation. Furthermore, that inflation was exacerbated by a rise in oil prices brought on by OPEC in response to the events of the Yom Kippur War of 1973. As a result, controlling inflation became a central issue, particularly as declining purchasing power led to a series of private and public sector strikes in the mid '70s. Rising commodity prices, such as wheat, oil, and gold, continued, particularly following the Iranian revolution of 1978-79 and the subsequent rise in the price of oil. In the United States, the response to these events was the election of Ronald Reagan and the introduction of monetarist policies. An emphasis on monetary policy means the use of interest rates to control inflation. As interest rates rise, investment declines and, ultimately, workers are laid off. The reduction in the demand for goods or services results in pressure to reduce — or at least not raise — prices, but it also results in economic recession. Canada was not immune from these economic forces. Indeed the Bank of Canada adopted similar monetarist policies, perhaps at first by necessity, but ultimately by choice.

However, as the private sector shrank during the recession of the early '80s, the public demand to **increase** public sector spending was high. But, as the government could no longer print money (that would be inflationary) it had to **borrow** money so as to meet its spending obligations and policies. As a result, the deficit increased dramatically by 1987 and remained high up to the present time. By 1994, the accumulated national debt exceeded half a trillion dollars.[3] What with interest rates averaging at about 10%, the cost of servicing the debt became the largest single expenditure of the Government of Canada. Had this national debt been owed to other Canadians, the consequences would not be so serious. In fact, much of this debt is owned by Japanese and German bond holders.

Public reaction to the mounting debt was at first slow. More serious perhaps were the pressures of globalization. NAFTA caught many Canadian companies in an uncompetitive situation. Similarly, resource-based industries, such as farming, fishing, and the forestry, were adversely affected by global declines in commodity prices. The resultant unemployment meant less revenue for government through taxation. (In effect, incomes declined, thus taxes declined.) It also produced more of a demand for unemployment insurance and even, if necessary, welfare payments.

The federal government by the early 1990s faced a dilemma. If it cut its social programs, then angry voters would "turf it [the government] out" at the next election. If it retained its social programs, then the national debt would rise and angry voters would "turf it out" at the next election. Confronted with such unpalatable choices, the government had to be seen at least to be fiscally responsible. The result was a "slight of hand" known as **downloading**.

[3]On a per capita basis, this is comparable to the U.S. Government debt of nearly five trillion dollars. Canada's national debt is about one tenth as large, but Canda has about one tenth the population of the United States.

Downloading is the transfer of fiscal responsibility from a senior level of government to a junior level of government. In effect, the Government of Canada warned, threatened, and then began to reduce its grants to the provinces. The provincial governments facing the same problem of declining revenues, among other strategies, reduced expenditures to local governments. Nevertheless, both the federal and the provincial governments sought to do more, or at least the same, with less. In effect, governments were looking for efficiency. The ideology of efficiency is captured in the phrase "economy of scale."

"Economy of scale" is intuitively easy to understand and difficult to measure in the aggregate. At the administrative level, an economy of scale is evident in fire services. For example, a payroll program must be adjusted to take into account a change in federal taxation. The personnel officer performs the same task whether the department has 1000 employees in a city or ten employees in a village. Thus, the ratio of administrative activity declines with increasing size. Similarly, clearly only one fire chief is needed in a consolidated department. Thus, the salary of one or more chiefs can be saved.[4] Aside from administration, the capital cost of service delivery can also be lowered. Consolidated urban transit or combined water and sewer services can be much cheaper depending on geography and density. For example, the average number of feet (meters) of pipe needed per household tends to be lower in larger communities reducing the magnitude of capital costs per capita.

Faced with the prevailing belief in economies of scale, the downloading of costs, and declining revenues from a federal government, it is easy to see why any provincial local government affairs department would seize upon local government consolidation as a solution to its financial problems. Another reason is less rational, more speculative, but equally compelling. Local government consolidation is a fad. Moreover, the fad justifies the work of provincial public servants working in local government affairs departments. Such justification is needed because these same public servants' jobs are also threatened by the worsening fiscal crisis. Whether consolidating local governments achieve economies of scale or not, provincial departments of local government affairs must do something. Consolidating local governments is at least a trend in other provinces and thus worthy for policy consideration. Currently, the local government consolidation move-

---

[4]Actually, this is not a guaranteed saving at all, particularly if the former chief becomes a deputy chief or if the former chief is a volunteer. We will explore these notions in greater detail later in this chapter.

ment has taken hold in nine out of ten provinces in Canada (O'Brien, 1993). Indeed, it is only British Columbia which seems to have the best economic prospects that has not seriously considered combining local governments.

So far we have seen that local government consolidation has been possibly a rational response to a fiscal crisis. Certainly, local government consolidation **appears** to be rational, justifying the jobs of provincial government employees in the various departments of local government affairs. However, policy issues of this magnitude are made by the minister of local government affairs, the premier of each province and cabinet, and all politicians. We must therefore ask: Aside from seeming rational, is there any political advantage in consolidating local governments? The answer seems to be "yes!" As the Canadian public begins to appreciate the worsening fiscal crisis, it has rewarded politicians who have cut expenditures and/or stood up to special interest groups.

Consider how consolidating local governments is raised as an issue. Typically, senior bureaucrats within a department of local government affairs will raise the subject with various mayors and CAOs during various meetings dealing with other matters. Similarly, the subject will be raised at conferences where local government officials are in attendance. The prime catalyst is the announcement of a task force by the minister of local government affairs. The task force will address local government change in some part or all of a province. Included in the changes is the option of combining local governments. Typically, the status quo is not regarded as acceptable. This announcement induces a "howl of protest" from local government politicians who are fearful (and who are accused of being fearful) of losing their own positions as councillors. The resulting conflict leaves the provincial government appearing to be on the side of cost cutting and opposing "grasping local politicians." This is a good strategy to win votes!

In summary, the province, as represented by its politicians and its bureaucrats, has the right to consolidate local governments. It sees it as a requirement to do so by virtue of a fiscal crisis. Its governing political party sees a political advantage in doing so as long as cost cutting is rewarded with votes. Now, let us briefly examine the response of the local governments and then the response of volunteer emergency organizations.

THE RESPONSE TO THE CONSOLIDATION POLICY

Most local government officials have rejected provincial initiatives to consolidate with an "ad hominem" argument.[5] They argue that local governments, through the prohibition against planning a deficit budget, are relatively financially sound. Therefore, they question, "why pick on local governments to solve a problem that originates with the senior levels of government?" This argument is well accepted among local officials, but is poorly understood by the general public. Recall that most citizens are unaware of the extent to which local government revenues are derived from provincial grants.[6] Thus, the "efficient" nature of local government is not appreciated by most citizens. As a consequence, most local governments have chosen to negotiate rather than fight the consolidation of local governments. In some cases, whole local government staffs of adjacent local governments have been required to reapply for a smaller number of jobs in a grand form of local government "musical chairs." Occasionally, the losers in a particular competition, say for the new CAO, apply for lesser positions, upsetting the incumbents at lower levels. Whatever the outcome, the process generates job insecurity among public officials who often serve in such jobs because of the security they used to provide.

At lower job levels the quest for job security rests upon union contracts. Occasionally, the staff complements of the local governments in question are blended onto one seniority list or one list within each department. The result is that junior employees are at the greatest risk of layoff. This is a serious problem within many career fire departments, because the junior firefighters are often the most trainable, and training will be a necessity as the department diversifies its services to include hazardous material response and special rescue and emergency medical service delivery.

The unfavorable response of fully career fire departments to the consolidation of local governments has been the same as the response of those same local governments. (Such is the nature of corporate strategic decision making.) Nevertheless, our particular interest is, after all, the suburban or rural combination or volunteer fire department, that is, an organization that we have already seen as not fully controlled by its local government.

---

[5]Ad hominem: Literally, "to the man." This method of debate attacks the argument by attacking the other debater. It is a logically fallacious approach but it is psychologically compelling in political debate.

[6]The reader may wish to re-examine Chapter Two which describes the typical government transfers of monies.

Many satellite local governments about to be consolidated with a larger local government fear their loss of identity and increased taxation for services which are not believed to be needed. Even worse, they fear for the loss of moveable property, such as public works vehicles.

As in the United States, satellite local governments, particularly if they are suburban, have higher incomes than the central city. Similarly, suburban taxation is lower than in the central city. Thus, many of these suburban communities are fearful that their taxes will rise.

Imagine the position of a volunteer department. It has just purchased, through hundreds of hours of fund-raising and hundreds of hours of committee meetings, a new aerial apparatus (around half a million dollars). This same department will fear that this apparatus will be transferred to the central city to optimize fire protection. In all likelihood, the larger consolidated community will be optimizing its fire protection but this will be cold consolation for the volunteers.

The few surveys done on volunteer firefighters reveal a desire on the part of the volunteer to help the community (Perkins, 1987a; Benoit and MacMillan, 1984; Thompson, 1992). Although this desire is not the primary motive for someone to volunteer, we can wonder whether volunteers of satellite communities will question their membership if the small community for which they volunteered has suddenly expanded. Indeed, several thoughtful fire chiefs and CAOs have speculated that this might be one dreadful consequence of consolidating local governments. Conversely, other CAOs and fewer fire chiefs have felt that the implied threat to quit is merely a bluff, part of the negotiating stance necessary before detailed reorganization talks are initiated. Later in this chapter, after specific cases have been presented, we will provide our judgment on the degree of credibility this threat provides.

If one assumes that most of these firefighters continue to volunteer, the next concern is what expectations have developed within these volunteers? Recall that in the past, whenever annexation had occurred, the large local government often offered career firefighting jobs to a number of the volunteers. Recognizing that some volunteers join volunteer departments to get the experience that increases the likelihood of getting a career firefighting job, these volunteers may be deluded that jobs will be offered to them. Recognizing that the intent of combining local governments is to **save** money, increasing the wage bill by expanding the number of career jobs is highly unlikely. Nevertheless, it is easy to see how such false expectations can be nurtured.

Finally, once departments are consolidated, how will the career and the volunteer force work together? This is particulary problematic if members of the career force have been laid off or if the threat of laying off such members is a credible one. Aside from savings at the administrative level, its primarily through the layoff of junior personnel that savings will be achieved. How will the "surviving" career firefighters view volunteers if their "brothers" have been laid off and replaced by these volunteers? This is the central management issue for the new "super chief" of the newly formed combination fire department. Initially, we can imagine that the chief, pleased by his or her recent appointment as chief, will exhibit strong corporate loyalty to the new CAO who likely was involved in the chief's appointment. Similarly, the "marching orders" to save money and to expect a reduced budget will have been issued. Under these circumstances, the chief must become the ultimate diplomat.

Faced with these questions raised above, this chapter now presents several cases where local government consolidation is in various stages of implementation. In each case, we focus on the effect of consolidation on the existing fire services. Several conclusions will be drawn at the conclusion of each case. After four cases, we will introduce the beginnings of a consolidation "movement" in the United States, concluding with a fifth case. Following this, several lessons will be posed based on the experiences provided by all the cases.

CASE ONE: CHARLOTTETOWN

Our first case is happening on the Canadian Province of Prince Edward Island (PEI), the smallest province both by geography and by population in Canada. PEI is a potato farming island with a population of 125,000 people. This province is heavily dependent upon transfer payments from the Government of Canada. It is, therefore, particularly anxious to reduce expenditures as revenue from the Government of Canada is projected to decline.

In the 19th century, farming, fishing, and forestry were the major industries of PEI. Charlottetown was the only urban area of note, its population exceeding 5000. It was the capital city providing government and serving the surrounding farms. Since 1945, the Charlottetown area had grown to include such suburban communities as Sherwood, Parkdale, Royalty, East Royalty, and West Royalty. In all, some 16 separate communities have grown on the fringes of Charlottetown, responding to the growth in government and the services needed for farming. Most of the population growth was migration from rural areas arising from the consolidation of farms and the mechanization of farm work.

Part of the growth was because the province fostered small community development, whether by intent or not. The province paid for road construction, maintenance, and policing. This resulted in lower local taxation than was the case in Charlottetown; thus, many Islanders were attracted to these suburban communities. Clearly, however, any casual examination of the province suggested an excess of local governments. The province contained 88 such governments, or about one local government for every 1500 persons.[7] A more careful observation would suggest that most of the councillors were essentially volunteering their labor and most staffs were very small (often only containing a part-time administrator). Nevertheless, a small provincial government (hoping to get smaller by reducing expenditures) need not deal with as many as 88 local governments.

In contrast to local governments, the fire service was already lean. The 88 local governments were served by 37 volunteer fire departments. Many of the local governments were served by contract with a volunteer fire department. Typically, a local government would enter into a contract with a volunteer fire department to provide fire suppression. In 1994, the 17 local governments in the Charlottetown area were served by five volunteer fire departments. Each of these departments maintained contact with each other, providing informal but relatively effective mutual aid. Nevertheless, increased efficiencies were possible. On one hand, the five departments had more apparatus than the average Canadian fire department in comparably sized communities. On the other hand, they would argue that this excess was more than compensated for by the low wage bill. The annual payments to volunteers were as follows:

FIGURE 7.1

PAYMENTS FOR VOLUNTEER FIREFIGHTERS

Department	1994 Annual Payment to Volunteers ($CDN)
Charlottetown	5500
Sherwood	2500
Parkdale	2500
North River	1500
Crossroads	unknown

[7]This compares with one local government for every 5000 persons in the sister province of New Brunswick and one local government for every 15,000 persons in Nova Scotia.

They were high payments for volunteers in Atlantic Canada, but they were clearly at most 12% of the average annual salary of a career firefighter in Atlantic Canada.

In the spring of 1993, PEI elected a new Liberal Premier, Catherine Kaulbeck. Within two months she called an election that was a landslide victory for her party, the Liberals, winning 31 of the 32 seats in the legislature. This victory was sullied by the disquieting news that the finances of the province had to be put in order. Provincial government reform (to be read as "civil servant layoffs") included local government consolidation. By the summer of 1993, the provincial government laid out a timetable as follows:

TIMETABLE FOR LOCAL GOVERNMENT CONSOLIDATION ON PEI	
Sept 93	Consultation wtih Local Governments
Dec 93	Report of Investigative Commissioner
Jan 94	Decision of Province
May 94	Elections in New Local Governments[8]
Fall 94	Establishment of New Local Government Organizations[9]

FIGURE 7.2

Most local governments protested against the speed of the process suspecting that the provincial government wanted to do the unpopular and painful changes early in its mandate so that the voters would forget by the next election (likely to be in 1997 or 1998). Nevertheless, the process moved along: Studies were completed, policy decisions made, provincial legislation passed, and new, local elections held. In the fall of 1993, an independent cost benefit analysis was conducted. After several adjustments to the data, the most knowledgeable people concluded that any savings through amalgamation would be questionable at best. (See the financial implications of the fire service issues below.) Nevertheless, other non-economic, indeed, political factors assumed greater importance.

[8]Ultimately delayed to November of 1994.

[9] Ultimately delayed to April of 1995.

Despite the growth of the greater Charlottetown Area, its political representation was rather weak. Although this Greater Charlottetown Area contained 36% of the population of PEI, it held only 19% of the seats in the legislature (6 out of 32). This discrepancy was challenged in court and, during this 1993-94 period, the court ruled that a redistribution of seats, based on population, was necessary. Now the Greater Charlottetown Area would be assigned 12 seats, double the previous number. Recognizing the increased political influence that the Greater Charlottetown Area would have, the Liberal Party of PEI (that is the Government) thought that consolidation was necessary in any case. However, one local government with 12 out of the 32 MLAs (Members of the Legislative Assembly)[10] was excessive. Consequently, the principal recommendation accepted by the provincial government was to combine the 17 existing local governments into three, using geographic criteria to combine them. (See map.) This way no one local government would have excessive power vis a vis the Provincial Government. Whether by intent or not, the provincial government was employing a "divide and conquer" strategy.

FIGURE 7.3

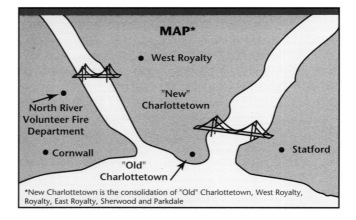

MAP*

- West Royalty

"New" Charlottetown

North River Volunteer Fire Department

- Cornwall

"Old" Charlottetown

- Statford

*New Charlottetown is the consolidation of "Old" Charlottetown, West Royalty, Royalty, East Royalty, Sherwood and Parkdale

Our principal interest is the middle peninsula that is consolidated into "new" Charlottetown. "Old" Charlottetown welcomed consolidation. It was expansionary and it brought the relatively rich West Royalty into its fold. For that same reason, West Royalty rejected amalgamation because it expected higher taxes.

---

[10]An MLA is roughly equivalent to a Member of Congress in a state.

These differences are reinforced by fire service delivery. On the one hand, the North River Volunteer Fire Department (see map) provides fire suppression service under contract ($125,000 CDN per year) to West Royalty. Response time to the industrial park is fairly good at 4.5 minutes. This response is faster than would be the case from any of the three key departments: Charlottetown, Sherwood, or Parkdale. As one might predict, before the province announced consolidation as certainty, West Royalty allied itself with the North River Fire Department. After consolidation was official (that is, once the legislation was passed), then West Royalty demanded expanded service from "new" Charlottetown. In effect, since taxes are going to go up, then "you might as well get as much service as possible." This "flip flop" by West Royalty disturbed the North River Volunteer Fire Department (NRVFD) somewhat. However, for a number of years the NRVFD anticipated the loss of the contract and therefore planned its actions based on this contingency. Moreover, North River recognized that West Royalty was merely reacting to the initiative of the far more powerful provincial government.

On the other hand, the three fire departments — Charlottetown, Sherwood, and Parkdale — chose a more proactive approach. Recognizing the inevitable effect of consolidation, they chose to meet together to develop recommendations consistent with provincial policy on consolidation. These recommendations would be submitted to the new council. In effect, they soon recognized that neither the new city nor the province had detailed policies. They knew that the province did not want to upset the volunteers because the current level of service was so efficient compared with any alternative. Similarly, they already had much contact with each other. The relations were sufficiently cordial that each department wanted to at least communicate and see if a common approach could be developed. In February, March, and April of 1994, chief officers from each department met with a facilitator who moderated discussions and sometimes mediated differences. The facilitator then developed a report listing 35 recommendations to be considered by the council of "new" Charlottetown.[11]

The report recommends that a substation be established in West Royalty (a site may be donated). Many volunteers from Parkdale and

---

[11]The province willingly funded much of the report's costs under the provincial Fire Marshal's Office. The report is entitled: *Report on the Amalgamation of the Charlottetown, Parkdale, and Sherwood Fire Departments Submitted to City Council September 1994.* (Fire Service Planning Committee, 1994.)

Charlottetown have already agreed to consider responding to that sub-station. Thus, it would be possible to meet West Royalty's suppression needs with little expenditure. Also included in the Report is a recommendation to raise the volunteer stipends in Sherwood and Parkdale to that of the level of "old" Charlottetown ($5500.00). The total cost of this recommendation is $225,000.00 per year. Whether this recommendation will be accepted is yet to be determined.

In general, the three departments have responded well to the challenge of local government amalgamation. Part of their success to date arises from the following factors:

1. Senior personnel in each department knew each other and, whatever their differences may have been, they could form a coalition to lobby with the new local government.

2. The province was always the "bad guy," given its initiative and power; nevertheless, the province "turned the other cheek," maintaining its sensitivity to the needs of volunteer fire departments.

3. The amalgamated department would be almost entirely volunteer (100 volunteers, eight career, of which six are in suppression); thus, career/volunteer conflict was not anticipated.

This last factor will become more important as we review the next few cases where career firefighters are already employed in significant numbers.

CASE TWO: MIRAMICHI CITY

In our judgment, the Province of New Brunswick has developed the most successful local government consolidation process in Canada. However, this province faces the toughest challenges. Unlike Prince Edward Island or Nova Scotia, New Brunswick is a bilingual province. Of the 750,000 citizens, about 300,000 are French-speaking Acadians. Unlike many Québécois, most Acadians are Canadian nationalists. To a degree this is because the Federal Government supported the Acadians' efforts toward building an officially bilingual province during the 1960s.

The rationale to consolidate local governments in New Brunswick is the search for economies of scale. Nevertheless, in some areas this may require the consolidation of French-speaking and English-speaking communities. This might incur more problems than the benefit provided by achieving an economy of scale.

As of 1995, the province explored the possibility of amalgamation in two areas: the Miramichi Region and Greater Moncton. Let us examine the effect of these two different processes on the fire departments. The Miramichi Region is considered first.

The Miramichi region is a collection of towns, villages, and local service districts on both banks of the Miramichi River in northern New Brunswick. The principal community on the north bank is Newcastle; its principle employer is an integrated pulp mill. The principal community on the south bank is Chatham; its principal employer was Canadian Forces Base Chatham, once a major airforce base. Until recently, the economy would ride the boom and bust cycle of the pulp and paper industry. These cycles were dampened by the steady employment of the military base. However, this condition began to change in the early 1990s as Canadian Forces Base Chatham was downsized and then eventually closed in 1994.

The Province of New Brunswick was conscious of these changes as it began to explore consolidation. In 1992, the Department of Municipal Affairs, Culture and Housing produced a discussion paper which examined consolidation, regionalization of service, and the status quo. The Department favored consolidation as a policy option and rejected the status quo. Despite these preferences, the province embarked on a slower consultative process with the communities in the target areas. Unlike the other two Maritime Provinces, New Brunswick had begun to talk about its fiscal problems as early as 1987. Its relative success allowed it to use a slower approach. If nothing else, the province could not use a fiscal crisis to speed up the process, as was the case in PEI.

In the summer of 1993, the province appointed John Robison, the former CAO of Fredericton, to develop a team of commissioners who would investigate the feasibility of consolidation in the Miramichi and the Greater Moncton Areas. In the Miramichi Area, John Robison formed a team with some input from the local business community and some input from local government officials. The team held public hearings over the fall of 1993 and developed its report in Jan./Feb. of 1994. In April of 1994, the report was released to the public recommending the full consolidation of local government and services, including the existing local government and volunteer fire departments. By August of 1994, the province announced acceptance of this report calling for the disbanding of existing councils and the election of a single council for the new Miramichi City in the spring of 1995. Let us now examine the effect of these events on the various fire departments.

The two principal departments are both combination in Chatham and Newcastle. In the early fall of 1994, the career chief in Newcastle and the career deputy chief in Chatham, the obvious contenders for the new chief's job, met to discuss the future. They quickly reached an accommodation resulting in harmonious relations. Later, unforseen events made this relationship even more important.[12] At these early stages, the absence of information fuelled the "rumor mill." For example, the fully volunteer department of Logieville expected that it would be disbanded.[13] It had a poor relationship with the Logieville village council and the membership assumed the worst. Far from the worst, the intent of the council was to revitalize the membership by providing additional training and resources. In general, the various fire departments adopted the strategy to use the opportunity of consolidation to garner more resources from the new local government. For example, the two union locals (both from the Canadian Union of Public Employees — CUPE not IAFF) agreed to combine the better clauses of each contract. Of course, subsequent collective bargaining will determine the outcome. Similarly, the various departments agreed to raise the volunteer stipend to the level of the highest department requiring an overall increase in the local government budget of $130,000.

Whether the new local government of Miramichi City allows for these budget increases remains to be seen. Nevertheless, Robison clearly recommends that the volunteer firefighters were already an efficient asset prior to the amalgamation. Consequently, he regarded it foolhardy to allow the consolidation process to interfere with the activities of the volunteers. Thus, the volunteers have support from the province. In the final analysis, however, we await a decision by the new council of Miramichi City.

---

[12]In the fall of 1994, the province appointed an interim council that was to make appointments prior to the election of a Miramichi City Council in April of 1995. Because this interim council was appointed rather than elected, some critics challenged its legitimacy in court. To the embarrassment of the province the court agreed, invalidating every decision the interim council made. Thus, the fire chief was appointed and then told his appointment was invalid. This can be very frustrating. Fortunately for him, elections were held in the winter of 1995 and his appointment was subsequently confirmed by the newly elected council.

[13]Logieville is adjacent to the Chatham airport. While the consolidation process was going on, Transport Canada, in order to reduce costs, downgraded the level of the airport removing the airport firefighters. Now any crash or structural fire is the responsibility of the local government. The local government response is to upgrade the volunteer firefighters in Logieville. Thus, the decisions made by a federal department in Ottawa have consequences in a small, hitherto independent, volunteer fire department.

CASE THREE: MONCTON/DIEPPE/RIVERVIEW

Changes to local government in the Greater Moncton Area of New Brunswick are the most significant at the fire service level. This case introduces the classic notion of combining an essentially fully career fire department with composite departments containing major volunteer contingents. However, it is first necessary to provide the economic and cultural context of the area.

Greater Moncton contains three local governments: Moncton (population 54,000), Riverview (population 18,000), and Dieppe (population 12,000). Riverview is a suburban "bedroom" community on the south bank of the Petitcodiac River, connected only by a causeway. Dieppe and Moncton are fairly similar in composition, both having a mix of industrial, commercial, and residential property. Since Dieppe and Moncton on the north bank of the river are so similar and geographically contiguous, the reader might wonder why they have remained separate? The answer is language and culture. Moncton is about 70% English Canadian and 30% Acadian French. Dieppe, however, is 90% Acadian French. Historically, these differences would also imply differences in social class, favoring the English Canadians in Moncton. Since the 1960s, however, this difference has reversed itself. Dieppe, building on an essentially bilingual workforce, has acquired a number of small- to medium-sized commercial and industrial establishments. The result is that it has built a tax base analogous to West Royalty in PEI. Unlike West Royalty and Charlottetown, however, Dieppe is distinct in language and culture.

In the fall of 1993, the distinctiveness of Dieppe was constantly presented to John Robison and Louis Malenfant, the principal restructuring commissioners.[14] As a result, the commissioners proposed greater inter-local government cooperation, particularly in the areas of policing, emergency preparedness, and fire services. The province chose to adopt the report in August of 1994 proclaiming that it would review the extent of cooperation after two years — in September 1996. Many local officials believed that they had a two-year "window of opportunity." They reasoned that the province would not want to push for consolidation until it had a new mandate following the next provin-

---

[14]Recall that John Robison, former CAO of Fredericton, was simultaneously examining the Miramichi Area described above. Louis Malenfant is the Vice President (Academic) of the Université de Moncton.

cial election (actually about one year later on September 12, 1995). After the election, if cooperation was not successful, the province would be able to force consolidation.

At first glance, it would seem that cooperation would be impossible. After all, on the surface, Moncton, the largest city, is also the poorest of the three communities. Thus, it had the most to gain from outright consolidation because it would be enriched by Riverview and Dieppe. Consequently, if Moncton chose **not** to cooperate with Riverview and Dieppe, then Moncton would be rewarded by the province forcing consolidation within a couple of years. Conversely, both Riverview and Dieppe, wanting to retain their autonomy, had everything to gain by cooperating now so as to avoid consolidation later. However, cooperation among any three parties is only possible if all three parties have incentives to cooperate. In this case, Moncton lacked that incentive. When the dance of cooperation among three local governments is desired, it only works when all three governments want to cooperate. In other words, "it takes three to tango."

However, during the fall of 1994, Dieppe tried to convince Moncton that Dieppe was not so attractive a partner in consolidation. Dieppe argued that it would require a higher level of service (such as street lights and fire protection) if it were to be consolidated with Moncton. Since this higher level of service would require expenditures, the additional revenue from Dieppe would be counteracted by the greater expenditures in Dieppe. So far it seems that Moncton is willing to cooperate, but it is too early to tell whether this cooperation will be sufficient to stave off the Provincial threat to consolidate.

How have these events affected the respective fire departments? There is no simple answer. In Dieppe, the volunteers within the combination department (28 volunteers and 12 career) have threatened to resign if consolidation takes place. This threat supports the position of the local government in Dieppe. Conversely, the employees of Dieppe and the career firefighters welcome consolidation because they believe that their salaries will be raised to that of the level of Moncton's firefighters (a raise of about $7,000 CDN per year). Riverview's career personnel welcome consolidation for the same reason; however, Riverview's volunteers do not see consolidation as a threat to their own existence. The reason is because most of these volunteers are trained as emergency medical technicians.

As the province has cut back on its funding to hospitals, these same hospitals are seeking other sources of revenue. Recognizing that there is more money in patient transport than emergency response, the Moncton General Hospital transports patients to Halifax, Nova Scotia during the day. Consequently, the hospital ambulance service is not so readily able to respond to emergency calls during the 10:00 a.m. to 3:00 p.m. period. It is at this time that the Riverview Fire Department responds to emergencies as a backup for the Moncton General Hospital. For this backup the Riverview Fire/Rescue Department receives a fee from the province. It is as if the province has transferred funds from one department to another. Since this need is likely to grow, the volunteers in Riverview will remain in high demand.

The Moncton Fire Department (MFD) is of two minds about local government cooperation, depending on the position within the organization. The senior officers welcome greater cooperation. Indeed, by the winter of 1995 the Moncton Fire Department had just purchased defibrillators to place on the apparatus. The Moncton Fire Department was taking the first steps to move into EMS delivery. Similarly, cooperative hazardous material response was beginning to be developed, encouraged by funds from the Provincial Department of the Environment. Finally, the volunteer force, which in recent years was fairly dormant, was beginning to be reactivated in 1995. It is the impact of volunteers that most disturbs the rank and file of the MFD. As many junior officers maintain, amalgamation will lead to a greater use of volunteers. These junior personnel fear that the volunteers may end up replacing those firefighters in the MFD who have low levels of seniority. Thus, the volunteers are a threat to job security. Recognizing this attitude, it is little wonder that career and volunteer firefighters might have problems interacting.

CASE FOUR: INDUSTRIAL CAPE BRETON

This case is located in Nova Scotia. Thus, the particular agenda of this province comes into play. This case will start with a brief history leading up to consolidation. Then, the unique features associated with Industrial Cape Breton will be described.

Nova Scotia has a population approaching 950,000. The two major urban areas are metropolitan Halifax with a population of 325,000 and industrial Cape Breton with a population of 125,000. Altogether, Nova Scotia had 66 local governments before consolidation. Consolidation in Cape Breton will reduce 11 local governments to one.

Consolidating local governments is not a new idea. In the early 1970s, John Graham presented a royal commission report recommending similar combination (Graham, 1974). At the time, the rural areas, and particularly the volunteer fire departments, successfully resisted any change. However, the trends which now motivate change were absent in the '70s. The forces which encouraged the most recent impetus to combine local governments are only about five years old. In the winter of 1991, Don Cameron was elected leader of the Conservative Party of the Province of Nova Scotia. Since the party held a slim majority in the Legislature, Don Cameron was automatically Premier of Nova Scotia. By that time, the Conservative Party was on its fourth term in office having won the previous four elections since 1978 — the elections in 1978, 1981, 1984, and 1988. Such one-party tenure in office was almost unprecedented in Nova Scotia's history. Few observers expected that Cameron would win the next election. Nevertheless, Don Cameron proceeded to govern. He argued that local government was far too wasteful and thus a consolidation process would be necessary to provide a more efficient service. The Department of Local Government Affairs (DLGA) began to consider boundary changes and, in December of 1991, several senior appointed officials representing local governments met with several DMA officials. The result was a task force report in April of 1992 that sought to achieve two objectives:

1. An exchange of service between local governments on one hand and the province on the other. In particular, they proposed that local governments pass welfare services back to the province in return for assuming responsibility for roads and policing. (This is based on the principle that provinces should serve people and local governments should serve property.); and

2. A consolidation of local governments in several areas, particularly Halifax, Industrial Cape Breton, New Glasgow, Truro, and Kentville. Other consolidations would arise two years later.

The initial response by local governments was neutral or positive. They were initially heartened by the process wherein the Union of Nova Scotia Municipalities (UNSM) was an equal partner in the process. However, by the end of 1992, the view became more negative, with some notable exceptions. Let us see why this happened. First of all, the service exchange proposal favored a few large urban local governments and harmed many rural local governments. The cities were already paying for roads and policing, so they welcomed surrendering the burden of contributing to welfare, particularly in a recession which forecasted increasing expenditures. However, the rural local governments had many more miles of roads to maintain and relied on the province paying the cost of policing.[15] Since there are many more rural local governments than urban ones, the overwhelming opinion was negative against change. Second, for tragic personal reasons, the Minister of Local Government Affairs, Sandy Young, could not fully attend to his duties at this time.[16] The responsibility for consultation fell on a recently appointed deputy minister. As a result, the UNSM felt estranged from the process and ended its cooperation.

In the meantime, John Savage, the President of the Union of Nova Scotia Municipalities and the Mayor of Dartmouth, (likely to be combined with Halifax), became the leader of the Liberal Party of Nova Scotia. He opposed the local government consolidation initiatives hoping it would become an election issue. By the spring of 1993, an election was called and the Liberals won by a landslide (40 of 52 seats). John Savage became Premier of Nova Scotia. Within 36 hours of his election victory, John Savage announced that any consolidation of local governments would **not** be forced by the province. It would not be a "shotgun wedding."

After the election, a new Minister of Municipal Affairs, Sandy Jolly, examined the Municipal Reform initiative of the previous government, concluding, after a six month review, that service exchange was a useful policy despite the objections from rural areas. Similarly, early in 1994, at the request of a number of the local governments in Industrial Cape Breton, she agreed to initiate the consolidation of 11 local governments (six of which were receiving emergency funding) so as to resolve the fiscal crisis there. This initiative is elaborated upon below.

Unlike most local governments in Nova Scotia, many local governments in Industrial Cape Breton welcomed the advent of consolidation. By 1994, several of the local governments were subsisting on emergency funding from the province. The problem is not surprising since Industrial Cape Breton is one of the poorest local areas in Canada. The Nova Scotia Department of Municipal Affairs appointed a com-

---

[15]For example, the rural Local Government of the County of Richmond (population 12,000) has more miles of road to maintain than the miles of streets in the City of Halifax (population 120,000). Thus, the burden is major.

[16]The Minster's daughter was accidentally given a medically induced disease. Heroic attempts at treatment prolonged her life during 1992. Many local government officials sympathized with the Minster's plight but felt that a different minister ought to be appointed. This eventually happened — too late.

missioner to plan for, and oversee, the initial stages of the transition. The province passed legislation creating a consolidated community from 11 different local governments. Although the legislation specified that the competition for positions would be closed only to employees of the pre-existent local governments, a strong impression was left that not all employees would be hired. After all, the existent tax base was not able to support those local governments. Otherwise, emergency funding would not have been needed.

Partly because of the magnitude of the task, the senior administrative positions began to be filled in the early months of 1995 **before** the election of council. The process of consolidation faced a dilemma. On one hand, Industrial Cape Breton could wait until after the election to select senior administrative personnel. This would allow input from the newly elected council. On the other hand, senior personnel could be selected beforehand, which is what happened. Positions were filled from top down in the new hierarchy. Once the CAO was hired, that person had input into the selection of department heads. A major advantage of this approach positively affected the fire service. The relatively rapid selection of a director of fire services ended any jockeying for position which preceded the appointment.

The position of director rather than chief of fire services is not in name only. Of the 37 fire departments in the area, only the largest in Sydney is fully career. A few departments are combination and the vast majority are fully volunteer. Cognizant of the need to preserve volunteer involvement, Industrial Cape Breton wisely opted for a decentralized fire service for the consolidated community. In this fashion, the principal role of the director is to coordinate the activities of the many fire departments. So far there is no evidence of disaffection among the volunteer firefighters or the volunteer chiefs. One additional reason for this was the creation of a fire service board containing volunteer chiefs. The fire service board sets policies to be implemented by the director. At these initial stages, priority has been assigned to upgrading training and standardizing equipment acquisition. The tangible involvement of the chiefs has succeeded in co-opting them toward a goal of fire service delivery for Industrial Cape Breton.

Co-optation is a process whereby a new, often externally imposed organization, reduces its conflict with local influential resisters by incorporating those resisters into the decision making of the organization. The initial effect, as Selznick (1966) discovered when he studied the Tennessee Valley Authority, is to mollify these resisters. However, as Selznick discovered, co-optation is a "two way street." Just as the resisters take an about-face with their attitudes and support the new organization, the organization must adjust its activities to fit **some** of the desires of these local influentials. Given this observation, we can ask how the local fire chiefs will influence the new fire service now that they are members of the board.

One way is to consider the movement of apparatus. Despite "efficiencies" that might be achieved with improved response time, it is likely that any movement of apparatus will be delayed so as not to upset the sensibilities of the volunteer chiefs and their departments. Inevitably, changes will be sought, but the role of the director will be to persuade rather than to order.

THE CONSOLIDATION DRAGON IN THE UNITED STATES

We would like to highlight some of the stresses and strains associated with various types of consolidation which involve volunteers. The kinds of consolidation we will examine are:

1. Initiatives from the departments themselves to consolidate;

2. Consolidation of independent volunteer departments under a specialized government agency, such as a department of fire and rescue that serves as a coordination function but does not have supreme authority;

3. The move from "functional consolidation," based on coordination by local government and where departments retain their autonomy and authority, to a consolidation of authority. This is very difficult to accomplish without great pain. (We will consider a case in some length.)

Consolidation of any sort is a shift in the traditional, familiar, and habitual way organizations work with one another. The reason we have called it a dragon is that consolidation often requires at least one organization to give up something. This process, regardless of its origin, can become ugly. The Queen County case is an example.

Many volunteer organizations operate like little empires or "fiefdoms." They have territory that they guard, rivalries that they nurture, and a general sense of monopoly as to their services. Also, there is a high degree of comradeship and fraternity that these organizations display, as was noted in Chapter Two. Many leaders believe their organizations are beyond criticism since there are so many sacrifices in time and energy from the members. All this is understandable in light of the tremendous personal investments members make in these organizations, even to the point of over-commitment. These organizations are, as one fire chief put it, "like children we collectively gave birth to, and we don't want them to leave home." Thus, volunteer departments, especially those that are organized as legally autonomous corporations, can be very stubborn when it comes to merging in any way with another department, not to mention any attempt by government toward this end.

At the same time, the economic reality and the great need for effectiveness of a fire and/or EMS system often make consolidation a necessity. Funding formulas change, suburbs grow, public expectations increase, and businesses demand a certain level of service. And, when volunteer departments take on EMS, they create risks for change since EMS brings with it a whole set of new challenges to the organization, such as cross-training, increasing call volumes, involvement with hospitals, increased costs of operations, material, and apparatus, more legal liability, and, often worst of all, paid personnel. The presence of paid personnel in a volunteer system creates momentum for consolidation, as we will see in the Prince William County case discussed below.

Consolidation Without Government Involvement _____

The Queen County case described in Chapter One is an example of a consolidation initiative generated by volunteer organizations themselves. The government actually had nothing to do with it. One unit, the Queen station, wanted to take advantage of the offer of a private citizen of a nice parcel of land located half the distance between the Queen and Minerville units. What seemed like a good idea to the Queen group was resisted strongly by the Minerville unit. The Minerville group did not want to give up its name. It wanted its own independence, autonomy, and identity with its own community. These people did not like the people in the Queen unit and were determined to block the movement toward consolidation at every turn, including filing a civil suit and sabotaging equipment. It did not matter that both Minerville and Queen were legally the same organization. (Remember, only one set of by-laws applied to both units.) We suspect that if the local government had threatened to make its own fire and EMS unit with paid employees, the picture would have been much different.

What was lacking in the Queen case was an external threat to the survival of the volunteer system. The Wayne Township Fire Department, just outside the city limits of Indianapolis, Indiana, provides a good example of what can happen when there is an external threat. This all-volunteer fire department (with some paid administrative staff, but not any paid firefighters or EMS personnel) is an example of a highly effective volunteer system in a densely populated area. Its organizational history began as seven separate volunteer fire corporations. The perception that the career department of the City of Indianapolis had designs on moving into the volunteer territory caused leaders of the seven autonomous corporations to vote to become one.

One corporation, not seven, could do a much better job at strategic planning for new stations, initiating retention and recruitment program development, training, and budgeting. Without the external threat, consolidation would have been hard to sell. Under the cloud of potential takeover by a career department, every chief of the original seven corporations gave up something, but also received something in return, that is, a sense of survival and pride in being a volunteer system in an area where few would expect an all-volunteer emergency organization to survive.

It is very difficult for a community-based volunteer department or EMS squad to think beyond its own district or protection area. These organizations are typically very locally oriented and have been known to resist attempts, even by a county or local government association of chiefs (men and women of their own stripe), to standardize dispatch or number stations. In the department of one of the authors of this book, one person said at a regular monthly meeting that "a station is not the same thing as a fire department." Agreement abounded among the members present. This was in response to an effort by the county-wide association of chiefs to increase dispatching effectiveness. The perception of this benign effort to call departments "stations" and to give each a number was loss of autonomy.

To many readers unfamiliar with internal politics and the culture of volunteer departments, all this probably sounds silly and juvenile. However, anything that looks like it will be taken away quickly comes to symbolize something big and important, such as departmental identity. Remember, most of these organizations were created not by government, but by members themselves. Change is very disturbing, especially to the old-timers (the keepers of the history of the organization). An external threat that forces leaders to agree that it can only be dealt with by consolidation, serves to neutralize objections and move the process forward.

Government Initiated Consolidation: Coordination Versus Control _____

We are going to use the terms "coordination" and "control" to refer to two general kinds of consolidation involving government. Many local governments with a volunteer system (including those with some paid personnel) have such agencies as bureaus of fire and rescue. Much of the function of these offices is coordination. Some of the main duties include training, administering a retirement program, arson investigation, public education, administering recruitment efforts, and providing leadership training. The control, or authority, for fire suppression resides unquestionably with the volunteer chiefs. Such a situation has been referred to as "functional consolidation" (Pittard, 1992). Departments maintain their legal status and identity, but agree to operate according to mutual aid plans worked out by the local government. In some cases, fire departments agree to allow equipment not owned by the corporations to be transferred to wherever the local government deems necessary. This is about as far as this kind of consolidation can go without creating anxiety among volunteers as to the government's real intention.

CASE FIVE: PRINCE WILLIAM COUNTY

The point at which a local government, or the departments themselves see the need for consolidation of authority, is not easy to know. It would appear that most of the time departments lag far behind local government in seeing this need. As one might expect, the idea of government having the heaviest hand in making policies for a volunteer system is hard to swallow for volunteers. One case in point occurred in a rapidly suburbanizing county in northern Virginia. This case has many twists and turns, and does not end up with a clear victory for any side. It does, however, show the intense political nature that such a move can have. And it shows how such a move can originate. Before we say any more about this case, we should note that consolidation of authority was not completely accomplished in this county.

Our research of the situation in Prince William County began rather oddly by a call from a former student who was working as a career firefighter in this county. At the informal invitation of the union local, we began to learn how painful consolidation of authority actually could be for all parties. This case is almost worth an entire chapter on its own, but we will keep it brief. In addition to our observations that included a dramatic public hearing which pitted career personnel against volunteers, we have been aided by a lengthy report by a consulting firm (TriData Corporation of Arlington, Virginia) that was called in by the county to assess the county's fire and EMS system.

The whole effort toward review and change of the Prince William fire and EMS system came partially as a result of a civil lawsuit against one of the fire departments for its untimely response to an EMS call that was said to result in the death of a citizen (TriData, 1994). This situation, which occurred during the time volunteers were on duty, called into question the effectiveness of the volunteer system.

Discontent with the system was present prior to this incident and career firefighters added "fuel to the fire" because they felt that their working conditions were hampered by volunteers, as well as by salary concerns. County career firefighters, who were only allowed to work day shifts in the volunteer stations, (and were members of the International Association of Fire Fighters), noted that volunteers gave them little respect to the point where they expected the career firefighters to clean up the fire houses after the volunteers left in the mornings. Both the union local and volunteers became political actors, lobbying with individual county supervisors and with the local newspaper for their respective positions.

What was at stake was the question of who had the most authority — volunteers or a paid chief **with increased authority to make policy on his or her own**. At that time, there was a paid fire chief, but his authority was based on the will of the county-wide association made up primarily of volunteer chiefs, with one career firefighter. However, this position reported to the county executive who, as a bureaucratic agent of government, was unlikely to see the world as the volunteer chiefs did. Thus, this situation describes the proverbial rock and a hard place.

Perhaps we should pause from our narrative and sample the local newspaper headlines for some of the flavor of how intensely political this situation became. These headlines and lead sentences (by Steve Bard of the *Potomac News*) were published several days leading up to a vote by the county board of supervisors on the issue of authority:

"Spending by volunteers comes under fire." (July 19, 1994.) While many Prince William County residents live on beer budgets, volunteer fire and rescue departments here spend tax dollars on champagne-priced equipment. (Bard, 1994b.)

"Board said to be clouded by politics." (July 19, 1994.) [The] Prince William County supervisors' reluctance to strip fire and rescue volunteers of much of their power shows they are bowing to political pressure, some former and current supervisors said. (Bard, 1994b.)

"Union: don't work at county stations." (July 17, 1994.) A Prince William County professional firefighters' union is asking fellow members in other jurisdictions to refrain from volunteering in Prince William, drawing sharp criticism from county officials. (Bard, 1994a.)

"Department sets record straight: OWL [Occoquan-Woodbridge-Lorton Volunteer Fire Department] says it's frugal with equipment." (July 17, 1994.) Media reports claiming Prince William County volunteer fire departments own about the same number of fire engines as more populous Fairfax County and more ambulances than Washington, D.C., are misleading, officials with the Occoquan-Woodbridge-Lorton Volunteer Fire Department said Saturday. (Bard, 1994a.)

"Board puts fire out with compromise: Volunteers in control; paid ranks get boost." (July 20, 1994.) Volunteers will remain in charge of Prince William County's fire and rescue system...But supervisors did not leave paid firefighters out in the cold." (Bard, 1994c.)

The end of this story, at least for now, came at a public hearing on two different "plans" for the county's fire and EMS system. The impetus for formulating plans was a recommendation by TriData:

"The County Fire Chief lacks the authority that is needed to fulfill all of the responsibilities that are assigned to the position. Also, the Chief is accountable to the County Executive and bound by the policies established by the [Fire and Rescue] Association, which creates a potential conflict. One of the most important recommendations...is for the Board of County Supervisors to make a decision on granting additional authority to the County Fire Chief or reducing the expectations from a manager to a coordinator level." (p.iii)

Basically, the first plan was to leave things as they were. The second was to increase the authority of the County Fire Chief. The compromise approved was to add two additional career firefighters to the Fire and Rescue Association. Thus, the county side-stepped this hot issue — temporarily.

Having read these five case studies on consolidation in local government the reader may feel overwhelmed with trivia. Indeed, any careful reader may be forgiven for forgetting most of the detail. Nevertheless, it is important to convey the complexity of the changes. In truth, each case study is a gross oversimplification of the recent history; moreover, each case ends barely in the middle. We lack the true perspective of history to know "how it turns out." Despite these problems let us summarize by listing some lessons.

Lesson One

At the state or provincial levels, officials should recognize that local governments are relatively cheap and effective. Thus, they should be given the latitude to devise effective and efficient means to satisfy broad goals set by the province or state. In other words, the state/provincial government should merely set the goals and evaluate the outcomes. Let the local governments choose the means. They can be held accountable to the state or provincial evaluation. The decision by New Brunswick to accept different solutions in Miramichi and Moncton certainly encourages other local governments within that province.

Lesson Two

Although economies of scale can exist, bigger is not necessarily better. Since optimum levels of scale vary with each local government service, then the most money can be saved by regionalizing each of the services. Thus, a fire department may merge with adjacent departments until the optimum efficiency is attained. The regional commission that might oversee this service would be entirely different from the commission overseeing a different service (such as public works). Initially, the services would be efficient but **not** accountable to the taxpayer, unless each commission was separately elected. Imagine electing ten representatives to its commission — each voter would vote about 150 times each local government election! In the long run, such a lack of political accountability could lead to even greater costs.

Lesson Three

"The devil really is in the details." Thus, any consolidation process is going to require much "bottom up" consultation. Unfortunately, those at the bottom may have vested interests (such as keeping their own jobs even if they are redundant). Therefore, such planning must be monitored by neutral outsiders. Industrial Cape Breton, facing job loss at management levels, nevertheless employed this technique with reasonable success. Despite this, any newly appointed CAO must be willing to accept the position as probationary, subject to change once a newly elected council is sworn to office. (If this tactic scares away good candidates, then it may be necessary to guarantee either a similar paying job or a generous severance/retirement package. Remember, the cost of a poor CAO will be far greater.)

Lesson Four

Recognize that the status symbol of the job title, fire chief, is important. Call the position with overall responsibility "Director" or "Coordinator of Fire Services." If this offends the ego of an applicant, then, in all likelihood, that same applicant will lack the diplomatic skill needed to do the job effectively. The director must use persuasion to convince the CAO and local government councillors, as well as volunteer fire chiefs.

Lesson Five

Select the Director of Fire/Rescue Services as soon as possible to reduce any overlap between planning and policy making and political competition for the job. Otherwise, key players bring politically hidden (and sometimes not so hidden) agendas to the planning table. Unfortunately, the qualifications needed to be an effective director may require more lead time to select the right person (who probably should be external to the area so as not to be seen to be biased). This suggests that CAOs should have at hand a network of qualified directors. Unfortunately, any such network is only informal at the moment.

Lesson Six

Co-opt potential conflict into a board. The co-optation itself will reduce conflict. Granted, more conflict will surface while policy making, but this is superior to conflict through the media or through small community gossip. Recognize that such co-optation will require compromise; thus, the director should encourage the development of the board's vision of a fire/rescue service rather than impose his or her own. This may be difficult because often candidates for the job are asked to provide a vision in the employment interview. This may then induce a commitment which is hard to break psychologically. Rather, the director should present several scenarios recognizing that the ultimate operative scenario will arise from the board's vision.

Lesson Seven

Maintain constant communication with subordinate officers and firefighters. Rumors abound in the absence of information. Unfortunately, the process will seem hectic to the decision makers and agonizingly slow for their distant subordinates. Particulary if layoffs are conceivable (see Lesson Nine below), then rumor is a major outcome. Similarly, recall that past annexation, or growth, often resulted in the absorption of volunteer fire departments to become fully career departments. This past history will misinform many volunteer departments. Thus, rumors are often negative (recall Logieville in Miramichi City). Conversely, many volunteer firefighters may falsely hope that career firefighter jobs are in the offing. Managing these expectations is necessary. Regularly scheduled meetings should be held even if there is no "news" to deliver. If a fire chief has nothing new to say, then that person needs to hear the rumors to dispell those that are wrong and investigate those that are uncertain.

Lesson Eight

Since the fire/rescue service will be a very low priority relative to other issues, then much decision making can be done by fire officials before the formal authority is delegated. The magnitude of the change gives all senior officers high influence on fire/rescue policies. The CAO and councillors will be distracted by other matters. However, those policies that require expenditures are less likely to be supported. Thus, officials from different fire/rescue departments should establish some policies with no, or negligible, financial implications. It is almost certain that such policies will be accepted. Thus, key officials will feel success in working together even if the CAO or councillors frustrate other initiatives. Both Charlottetown and Industrial Cape Breton have done part of this, but we fear the consequences of possible negative financial decisions. If local officials set broad guidelines on fire service planning, then the expectations of some fire service personnel can be contained.

Lesson Nine

Announce a no layoff policy, if possible. This will reduce some of the rumors mentioned above and prevent a drop in morale. The "catch" is the phrase "if possible." Nevertheless, it is amazing how often local governments unnecessarily induce fear by remaining silent, allowing silence to convert employee anxiety into fear. Since citizen service motivated by fear is rarely effective, then the quality of service is likely to drop.

THE COMBINATION DRAGON

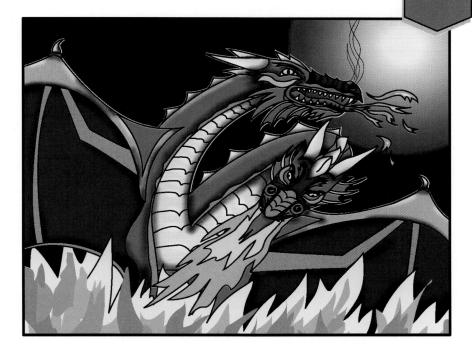

TYPES OF COMBINATION DEPARTMENTS

The previous chapter on consolidation sets the stage for a chapter on combination or composite departments. The definition of a combination (or composite in Canada) department is simple. A combination department contains a mixture of career and volunteer firefighters and/or EMTs. This definition masks a greater level of complexity. After all, by this definition a department with one volunteer firefighter and the rest career is the same as a department with one career firefighter and the rest volunteer. Intuitively, we would expect considerable differences between these two departments. Since little writing has been done on this subject, let us explore the variations in combination/composite departments shown in Figure 8.1.

Of these eight types of departments, clearly the fully career and fully volunteer departments do not fit our definition of a combination/composite department. For our purposes, we can also disregard the Career/Dying Volunteer Department as likely to disappear in the near future. Similarly, the Career Driver Volunteer Department and the Career Chief Volunteer Department have only one or two career per-

COMBINATION/COMPOSITE DEPARTMENTS

Name	Description
Fully Career Department (not a combination/composite department)	Usually large (40 to several thousand full-time employees). Usually found in large or moderately sized cities. Invariably unionized with an IAFF local or other union affilation.
Career/Dying Volunteer Department	Similar to the fully career department except for a dying volunteer component which is really an aging social club. Typically, the volunteers will only be called out for very serious fires, engaging in exterior activities.
Career/Infant Volunteer Department	A new phenomenon whereby the fully career department of a city establishes a volunteer force, trains it, and gradually introduces it to fireground operations. Usually this volunteer force is eligible for hiring once career firefighter positions arise.
Equal Career/Volunteer Department	A department containing a roughly equal number of career and volunteer personnel. Typically, the career force predominates because that force is always on duty, first arriving at the scene, thus providing the first-due officer who is incident commander. The remaining apparatus will be staffed by volunteers. Often these volunteers will engage in water transport in areas without hydrants. Until recently, this type was not stable, as it evolved to a Career/Dying Volunteer Department. Now, fiscal pressures assure the local government will preserve it.
Volunteer Dominant Department	This typically suburban force includes a significant minority of career firefighters who often work during the day when volunteers have commuted to the central city. During the day, the career personnel respond first and any remnant of volunteers may arrive later. At night, however, the volunteers provide the response including incident command.
Career Chief Volunteer Department	This is a hitherto fully volunteer department receiving significant funds from the local government. The government "buys" some control by hiring the chief.
Career Driver Volunteer Department	This is a hitherto fully volunteer department hiring a driver during the day to move the apparatus in response to an alarm. After the alarm, the driver will engage in the majority of cleanup so that volunteers can return to work. Fund-raising is often generated by the volunteers.
Fully Volunteer Department (not a combination/composite department)	This is found in rural areas, usually depending on fund-raising by the volunteers. Fire suppression and rescue are provided by the volunteers.

FIGURE 8.1

sonnel. These structures are interesting but not so much as the other three types of combination departments.

Our interest remains in the Career/Infant Volunteer, Equal Career/ Volunteer, and Volunteer Dominated Departments. Each of these serve as models for the future as far as local government is concerned. As well, each of these present nightmares to most fire chiefs whether career or volunteer. The next few paragraphs will address why local governments consider these departments the dream. The next section of the chapter will address the fire chiefs' nightmares. The final section will address ways of reconciling these conflicting perspectives.

THE DREAM OF LOCAL GOVERNMENT

In order to present the logic of why a combination department is so efficient, we need to explore the effect of time on fire losses. The discussion which follows is far too elementary for some of the readers; however, for those readers who are local government officials and are just being introduced to these issues, the next few paragraphs should be useful.

First of all, the chemical reaction in structural fires, such as houses, barns, and stores, is oxidation. Oxygen combines with the fuel to produce carbon dioxide and carbon monoxide (the greatest cause of death at fires). The rate of growth of this reaction is most important. At its early stage, such fires can be suppressed by rapidly removing the heat that is needed to sustain the reaction. Unchecked, the rate of growth of most structural fires is exponential. That is, growth is very slow following ignition in the first minute or so; however, as the fire spreads, it ignites more fuel, such as wood, paint, and fabric, producing more heat and increasing the fire even further. By about 60 seconds after ignition in a house, we would hope a smoke detector would sound the alarm, allowing the occupants to leave and call the fire department (about two minutes after ignition). At this point, the rate of growth of the fire continues to accelerate in the room. During the next five minutes after ignition, (minute two to minute seven from ignition), the temperature of the room begins to rise. Since hot gases and fire rise, the temperature will be highest at the ceiling. By about seven minutes, the fire will likely be visible in the corner of a room burning the fuel at that spot. During the next three minutes, the temperature will build until the gases at the ceiling are so hot that the rest of the room suddenly ignites, (this phenomenon is known as flashover). Once this happens, damage has increased considerably. Unless fire walls are built into the structure, the fire will spread within a minute to other rooms and the structure will likely sustain considerable loss. Clearly, the period from minute seven to minute ten is a critical one. If arrival and setup by the fire department can be achieved before minute seven, then knock down of the fire is virtually assured. The resulting losses on a $100,000 home might range between five and fifteen thousand dollars. Conversely, if arrival and setup is achieved after minute ten, then the loss to the structure is excessive.

Recognizing the crucial role of time, the fire service (including the fire engineers) have asked what can reduce the time interval as much as possible? Smoke detectors have been critical in this process. Many lives have been saved by waking and warning occupants at night before they succumb to carbon monoxide poisoning in their sleep. Similarly, at the other end of the time scale, constant training and practice by fire companies has reduced setup time to under one minute. For example, firefighters a few years ago used to don breathing apparatus on their back at the fire scene, usually a 30 to 45 second procedure. Now, pumpers are designed with the breathing apparatus in the seats so that as the firefighter sits in the seat, the breathing apparatus is put on within a few seconds.

Despite these improvements, one critical factor is response time, that is, the time from receipt of alarm to the time when the first apparatus arrives at the scene of the structural fire. The magnitude of response time, in turn, is a function of distance from the fire station to the structural fire and the availability of personnel in the fire department. The effect of distance is obvious. Despite sirens and warning lights, an apparatus can only move so fast. At 30 miles (50 km) an hour it can travel three miles (five km) in six minutes. Consequently, cities tend to place fire stations so that response time can be set at an acceptable level (usually four to four and one-half minutes) to nearly all the buildings of a city.

A fully career department will have its first-due pumper moving out of the station within 30 to 45 seconds of the sounding of the alarm. However, a fully volunteer department will require more time unless members are at the station. Let us consider two basic standard operating procedures that volunteer departments use.

First of all, the volunteers must receive the alarm (usually a pager or siren or both), proceed to the fire station in their own cars, park, don protective clothing, and get into the apparatus. Any fire attack will require at least three volunteers, so the unit will not proceed to the scene until the **third** volunteer is seated and belted in the vehicle. Despite practice, all of these steps may require three or four minutes. Thus, this procedure is already at least two and a quarter minutes slower than a fully career department.

The second type of standard operating procedure requires that nearly all of the volunteers on receipt of a pager alarm are given the address of the structural fire. Knowledgeable about addresses in the community, the volunteers proceed in their own vehicles to the fire scene. A few designated volunteers who live near the fire station will proceed to the station and drive the apparatus to the fire scene. At the fire scene, volunteers will don protective clothing and breathing apparatus, and proceed to set up the fire attack. This second procedure speeds up response time in comparison with the first procedure above. However, it requires better coordination, greater reliability of personnel, overall knowledge of addresses by all volunteers, and increased setup time.

It is clear that fully career departments usually have a considerable advantage over fully volunteer departments in reducing response time and, therefore, property loss from fire. McDavid (1986) has explored these notions in his research. Comparing fully career and fully volunteer departments, he measures response time and fire loss per capita. (See Figure 8.2 below.) These data confirm the arguments raised above.

THE EFFECT OF STAFFING ON FIRE DEPARTMENT PERFORMANCE AND COST
(Communities 10,000-50,000 Population)[1]

Staff Type	Operating Budget Per Capita ($CDN)	Response Time (Min.)	Loss Per Fire ($CDN)	Civilian Injuries Per 100 Fires	Department Cost Plus Loss Per Fire ($CDN)
Fully Career (N=14)	44.01	3.9	8,505	2.29	19,973
Combination (N=38)	34.51	4.2	6,634	1.48	12,447
Fully Volunteer (N=5)	9.81	5.4	10,166	1.17	12,936

FIGURE 8.2

[1]This figure is a modification of Tables 2, 3, 4, and 5 found on pages 381, 382, 383, and 384, respectively (McDavid, 1986). In addition, civilian injuries per 100 fires is provided within the text of the article on page 383. One of McDavid's conclusions is worth quoting: "Mixed [combination] fire departments, especially in communities between 10,000 and 50,000 residents, appear to combine economy and performance, making them less costly than full-time departments without sacrificing performance levels" (McDavid, 1986: p. 384).

Figure 8.2 gives us more information, however. This table also presents the response time of combination/composite departments as well. The reader will note that the response time of composite departments is only slightly greater than career departments. Why is this the case? The combination departments respond with career firefighters directly from the station once the alarm has sounded. The slight increase in time is explained by the fact that most (although certainly not all) combination departments are single station departments. Therefore, travel time is slightly greater. For all intents and purposes, we may conclude that fully career and combination departments are, on average, equally effective.

However, are they equally efficient? That is, is the ratio of fire loss per capita to the department budget the same? The answer is: of course not! Fully career fire departments are much more expensive, principally because the vast majority of a fully career fire department's budget is devoted to the salaries and fringe benefits of career firefighters. Conversely, the budget of a combination department is almost proportionate to the percentage of career personnel. Thus, Equal Career Volunteer Departments and Volunteer Dominant Departments will be particularly financially efficient.

As we have seen, particularly in the last chapter, local governments once could afford their fire departments to be financially expensive. Far more pressing concerns faced most communities. Throwing money at the problem by building more stations, buying more apparatus, hiring more personnel, and paying higher wages was acceptable when government revenues were on the rise. In the past, citizens did not significantly object to either an increase in taxation or an increase in borrowing to address these increased fire service expenditures. Now, however, citizens and local governments are demanding increased efficiency from their departments and, failing to achieve cost savings, are willing to reduce the fire service so as to reduce expenditures.

This motivation to find efficiencies makes the combination/composite department an extremely attractive alternative for the CAO and council. One consequence of this is the rise in Career/Infant Volunteer Departments. Over the short run, such a change from a fully career department is not likely to induce savings. Over the longer run, such a department is more likely to become an Equal Career Volunteer Department. It will be at that point when efficiencies will be realized.

THE MONTGOMERY COUNTY MARYLAND CASE
(BY DON FLINN) ▰▰▰▰▰▰▰▰▰▰▰▰▰▰▰▰▰▰
Power Is Nothing Without Control _____

Now let us examine how a combination department can develop by studying a large suburban example. Montgomery County, Maryland, an urban suburb of Washington, D.C., has struggled to maintain the balance of power with control over its unique fire/rescue and emergency medical services delivery system. The combination of full-time career and volunteer firefighter/rescuers, EMS, administrative, and support service members, have delivered a high quality service since the mid-30s. To appreciate and understand the development of the elements of power and control, the reader will need to follow the foot prints leading to this much publicized combination delivery system.

The Beginning _____

The oldest fire suppression service in Montgomery County began in the community of Takoma Park in 1894 with the founding of the Takoma Park Volunteer Fire Department. Proudly celebrating its centennial in 1994, the Takoma Park Fire Department welcomed the newest emergency service organization in Montgomery County, the Germantown Volunteer Fire Department, which was recognized by county and state governments in 1989.

Founded by need, following a disastrous fire, concerned citizens in the City of Takoma Park, Maryland, organized to provide firefighting services from within the community, rather than depend on the Washington, D.C., Fire Department. These same events occurred in other communities: from Silver Spring, immediately adjacent to Takoma Park, to the outlying areas of Rockville, Sandy Spring, and beyond.

Before we examine this fire/rescue service any further, we must delve into the history of Montgomery County that provides the setting for the fire/rescue service. From the arrival of the earliest settlers in 1634 to the early 20th century, Montgomery County prospered due to agriculture. Following the peace of the Civil War, the county profited from market gardening, fruit, and general farming. Also, the water power of the Great Falls of the Potomac River and the influence of the growing cities of Washington, D.C. and Baltimore led to prosperity. The opening of the metropolitan branch of the Baltimore and Ohio (B & O) Railroad brought passenger service to the county for the first time. Trolley cars were introduced permitting developers to begin building residential homes in the suburbs.

After 1900, the county experienced the effects of suburban growth in population and land development. Early recognition of the need for the orderly development of water and sewer resulted with the state legislature creating the Washington Suburban Sanitary Commission (WSSC) in 1916. Civic associations and community improvement organizations began to assume an important role in local government and were demanding better services. Except for school teachers, county government was a part-time operation. After 1926, the county began hiring full-time police officers, building inspectors, health workers, secretaries, and other employees.

In 1927, the state legislature created the Maryland-National Capital Park and Planning Commission (M-NCP&PC). A zoning ordinance, subdivision regulations, and building codes were adopted. A unique quality to the vision of the future was the regional approach taken by the political leaders of that day. Both the problems of planning and the expansion of water and sewer lines were approached with the emphasis on impact on the region, as opposed to the probems being viewed by more traditional and colloquial methods.

The Drive For "Home Rule"

From its inception, the county functioned under the county commission system that kept most of the power with the state legislators in the capital of Annapolis. For over a decade, civic organizations battled for more home rule (that is a movement to increase the autonomy of Montgomery County). In 1941, the Brookings Institution conducted a study recommending sweeping changes, including the adoption of a home rule charter. Following years of effort, which were interrupted by World War II, the supporters of the charter were finally successful when, in 1948, 56% of the voters approved the change. Montgomery County became the first county in Maryland to adopt a home rule charter.

The new charter established a Council-Manager form of government. In 1949, six men and a woman were elected as the first county council. In 1968, advocates changed the charter to an executive-council form of government. The seven member council **and** the county executive were all elected. The county manager, a full-time career position, was replaced by a chief administrative officer, appointed by the executive. A 1986 charter amendment increased the number of council seats from seven to nine. Five members are elected from geographic councilmanic districts and four are elected at large.

Keeping Pace In The Fire Service

Increased urbanization affected the communities with a recognized need for paid daytime department staff. In the 1930s, two departments, the Bethesda Fire Department and the adjacent Chevy Chase Fire Department (both operated by citizen boards), abolished their volunteer organizations and hired full-time paid career firefighters. Others hired staff, usually coming from their own volunteer membership ranks, to maintain the station, apparatus and equipment, and to serve as drivers for the initial apparatus response.

Gradually, additional paid staff were hired, and, in the early 1940s, the Silver Spring Volunteer Fire Department established, maintained, and operated with paid staff, the first central alarm for the receipt of telephone calls and the dispatch of equipment. With two-way-radio-equipped apparatus having direct communication to the central alarm system, Montgomery County established one of the first radio-dispatched fire systems on the East Coast. Despite these innovations, service was still focused on fire suppression and the pre-hospital emergency medical care was provided by other organizations.

Growth Trends

In the 20 years preceding the Great Depression, land values more than doubled. The large number of job secure federal workers living in the county cushioned some of the economic effects of the Depression. Montgomery County increasingly became a suburban community with a growing dependence on federal employment. World War II brought housing construction and suburban growth to a halt. The membership ranks of the fire departments, both paid and volunteer, were drained because many of the members served in the war effort.

After the war, the county embarked on unprecedented growth. The 1946 population of 87,000 nearly doubled by 1950 to over 164,000 and doubled again in the next decade. By 1960, nearly 341,000 residents called Montgomery County home. The automobile became a necessity and housing development soared. Much of this growth was in single-family homes. Most of the home owners were also new to the region, coming from all parts of the U.S. to work for the federal government.

The sixties saw a surge in garden-type and suburban high-rise apartments. During the seventies, the population growth rate slowed down from the dizzying pace of doubling every decade. Yet, continued strong suburbanization gave way to increased urbanization. By 1980, the population had reached 579,000 and climbed to 665,000 by the late '80s. There was no sign of slowing down. The school system had grown to be among the 20 largest in the nation. The census of 1990 totalled 757,027 people with the current population estimated at nearly 810,000. All this growth took place in nearly 500 square miles (1 250 square kilometers).

The Challenges Of Growth: The Fire Service Responds

The first half of this century found the communities abutting on Washington, D.C., relying on that Fire Department for suppression services. As the communities evolved, local citizens organized their neighbors into volunteer fire departments, frequently after a calamitous fire threatened their safety and well being.

After World War I, motorized pumping engines replaced hand-drawn hose carts and wheeled chemical extinguishers. Cisterns and wells supplied the essential water, and with the creation of the WSSC, water lines brought hydrants for fire protection. As stated earlier, paid staff were hired in the '30s and, except for the Bethesda and Chevy Chase departments, augmented the available volunteers.

Since World War II, growing and emerging communities bound together to form their own volunteer organizations. Generally, they followed a pattern of first providing fire suppression and then ambulance service with members trained in both firefighting and first aid.

The Challenges Of Growth: Government Responds

With the establishment of the Division of Fire Protection in 1949, Montgomery County played an official role in fire and rescue protection. The division was supervised by a fire marshal. Throughout the years, efforts to centralize all fire and rescue services under a county fire chief had been unsuccessful. A Fire Board, consisting of the chief of each department and an elected delegate and alternate delegate, was also created in 1949 to advise and make recommendations to the county government on fire and rescue matters including fire response and performance. The Fire Board's duties were increased twenty years later and included additional administrative and operational responsibilities including the approval of response areas and station locations, training standards, and communication procedures.

In 1972, the county council created the Montgomery County Department of Fire and Rescue Services to consolidate the various fire-related activities performed by the county, such as the fire marshal, communications and dispatch, and training.[2] The department was administered by a director, not a fire chief.

Throughout the years, the operating and capital budget of the individual fire departments were funded by separate fire tax districts. A tax levy was established by the county council on each $100 of the assessed value of taxable property in each fire tax district. This was set at a rate sufficient to fund the operations of each fire department, the district's share of the operation of the complete fire and rescue service delivery system, and, later, the Fire and Rescue Commission. When the required tax rate reached 26¢ per $100 of assessed value, the department was included in the Consolidated Fire Tax District. Initially, inclusion began with the highly urbanized communities with large numbers of paid staff but now it includes all of the fire departments. The two highly regarded volunteer rescue squads, Wheaton Volunteer Rescue Squad and the Bethesda/Chevy Chase Rescue Squad, receive little direct financial support from the county.

The structure of the volunteer and combination paid/volunteer departments permitted the augmentation of these monies with additional funds obtained through a variety of fund-raising efforts, including donations, raffles, appeals, and carnivals. This practice continues with the rescue squads generating the hundreds of thousands of dollars necessary to purchase equipment and maintain their vehicles and facilities. Some departments also provide paid daytime staff for the thousands of emergency responses and transport requests. Many of the volunteer fire departments also rely on financial support from their communities to purchase apparatus and equipment, and to provide for the recognition and support of the efforts and contributions from their volunteer members.

A major change to the organization and management of the fire and rescue services delivery system took place in 1979 with the enactment of Bill 15/16-79. Struggling to balance authority, control, and fiscal oversight, the bill provided for: centralized policy making in a newly created Fire and Rescue Commission; called for county-wide standardization of personnel administration for the firefighter employees

---

[2]This has resulted in increased specialization and an increased requirement for training. By 1995, personnel, whether volunteer or career, specialize as firefighter/rescuers, rescuers, or medical attendants. Each specialty has five levels of increasing competency, training, and experience. Furthermore, management personnel are differentiated as sergeants, lieutenants, captains, assistant chiefs, deputy chiefs, and chiefs.

of the individual fire departments; training and certification; directed the development of a master fire defense, rescue, and emergency medical services plan; and provided for a greater degree of oversight by the county executive and county council over the use of public funds. The council did not enact two major recommendations of the county executive. They are: the creation of a county fire chief and the transfer of all paid employees from the individual fire and rescue corporations to the county merit system. They remained employees of the various emergency service organizations, subject to the individual policies of recruitment, hiring, firing, and administration, along with general personnel oversight by the Fire Board.

Significant authority and control remained with the Fire Board as they were given the authority to approve a variety of policies and programs of the Fire and Rescue Commission relating to both career and volunteer personnel. Most importantly, the Fire Board appointed five of its members to the seven member commission. The volunteer chief-dominated Fire Board exercised this appointed authority and controlled the direction for the fire and rescue service delivery system until 1987. After 1987, council legislation gave the appointment authority for all seven members to the county executive with approval by the council.

With a last gasp of recognition for the contributions of the volunteers, the Fire Board was permitted to submit a list of at least ten volunteer firefighters to be considered for appointment to the commission. The legislation further directed that the executive consider at least one member from the list when making the commission appointments.

By the late '80s, the burdens of an expanding system left the delivery system struggling. It was necessary to direct a combined workforce of over 2,000 career and volunteer personnel. Regulatory oversight at the county, state, and national levels was becoming increasingly complicated. In addition, declining participation by trained and experienced emergency service volunteer providers, greater reliance on paid staff, and an increasingly active firefighters' union with its own agenda combined to bring about a great and significant systemic change.

That major systemic change was a change in the employed status of the career firefighters. In January of 1988, the career firefighters and EMTs, hitherto working for the various departments within Montgomery County, became employees of the Department of Fire and Rescue Services of Montgomery County. This was the "high water mark" for the centralization of fire and rescue services within the county. Despite this centralization as of 1995, of the 33 fire/rescue stations within the county, 29 of them are still owned by separate corporations, many of which still raise funds. It seems that Montgomery County has gained control and yet has minimized the cost.

Concluding The Case

From your reading of the Montgomery County case, you will note the features of the suburban volunteer emergency organization we described in Chapter Two. Standards of training for career **and** volunteer personnel are high. Reference to rules is high. Supervision is present, but it is not the dominant way to control worker behavior. Montgomery County has experienced high growth, bringing into its fire/rescue service many newcomers to the county who have a relatively high formal education as compared with the traditional rural volunteer fire department. Despite a community history of residential segregation, the organization is fairly integrated by race and gender. However, do the career and volunteer personnel get along? We examine this question below.

THE NIGHTMARE OF THE FIRE CHIEF

At this stage, it should be evident to the reader why a combination/composite department is a local government's dream. Unfortunately, it is also a fire chief's nightmare. Let us see why this is true. The principal problem is the natural human tendency to seek fairness. When we feel that a relationship is unfair, we tend to feel upset and aggrieved if we are disadvantaged and (to a lesser extent) guilty if we are advantaged (Homans, 1961; Adams, 1965). The easiest way to proceed with an explanation of the fire chief's position is to consider two firefighters: Person C (Career) and Person V (Volunteer). In any relationship, including their relationship with the combination fire department, Person C and Person V each have rewards (R) and costs, or investments (I). For example, Person V is rewarded by being in the parade every July. Similarly, V is rewarded by excitement at fires and skill mastery during training. However, Person V hates fund-raising and boring training (I). As long as the reward, R, is sufficiently greater than the investment, I, then Person V will tend to remain a volunteer.

Similarly, Person C also compares R and I. For example, Person C likes, or is rewarded by (R), the salary, the job security, and the excitement of fires. However, Person C hates, or invests in (I), the paperwork, the station discipline, and the platoon chief. In all likelihood, R will be significantly greater than I, despite the necessities of I, or else turnover within the fire service would be much higher. Rarely do career firefighters quit.

Aside from comparison within each individual's Reward and Investment, both Person V and C (and people in general) make comparisons among each other. For example, both Person V and C will consider it fair if:

$$\frac{R_C}{I_C} = \frac{R_V}{I_V}$$

In effect, fairness does not require equal rewards or equal costs, but it does require an equal ratio between the two.

Unfortunately, we rarely develop standardized calculations of reward and investment unless all rewards and investments are expressed through a medium of exchange, such as money. Consequently, we have a tendency to see the other person as somewhat better off. Thus:

1. Volunteers tend to feel that they are donating their time to the department whereas career firefighters are mercenary;

2. Career firefighters tend to feel that they have invested a great deal of time in training whereas volunteers are merely playing at training;

3. Volunteers believe that only they have significant firefighting experience because they respond to all alarms whereas career firefighters only respond to those alarms during their shift; and

4. Career firefighters believe that since they arrive at the fire scene first, they bear the risk and burden of interior attack.

The first tendency, therefore, is for each group (whether volunteer or career) to minimize its own perception of its rewards and maximize its own perception of its investments. Conversely, the second tendency is to maximize its perception of the rewards of the other group and minimize the perception of that other group's investments. These tendencies are reinforced because volunteers talk among each other and career firefighters talk among each other. Rarely do career personnel interact with volunteers. When such interaction does occur, it is either routinized (although significant) at the fire scene, or very formal, such as in a committee meeting or ceremony.

Aside from the bitterness, and sometimes anger, that arises between volunteer and career firefighters over the failure to perceive fairness, other factors have recently risen that intensify the negative relationship. One of these factors is the tendency to create Career/Infant Volunteer Departments by recruiting and training a core of volunteers to be added to the hitherto fully career department. Most union locals (usually IAFF) perceive these volunteers as "the thin edge of the wedge."

They reasonably fear either job loss or at least reduced hiring once volunteers take on a greater role.

More dramatic still is the impact of local government, or at least fire service consolidation, as was explored in the last chapter. The consolidation of a fully career (or even a career/infant volunteer department) with a fully volunteer, or volunteer dominant department in an adjacent suburb or rural area, is a major threat to job loss through layoffs as well as death, retirement, or exhaustion.

To illustrate the tension between the two groups, consider the research of one of the authors (Benoit, 1992). The firefighters and fire officers of the Surrey Fire Department were surveyed. This department is a naturally consolidated force arising from the consolidation of a number of suburban communities into the City of Surrey (population 300,000, a satellite city of Vancouver, B.C.). The Surrey Fire Department (SFD) had, in 1992, 13 fire stations. Of these, six were composite and seven were fully volunteer. In all, the SFD had a complement of 210 career firefighters, or officers, and 275 volunteers.

One hundred fifty-six career personnel and 76 volunteers responded to a questionnaire that included the scale of items shown in Figure 8.3 below. Respondents were asked to indicate the extent of agreement with the following statements. The statements and the mean (average) response to each statement provided by career and volunteer personnel is indicated in Figure 8.3 below.

ATTITUDINAL DIFFERENCES AMONG PAID AND VOLUNTEER FIREFIGHTERS: MEAN RESPONSES[a]			
Item	Paid Firefighter Mean (n=140)[c]	Volunteer Firefighter Mean (n=57)[c]	Overall Mean (n=197)[c]
a. Career firefighters just want job security.[b]	2.24	2.56	2.33
b. Volunteers mostly join up just to get a career job.	2.97	2.73	2.90

[a.] The scale scores range from strongly disagree (1) to strongly agree (5).

[b.] These items exhibit statistically significant differences between the mean responses of paid and volunteer firefighters, (p<.05).

[c.] The value of n is at a minimum that ranges from: 156 to 140 for paid firefighters; 76 to 57 for volunteers; and 232 to 197 for the total. The value of n varies depending

FIGURE 8.3 *Continued on next page*

FIGURE 8.3 CONTINUED

ATTITUDINAL DIFFERENCES AMONG PAID AND VOLUNTEER FIREFIGHTERS: MEAN RESPONSES[a]

Item	Paid Firefighter Mean (n=140)[c]	Volunteer Firefighter Mean (n=57)[c]	Overall Mean (n=197)[c]
c. Career firefighters are mostly interested in their second jobs.[b]	1.87	2.26	1.98
d. Volunteers are not trained well enough to perform effectively on the fireground.[b]	2.78	1.91	2.53
e. Sometimes the union is a bad influence on career firefighters.	1.78	2.50	1.98
f. Volunteers are taking away jobs and promotions from career firefighters.[b]	3.24	1.89	2.85
g. Career firefighters would prefer to see the volunteers disbanded and be replaced by career firefighters.[b]	3.75	3.22	3.60
h. Volunteers just want to be seen wearing turnout gear and driving around in fancy apparatus with the siren blaring.[b]	2.87	1.59	2.50
i. Career firefighters are the backbone of the Surrey Fire Department.[b]	4.45	3.00	4.03
j. Volunteer firefighters are the backbone of the Surrey Fire Department.[b]	1.81	2.96	2.14
k. Volunteer firefighters leave the equipment in a mess after training.[b]	2.30	1.40	2.04
l. Volunteer firefighters provide a great help to Surrey.[b]	3.74	4.70	4.02
m. There are few things more exciting than responding to an alarm.[b]	2.91	3.35	3.03

[a.] The scale scores range from strongly disagree (1) to strongly agree (5).

[b.] These items exhibit statistically significant differences between the mean responses of paid and volunteer firefighters, ($p<.05$).

[c.] The value of n is at a minimum that ranges from: 156 to 140 for paid firefighters; 76 to 57 for volunteers; and 232 to 197 for the total. The value of n varies depending upon the amount of missing data.

What is particularly surprising is the comparison between volunteer firefighters, career firefighters, and career officers. The research found that volunteer firefighters have negative views of career firefighters. Similarly, career firefighters (not officers) have a negative view of volunteer firefighters (no surprise here). Nevertheless, career officers have a relatively more positive view of volunteer firefighters than career firefighters do. Moreover, senior officers have a more positive view of volunteers than junior officers. Why is this so?

It seems that these senior officers started as volunteer firefighters some 20 to 25 years ago. They probably had a positive view of themselves and a negative view of career firefighters. However, some 15 to 20 years ago they became career firefighters and by adopting the views of their fellow career firefighters, they "scorn[ed] the base degree by which they did ascend." However, some five to ten years ago, when they became junior officers and started bearing the brunt of the firefighters' discontent, they began to react negatively to career firefighters, seeing volunteers more positively. Finally, now as senior officers, they are fraught with budgetary constraints and are socialized to identify with the interests of the Surrey Fire Department and even the City of Surrey itself. Consequently, they appreciate the value of volunteers as an efficient alternative.

PRACTICAL SUGGESTIONS

Over the last two chapters on consolidation and the combination department, we have described organizations reacting to societal pressure. Whether it is a local government or a combination department, the dominant coalition is reacting to powerful external forces. Let us examine each organization, summarize the key concerns, and prescribe advisable action.

Questions A Local Government Might Ask

Q. *How do we live within our means and yet maintain the morale of the career firefighters?*

A. The answer depends on the wealth of the local government. If the local government is relatively well off, then it needs to make a policy statement that it values its career firefighters and does not intend to lay any of them off. Savings are thus achieved through the following strategies:

1. Move the apparatus to suit the fire protection need. Since many volunteer departments have an excess, then such redeployment will reduce capital expenditures over the next five years or so. Announce that this is intended.

2. As (rare) resignations and retirements occur, replace the worker with the most qualified replacement, whether that person is career or volunteer. If that replacement is a career person, then a vacancy chain is created by typically moving down the hierarchy until a replacement by a volunteer(s) occurs. Announce that this is intended. The rate of savings greatly depends on the age structure of the career fire department.

3. If retirement is infrequent over the next few years, investigate early retirement policies. Consider retaining those effective personnel as advisors at a much lower fee. In this way, crucial expertise is not lost. Moreover, an early retirement practice will enhance the promotion opportunities and, therefore, morale among a significant number of career personnel.

4. Making a policy implies that it is in writing and further implies that the policy is made public. This guarantees the commitment and makes reversal of the policy more difficult. The local government surrenders flexibility and, hence, some power by making such policies. However, this should be a small price for maintaining morale.

If the local government is relatively poor, then it may have to lay off career firefighters. How it does so will depend on the existing collective bargaining agreements. Most of these agreements include provisions for layoffs based on reverse seniority, as described below:

1. Since layoff is painful and bad for morale, plan for an excess of layoffs when it occurs so that it need not be revisited every year during the budget process. If possible, engage in layoffs so that the survivors can be assured a security of five years. Then, it is possible to adopt the strategies outlined above for relatively rich local governments. (The adoption of the strategies does not apply to the next suggestion.)

2. Since structural firefighting (particularly interior attack) is a young person's "game," ensure that the physical fitness of the firefighters (both career and volunteer) is maintained at acceptable standards. In all likelihood, in a policy of layoff by reverse seniority, the firefighter that has just been laid off, was, ironically, engaged in the most strenuous aspects of firefighting.

Q. *How do we increase our control over the volunteer fire departments without alienating the very volunteers whose services we need?*

A. The answer depends primarily on what relation develops within the newly created combination department. To a great extent, this likely will rest on the shoulders of the new fire chief. Since this chief will invariably be career as well as a department head, then council and the CAO must give that person direction. That direction should be:

1. Foremost, the chief must not favor or not even seem to be favoring the volunteers over career personnel, or vice versa.

2. Second, the chief must meet with each volunteer station to determine their concerns during the consolidation process. Many of these concerns will be irrelevant to the local government. Knowing them will prevent inadvertent conflict. Problems arise if these concerns are in conflict with local government policy or with each volunteer department. The resulting agreement must be in writing and publicized to council, career staff, the volunteer memberships, and the public. It is desirable that council and the volunteer members ratify the agreement.

Questions A Combination Fire Department Might Ask

Q. *How do we protect our budget in order for us to deliver the same, if not an even greater, level of service for the community we serve?*

A. You cannot protect that whole budget. However, you should expect a predictable base budget over the next five-year period. Given the answers to the questions raised by local governments, the minimum career complement (which is 90% of the budget) should be evident. Moreover, the capital needs of the department should be more easily addressed by redeploying apparatus among volunteer combination and career stations.

Since most volunteer departments underutilize their volunteers (see the justification below) then an **evening** resource is available for fire prevention. Many volunteers can be initiated into pre-fire planning. As they become knowledgeable of the fire code, they can advise the owner/occupant on fire safety and report code violations to career fire inspectors for follow-up work. Since the volunteers will have a reduced fund-raising need, then they will not be caught in the conflict of interest that currently exists.[3]

Q. *How do we keep the autonomy our volunteer membership wants?*

A. "You win some. You lose some." Unfortunately, the losing is more evident than the winning. On one hand, by losing title to appara-

---

[3]Often, volunteers are reluctant to give advice on fire protection when so many other visits are made in order to solicit funds for the department.

tus, the possibility of loss of apparatus increases but then so does the possibility of gain. The policies and procedures of the volunteer group are constrained by some need for standardization. On the other hand, the risk of lawsuit is transferred to the local government. However, as has already been shown in Chapter Four, a risk management program is required.

Nevertheless, the greatest gain in autonomy is the reduced reliance on other sources of funding. This provides more volunteer time to engage in service activities, such as prevention. This allows for a scheduled service activity that increases the predictability of meaningful work for the volunteers.

Irrespective of these advantages, the major role of the senior officers of the volunteer department is to perform rumor control and disseminate accurate information. For example, the importance of rapid response time still means that volunteers will respond with their stations at evening calls. It may also mean that volunteers will be available in the central city to respond from their workplaces.

The social aspect of the volunteer membership will remain. Decisions must still be made. Fund-raising (although at a reduced level) will still be necessary. Volunteer auxiliary organizations will still be required.

Q. *How do we get volunteer and career fire/rescue personnel to get along with each other?*

A. This is the toughest question of all. Indeed, so tough that we are devoting the next few years of research time to examine this question. It may be necessary to distinguish between stations or halls which are fully career, combination, and fully volunteer. Thus, for example, a combination department, by having only fully career and fully volunteer stations, may avoid the conflict that often arises between career and volunteer personnel. Where overriding planning issues require combination stations, then perhaps volunteer and career personnel can be segregated by time if not by space. Career personnel respond to daytime, weekday incidents. Volunteer personnel respond to evening, night, and weekend incidents.

This type of answer is not satisfactory, however. Thus, we intend to conduct more research. We believe that some combination departments are, at least, somewhat successful in integrating career and volunteer personnel. We intend to find these departments and learn what their successful practices are.

EMS: THE BIGGEST DRAGON OF CHANGE

INTRODUCTION

There is probably no single phenomenon that has had a greater impact on volunteer/local government relations than EMS.[1] EMS stands to have even more influence on governments, fire departments, and EMS squads. This chapter intends only to cover what we see as the basic issues faced by volunteer fire and EMS organizations and their local governments as they attempt to adapt to the complex environment forced upon them by the provision of EMS.[2] The economic features of this service are changing so rapidly that we must readily admit our research may be incomplete. However, from our interviews, surveys and literature research, some trends are noticeable.

---

[1] We must note how helpful the Florida EMS Clearinghouse (1317 Winewood Boulevard, Tallahassee, Florida, 32399-0700) and its employee, Ms. Sue McCauley, have been to this chapter. This organization graciously provided us with current published material on EMS.

[2] Several of these issues were discussed in a 1990 report of the Office of Rural Health Policy, U.S. Department of Health and Human Services, entitled: *Success and Failure: A Study of Rural Emergency Medical Services.*

What can happen to volunteer EMS organizations in the face of great internal conflict? Here we examine the published case of the Lexington Lifesaving Squad, a case which has shades of the Queen County situation introduced in the first chapter.

What practical strategies might exist for a volunteer system facing the reality of a paid county EMS agency that is only supposed to augment them, but in fact greatly threatens them? We look here at another published account, a two-part newspaper article that aired one county's EMS woes to a whole state. This case is an example of the all-too-common situation where demand exceeded the best efforts of a volunteer system to meet it.

What future do volunteers have in an environment of managed health care that is economically more favorable to private EMS transport businesses? The issues of internal conflict and coping with change presented by a local government's creation of its own EMS agency are indeed crucial and has immediate concerns for volunteers.

What changes will be faced by local governments? Many suburban and rural "health markets" are becoming attractive to health maintenance organizations (HMOs) and private providers of EMS. The prevailing model of government providing EMS (or seeing that it is provided by volunteers) may well be eroding and the responsibility transferred to HMOs. The wearisome problem of public demand for EMS may be redefined also, due to changes in the role of paramedics toward more in-home care with less transport.

Qualifications About Volunteer Organizations

We should make some qualifications before we continue about the types of organizations likely to be caught up in the changes we are considering. The case examples in this chapter are about volunteer organizations that provide only EMS, often called rescue squads. This is in no way to suggest that volunteer fire departments, which have adopted EMS as a mission, are immune. In most cases, it would be accurate to say that many volunteer departments have become EMS providers that also run fire calls. This fact has been a bitter pill to swallow for many traditionally oriented firefighters. The changes may be somewhat less threatening to all-volunteer fire departments that provide EMS simply because their mission is not threatened to the same degree as with a volunteer organization that is solely devoted to EMS.

Combination departments (volunteer and paid personnel) that provide EMS are considered likely to suffer the most disruption. This would be less from internal conflict and more from the uncertainties faced by government in the context of migration of EMS responsibility to HMOs and private providers. Fully paid government fire and EMS systems have already been in the national news about their struggles with private providers. (See Robert Tomsho's December 27, 1994 article in the *Wall Street Journal*, "Ambulance Companies Fight Municipalities for Emergency Market," and Mark Fritz's October 30, 1994 Associated Press article picked up by the *Richmond Times-Dispatch*, "U.S. firefighters working to save their livelihood: They're battling corporations for paramedic work.") It seems to us that combination fire departments are in a direct line for confrontation with private providers seeking EMS contracts from HMOs. We will take up this subject near the end of this chapter. Before we return to real-life issues, allow us to note a few somewhat abstract points about EMS as we see it.

FOOD FOR THOUGHT: SOME BACKGROUND FEATURES OF EMS

EMS is fundamentally different from fire service. Differences are in the skills and training needed, the theoretical knowledge upon which these skills are based, the professional control of this knowledge, and, most importantly, the economic costs of these services. EMS is a medical specialty and requires skills that are deemed to be so important that they have extensive oversight by physicians and state level bureaucracies. It is part of the health care industry in the United States, and, thus, subject to changes in this industry.

Unlike fire service, EMS now is a means to an end served by a hospital. The goal of fire service when something is undergoing rapid oxidation is to suppress the fire, which it is uniquely equipped to do. At present, rescue, stabilization, and transport of a "patient" are means for the injured, or otherwise sick person, to regain his or her normal health status in a hospital setting. The health of the person can be thought of as in a constant state of risk.

EMS is increasingly seen as a panacea, or universal cure, for all sorts of messes in which people find themselves. Before we examine specific problems that seem to be inherent in the volunteer provision of EMS, we will highlight several general background ideas that may be helpful in becoming oriented to problems attendant to this service.

The "Fountain of Youth" Myth

The legendary Fountain of Youth, a spring with the powers of rejuvenation, was the object of exploration into the New World by brave navigators like Ponce de Leon who, in 1513, discovered Florida. This myth of finding a fountain that could rejuvenate one's youthful vigor and forestall death sounds silly. However, we suggest metaphorically that the public's thirst for high-tech medicine — EMS in particular — may be understood in light of the ancient quest to defeat aging and death.

Could it be that EMS symbolizes a modern technological version of the Fountain of Youth? Certainly, it seems that the public puts a great deal of trust in EMS, evidenced by the volume of calls to 9-1-1. The public does see EMS as a way to defeat all kinds of accidents, diseases, and violence that afflict people.

The Expanding Definition Of "Emergency"

While there is no natural ceiling to the number of calls to 9-1-1, there seems to be an expansion of the kinds of crises EMS is expected to resolve. In a recent issue of *Annals of Emergency Medicine* (Williams, 1993: p. 125), the president of the American College of Emergency Physicians, R.M. Williams, wrote: "AIDS, trauma, domestic violence, substance abuse, elderly abandonment, access to care for the homeless, and the uninsured: the specialty of emergency medicine is truly on the cutting edge of the most important issues facing our society."

The Little Sister Phenomenon

EMS has never really belonged to any single kind of organization, unlike fire service. Perhaps this is because its modern history only dates back a few decades (Boyd, 1983; Mustalish and Post, 1994). It can commonly be found in a wide variety of configurations involving fire departments, volunteer EMS squads, private providers, hospitals, funeral homes, and even civic clubs.

EMS's historical relationship with fire departments can be described as that of a stepchild. Early on, it was not fully embraced as part of the overall mission of these organizations. There is an argument today about how well integrated and respected it is by the fire service (Gresham, 1994; Page, 1990). One former president of the IAFC even described EMS as the "little sister" of the fire service.

Fire departments have now been drawn into the health care arena in ways few expected. EMS is essentially the main business of most of the departments (career and volunteer) that provide it. At the same time, the number of structure fire calls have decreased such that EMS, ironically, represents the livelihoods of many career firefighters (Page, 1990; Fritz, 1994). Volunteer departments often become dependent on it as a means by which to acquire greater funding. (This strategy for growth is not without side effects, as we will note below.) While EMS is likely to be the dominant service in departments that provide it, (whether it is done so gladly or begrudgingly), it is essentially a medical concern. And, as we have suggested, health care economics are causing considerable uncertainty about the fire service's role in EMS provision (Murphy, 1986; Ludwig, 1994; Garza, 1994a).

Future Power Of Hospitals And Private Providers

EMS is ultimately controlled by the medical profession. This profession is firmly affiliated with hospitals and related organizational variations particularly like health maintenance organizations (HMOs).[3] Along with its large base of abstract knowledge, this profession has the power and organizational resources to dictate the direction of EMS. Furthermore, as we noted in our chapter (Chapter Four) on legal issues, there is no historical tradition of any **duty** of government to provide EMS. Although, most governments for political reasons try to provide it, or provide for it, in the form of a public utility.

Unlike fire service, which has traditionally had a much closer relationship with government (such as appealing to governmental immunity for tort lawsuits), EMS is more sensitive to economic pushes and pulls. Economic factors now seem to be pulling EMS toward whomever can perform the service at the lowest cost and according to standards set by large, regional, hospital organizations and insurance providers. The guiding philosophy of these hospital organizations is health care that is cost effective and "managed" by the health organization or its contracting agent. This philosophy assumes that to maximize cost effectiveness, the management of health should begin at the time a health crisis first occurs. We will see below that such a perspective will most likely mean less transport, more in-home care for "patient-

---

[3] According to Sorkin (1986), HMOs are: "integrated organizations of various health care providers responsible for providing and overseeing the comprehensive health care of their enrollees." The type of payment is an important distinction in understanding these organizations. The traditional method of paying for health care had been to pay a fee for some service. HMOs use a system of advance payment for care. This system is referred to as capitation or capitated system, where a fixed rate per person is paid — often by an employer — to the HMO before services are given. Hospitals often contract with HMOs to deliver services to enrollees. There are strong incentives to reduce utilization, particularly in-hospital care. EMS transports to the hospital as part of an HMO would be the kind of utilization the HMO would seek to discourage.

subscribers," and new patterns of relationships between EMS providers and health organizations (Criss, 1994; Garza, 1994a; Kuehl, 1994; Wolff, 1994).

A public utility approach to EMS delivery implies that economy of scale is so important a factor that competition will result in inefficiency.[4] Jack Stout and the American Ambulance Association (1994) have suggested this. Since efficiency requires a local monopoly, they argue that the deliverer of EMS be regulated by contract incentives and penalties that ensure high patient care at a competitive cost. Ambulance companies will not compete to arrive to the patient, but they will compete when they bid on a multi-year contract with a large local government or a consortium of small ones. Failure to perform to contracted standards, such as response time, may be sufficient to cancel the contract. This keeps the deliverer "on its toes." It also tends to encourage larger EMS firms that can demonstrate a history of complying with the contracted standards. Thus, the EMS industry tends to concentrate its ownership in fewer and fewer firms.

STRAINS OF SUPPLY AND DEMAND IN VOLUNTEER SYSTEMS

Just as there is uncertainty when we think of national level EMS economics and contests for control, there is also considerable ambiguity on the local level of how to provide EMS and at what quantity (and quality). Philosophically speaking, most people would argue that a society could never have too much medical care. But, speaking practically, it is a matter of what can be afforded.

Volunteers complicate the economics of provision. In a world of strictly paid labor, it would seem to be relatively easy to know when financial limits have been reached in service provision. In a system that is based on volunteer organizations, and local government believing it has some responsibility for this provision, the goal of achieving a stable service seems to us to be a hard one to reach. Governments want to be responsive to voters and provide the greatest good for the greatest number. Volunteer fire and EMS organizations want to do this also.

---

[4] If the population served is too small, then the public must either pay a large subsidy to the EMS provider or accept excessive response times resulting in more patient deaths. A larger area and population permits sufficient transport calls to pay for the cost of maintaining acceptable response time (such as ALS care which is delivered within eight minutes, 90% of the time).

The limits of service in a volunteer context are not so much economic as they are limits of human sacrifices of time and energy. We should remind the reader that this public service by members of volunteer organizations is something in which they have tremendous pride and emotional investment. It has deep meaning for both the individuals and the organizations. This meaning often encompasses religion and patriotism. Thus, we can begin to understand the reactions of volunteer organizations in the face of demand for EMS that is beyond their capacity to meet.

Allow us to make one more point about volunteer organizations before we present some actual case examples. This point was brought out in Chapter Two. Because volunteer organizations embrace the ethic of democracy in much of their business affairs, they can be inefficient compared to a purely corporate or bureaucratic model. Leaders are often elected who have little leadership ability. And democracy, by definition, produces opposition groups and factions that can, among other things, erode retention and leadership effectiveness. Also, democracy has the ironic tendency to produce a small group of individuals who seek to build their own little empires. Conflicts can become bitter and long lasting. What appears to the outsider as a relatively simple organization, to those of us who are attentive members, we recognize it as very complex.

CASE: UGLY INTERNAL CONFLICT SPILLS INTO PUBLIC VIEW

"Squad squabbles cause resignations" by Doug Harwood (*The Rockbridge Advocate,* "Independent as a Hog on Ice," Volume 3, No. 8, October 1994). (Minor deletions have been made with permission.)

Conflicting volunteer fire and rescue squad politics are nothing new. But rarely do they spill out into public view.

About a year ago, Lexington police were called to break up an argument between two women. One of them was charged — and later convicted — with curse and abuse. Such things happen all the time. But this time, the call was unusual. First of all, it was to the Lexington Lifesaving and First Aid Crew Building. Secondly, the argument was between two members of the squad, Nancy Wade and Theresa Moore. And Moore, the woman charged in the incident, is a police dispatcher.

It is not uncommon for volunteer organizations to have their internal bickering. But, largely because of them, the Lexington squad has been losing members — at least 20 since 1990.

Captain Roy Smith, who has been with the squad for 27 years and who answers nearly every daylight call, distinctly does not want to talk about the bickering. "I think it's very childish," he says. "We don't have a problem. We have a problem with one member. That is no different from any other organization in the world. It will eventually work itself out."

"You get burned out," says former 1st Lt. Mickey Cochrane. "You get gruesome calls. Drunks and druggies fight you all the way to the hospital. You have difficulty getting to sleep when you're on call." Cochrane had been a member of the Glasgow Rescue Squad for ten years when he joined Lexington's in 1979. "A lot of people resented that," he says.

Cochran's [sic] resignation came six months after he questioned squad secretary Theresa Moore's accounting of the number of calls he answered. (Squad members are paid $2.50 per call.) Moore responded with a sarcastic letter that ends with, "Mickey, in other words, get off my ass!"

And [Cochrane's resignation letter] came two days after [Captain] Smith sent out a long letter saying: "We have members that are hell bent and determined to do everything they can possibly do to defy every rule, by-law, minutes, policies, or anything this organization has worked for or stood for, for the last fifty-eight years. Their policies, rules, and by-laws were not made by me, but by members that worked hard so we — the present members — can have the vehicles, equipment, and building, that some of you as members refuse to keep clean, or take care of anything that is in this building."

After complaining about some members being lazy, Smith wrote: "I gave everyone a new lock for their locker, so everything would look uniform. In order to defy that to this date, three members have installed three different lock types. Anything to be different. Well, as the saying goes, the worm will turn. I'm tired of cleaning up behind you, swallowing everything said about me, and being one of the members to cover all the daylight calls and weekend calls. It's your turn now...I tried to run the crew the way it has been run for the past fifty-eight years. We have a quarter of a million dollars in the bank, three-quarters of a million dollars in equipment, and over one half a million dollars in a beautiful building. You are paid now for each call you answer, and we are working on a retirement system for active members. I question, what changes does the crew need to make?"

Joan Daniel resigned in response to that letter. She told Smith, "You have a very critical situation on your hands with our Rescue Squad members and I am truly sorry you have been placed in that position." She goes on to say, "It has been called to my attention that certain personality conflicts within our membership has reached a stage of explosion. I am extremely sorry that this has not been brought out in the open before now to get the facts straight before it reached the present level of conflict. I can sympathize with you, but for what it is worth, you have no choice but to remain neutral in whatever develops. If you take sides now, whatever occurs will surely ruin what you have built up for yourself during the years of your tenure. This situation has now gone beyond a peaceable solution; it is way too late for that...

"No one told me when I requested to join the crew that gossip and unfounded rumors would be the criteria used to keep me as a squad member. No one said that my every move was to be analyzed and how I reacted toward one person or another would determine whose side I was on. Are these the qualities expected of our members? Are we to find fault with everything anyone does in order to remain in the good graces of others. Should we criticize and make fun of other members for the sake of staying on the crew? If so, what is the Lexington Lifesaving and First Aid Crew all about? There is no future for anyone on the squad without trust and respect for each other."

One woman who quit the squad after a few years, despite what she says is her love of the work, says personalities have a lot to do with the squad. "Roy Smith feels like it is his squad. He takes a personal interest in it." And, she says, some of the tasks assigned to her were degrading. "Hell, I spent more time cleaning their bathroom than my own. He wanted us to look professional, but we're volunteers."

"Most are leaving for the same reason," says another, who was in the squad for more than a decade. "It's dissatisfaction with the management of the squad. It has nothing to do with the people or the training. To tell you the truth, there's not a Lexington rescue squad. It revolves around two certain people. Everything centers around them."

If there's one thing that nearly everyone interviewed about the squad can agree on, it is that the days of volunteer squads are numbered. Too many employers will not let their employees go out on calls. And fewer and fewer people are willing to volunteer for what can turn into a nearly full-time job for little or no pay.

"I've been concerned about the number of members," Lexington City Manager Jon Ellestad says. "There are not that many people who are that interested in rescue squad work."

He's heard a number of complaints about the management of the squad. They vary, he says, "from somebody who just doesn't like something," to Smith's insisting that squad members come to training meetings. "Does he rub some people the wrong way? Well, yes, he rubs some people the wrong way."

He hopes that the city squad can continue to keep old members and attract new ones. The alternative is a paid squad. If one started, it would begin with two employees to answer daylight calls. Ellestad figures they would have to be paid, with fringe benefits, between $30,000 and $35,000 each. Once that happens, a full-time paid squad is inevitable, he says, because of the inevitable friction between volunteers and the people who are being paid to do the same work the volunteers are. And the price of a full-time paid squad, Ellestad says, "is substantial."

The Strain Of Great Internal Conflict

We selected the article about the Lexington Lifesaving and First Aid Crew because it represents an extreme, but not uncommon form of stress that can happen inside a volunteer organization. What is uncommon is for reporters to have access to such poignant written correspondence from these groups.

The squad in the present case was all volunteer and in a relatively rural setting, but with pockets of industrial and housing developments. This organization had the misfortune of media attention to its "dirty laundry." There seemed to be nowhere for the conflicts of the informal relations inside the organization to go. The members seemed to be intensely focused on themselves as hurt individuals, rather than as members holding positions in a professional-type organization. This organization was absolutely dedicated to its mission of EMS but seemingly unable to handle its own "health crisis."

It would be easy to blame the individuals for a variety of indiscretions and blunders, but this is not appropriate. The problem as we see it is that these organizations are so focused on delivering EMS, often intentionally isolated from other organizations, that they are not equipped to deal with internal conflict.[5] If we add to this the problems of leadership selection and inefficiency in a context of providing a demanding service, then we see a troubling picture.

We do not wish to suggest that only EMS squads have serious internal conflict. No organization is immune to this. However, in light of the number of calls to these squads, the human misery to which volunteers must attend, the extensive training requirements, along with the internal organizational weaknesses, it does seem logical to expect that volunteer organizations devoted to EMS would be at great risk of explosive internal politics. Perkins (1989, p.8) found in a study of 1202 volunteers from 92 all-volunteer EMS squads in Virginia that internal conflict was the answer most often given to an open-ended question about the greatest problem in the squad. He stated: "The [volunteer EMS] service is being performed at a dangerous level of high output by organizations that are plagued by tremendous internal conflict..."

Nor do we wish to paint an overly negative picture of these groups. We do want to say, however, that many leaders and government officials seem to take these groups for granted and have very little understanding of their nature. In some cases — like the Queen County squad — the government does not want to know anything.

Short of the government getting into the EMS business by creating its own agency of paid EMTs, what can be done to address such conflict that drains off personnel and lowers the organization's level of service? A number of possibilities come to mind, most of which would not work. Here is a short list of tempting but dubious moves to address internal conflict:

1. Formation (by whom?) of an external conflict resolution team from the community to arbitrate the grievances.

2. A sudden threat by government to link funding to accountability and performance (likely to be easily read as a hollow threat and make problems worse).

---

[5] See Rich Adams' (1995) article in *Firehouse*, "Rural Responders," for a sensitive treatment of some of the stresses of providing EMS in small communities.

3. Calling in sociologists as consultants to the leaders. (A dubious move to have outsiders of any stripe get into it).

4. Visitation by state EMS officials with a thinly veiled threat to revoke license. (This might work for paid people).

5. Renewed efforts at recruitment to replace the quitters (who have likely poisoned the recruit pool).

6. New elections to install fresh leaders. (This has some promise.)

7. Requiring all members to take a class in civility. (This has promise as a preventative measure.)

There are some positive implications from all this, that we will present below, related to prevention of internal conflict on a large scale. These have to do with changes in the internal structure of the organization and the linkages to other groups. Let us now turn to another typical EMS scenario. This is the situation where a county government gets into the EMS business.

CASE: SMALL COUNTY GOVERNMENT GETS INTO EMS BUSINESS
Part One

A two part "Special Report" in Virginia's state-wide newspaper appeared on the front page of the *Richmond Times-Dispatch* on November 27 and 28, 1994, with the following headlines:

"Calls for help now always answered: Despite progress, Dinwiddie's EMS system is ailing" by M. W. Goodwyn

"Change key to curing EMS ills" by M. W. Goodwyn

(With the permission of the *Times-Dispatch*, we have made minor deletions to shorten the text of these articles.)

When an early morning car crash on Interstate 85 in May left three people dead and one injured, only two rescue squad workers were on duty in the county.

The crash occurred at a time when Dinwiddie typically has few volunteer rescue squad members available for duty. Rescue units from two nearby localities and a state police Med-Flight crew assisted with the wreck.

"We could have used more help," said Dinwiddie County Administrator Charles W. Burgess Jr. "A catastrophic event like this exceeded our ability at that moment. This is the type of situation that can be improved."

The crash highlighted Dinwiddie's long time problems with emergency medical coverage, especially during the day. Problems of coverage gaps and a shortage of volunteers are common throughout the state. But the problems are keenly felt in a county the size of Dinwiddie — 502 square miles — with vast ribbons of secondary roads and Interstates 85 and 95.

"You can't tell people that they can dial 911 and not have help 24 hours a day," said Jon R. Donnelly, executive director of the Old Dominion Emergency Medical Services Alliance, a regional agency that works with the state Office of Emergency Medical Services and local rescue groups.

There are two volunteer rescue squads in the county — Dinwiddie Fire and Rescue Company 4... and Dinwiddie Volunteer Rescue Squad. Last month, a [third] crew employed by the county started providing additional daytime coverage.

But the county's EMS system is still ailing.

During the summer, "it became apparent that 24-hour coverage was lacking in Dinwiddie," Donnelly said.

Dinwiddie officials called Donnelly to seek advice on staffing problems. They also asked him to serve on a task force formed in July after volunteers asked the county for staffing help.

Using the I-85 crash as an example of the problems the county must overcome, Donnelly said, "It's not to say that volunteers were the blame. It's to say it's something you don't want to ever happen again."

The task force, which included supervisors, county officials, fire and rescue volunteers, and a sheriff's department dispatcher, examined EMS deficiencies. "The situation didn't happen overnight," said task force member Edward B. Titmus, a farmer and lifelong Dinwiddie resident who served for 21 years on the board of directors of the Dinwiddie Volunteer Rescue Squad.

The task force discovered response times that were too long, a shortage of round-the-clock basic and advanced life support personnel, and an inability to help neighboring localities as much as they were aiding Dinwiddie. "There were times when there was actually no one on duty in the county," Titmus said.

Anne Scarborough, a task force member and long time Dinwiddie resident, said, "I've been concerned about this for years. It's a top priority as far as I'm concerned. People have been questioning [the county's emergency] services for a long time. From listening to my [police] scanner and what other people had said, I felt that there were hours we didn't have any coverage. Every citizen in Dinwiddie deserves EMS coverage."

One county woman said when she called 911 on a recent afternoon during a life-threatening emergency, rescue workers "seemed like they took their time coming. It may have been anxiety on my part. But I had to call a second time." The woman declined to be identified because she was concerned about offending rescue squad personnel.

"The problem was they came, they checked [the patient], but they didn't have anyone that could start an IV [intravenous procedure]," she said. "They called ahead for a volunteer to meet them down the road who could start the IV." The patient was successfully taken to a hospital.

Part Two _____

Disagreements about emergency medical services in Dinwiddie County have sometimes overshadowed the mission over the years, but county leaders and volunteer squad members realize that must change.

Dinwiddie officials created a task force in July to address rescue squad staffing problems after volunteers asked the county for help. In September, county supervisors adopted the task force's recommendations to "reinforce, not replace" volunteers.

"There's the perception that the county is saying [the volunteers] are bad people and is out to replace them, which is not true," said Jon R. Donnelly, a task force member and executive director of the Old Dominion Emergency Medical Services Alliance. "The Board of Supervisors took a brave step, realizing a potentially explosive issue."

Aubrey Clay, a Dinwiddie supervisor and task force member, is a long time supporter of an all-volunteer EMS system. He was torn in his decision to approve more paid help.

"We got into a situation where people had to be served," he said. "We'd have a wreck and nobody to cover it. The volunteers dwindled down to where they didn't have enough people to do the job. We have to do what we have to do."

Changes in Dinwiddie are a natural evolution of patient care, said Donnelly. "It's going to take some adjustment in attitude among all the people involved," he said.

The pool of one full-time and 11 part-time paid EMS providers includes three emergency medical technicians, six cardiac technicians and three paramedics. Under the new plan, paid staff will be able to support and supplement squads when no volunteers are available because of staffing shortages or because the volunteer crew is on an emergency call.

"Until volunteers are available in the evenings, residents have coverage," said Dinwiddie County Administrator, Charles W. Burgess Jr.

Some dissatisfaction among volunteers stems from ego problems, Donnelly said. "Volunteers are trying to do their best. They take great pride as a rescue squad person," he said. "But sometimes it is difficult for people to face reality. None of us likes to admit that we need help. Whether it's real or perceived, they don't want to feel they're being dumped on."

R. Bruce Archer, chief of Dinwiddie Fire and Rescue Company 4 and a member of the task force, said he had reservations about the panel's solution — more paid help to cover hours when volunteers were least available. "I felt certain individuals had already made up their minds and the task force was getting what they already knew they wanted," Archer said of the outcome. But now Archer has a different outlook. Volunteers "were a little leery at first because they thought the paid people were going to end up controlling the entire county," Archer said. "Now they're finding out that's not the case. We're doing the same job. I don't cringe anymore at nine in the morning when I hear an EMS call because I know [the paid workers are] in the county.

"I'm happy my [volunteers] are working with the paid EMS people every day and happy the county is putting out the money."

But some residents are concerned that bad feelings may result because of the paid-volunteer combination.

Elmer Jeter, a former volunteer squad member who started in the 1970s, said, "How are you going to pay ten and expect thirty to do it for nothing? It can lower morale."

Dawn Titmus said past relations among the squads sometimes were strained but are improving. Part of the tension was because Titmus is a relative of Edward B. Titmus, who served on the task force that recommended more paid employees. "It's better than it was," she said. "I think there was a lot of tension there."

Titmus is the only full-time provider on the county's EMS crew. She had been employed part time since January. In September, when the county decided to expand the paid staff, all four of the part-timers had to reapply.

The paid EMS workers recently sponsored a demonstration for Dinwiddie squads featuring the state's newest Med-Flight helicopter. The effort introduced EMS providers to differences between the new aircraft and the old ones. James McWatters, a Company 4 volunteer, said the demonstration was another step in bridging gaps between the squads.

"It's about time," McWatters said. "It's a good thing. Patient care is more important than politics. I think it's great that we have paid people during the day. That's what we needed. I don't feel like paid people should be a threat. They're there to help the volunteers."

Before the task force recommendations were implemented, paid EMS workers were supervised by Dinwiddie Volunteer Rescue Squad and operated under that squad's medical license. But liability questions were raised regarding that arrangement and the task force opted for the county to secure its own license to provide EMS.

"Dinwiddie Volunteer Rescue Squad was trying to do a good job of administering the [former] part-time people, but the county needed to do it," he said. "Supervision was the problem." Burgess, the county administrator, said, "I feel more comfortable as far as on-site supervision of county employees and structuring them. The county is in a position to be more responsive in overseeing their actions."

The county also applied to the state Office of Emergency Medical Services for a state grant to purchase its own ambulance for the paid providers. They now use an ambulance supplied by Dinwiddie Volunteer Rescue Squad. Word on the application is expected in January. The paid crew, operating as Dinwiddie County Emergency Medical Services, is housed near the county's government complex.

Each of the county's three EMS groups operate independently under the physician who supervises patient care services.

Floyd Wilson, a member of the Company 4 rescue squad, said he's OK with paid help "as long as it doesn't cut into our budget." He's concerned that county funds targeted for volunteer squads will be undercut by funds set aside to operate the paid service.

But Burgess said financing paid service will not impact allocations to either of the two volunteer squads.

One task force member, Anne Scarborough, said she hopes volunteers can muster the staffing and commitment needed to provide all-day coverage. "I'm waiting to give them a chance to regroup, seek membership and training. If they can't do it, I'm going to push for paid people," she said.

Donnelly said he would like to see the task force and county rescue squads reassembled to form an EMS advisory council.

"I see tremendous improvement compared to six months ago. It's time to settle down and begin the process of rebuilding manpower," Donnelly said.

"They've recognized the problem. Now they've taken steps to begin the solutions. They've decided against the Band-Aid approach. This is going to cure the patient."

Injecting County Employees Into A Volunteer System

We apologize to the reader for the length of the preceding case material, but we felt that a full reading of these articles was necessary to capture the complexity of the seemingly simple addition of paid personnel. What we have here is a fairly typical situation in which volunteer EMS squads and county governments find themselves. That is, the capacity for volunteer organizations to supply EMS has been surpassed by demand. Since the prevailing, unquestioned assumption is that EMS is a public utility, it is the government that is compelled to act. Ironically, there is no mention of any attempts by a hospital to give aid and comfort, though practically every EMS patient arrives there and is sent home with a large bill. Nor did there seem to be a serious consideration of a recruitment effort to find new volunteers.

Typical Model Of Governmental Response

The case of the Dinwiddie EMS squad provides us with a chain of six key events that might be seen, with minor variation, in many other localities. First, there was **a hidden but widely known history of problems** with response times and insufficient personnel. Second, there was a **precipitating event**, in the form of an interstate auto crash, where there was considerable public exposure of the response of the squad. Sometimes such an event is a lawsuit. Third, with the problem no longer hidden, **someone has to act officially**. The government appointed a **task force** for fact finding (although the facts are already known) and for unbiased recommendations. Fourth, there seemed to be considerable **retrospective interpretation** of past actions of the squad to fit the current definition of the situation. Fifth, by this time the only solution perceived by government is to expend resources for paid help. There was some paid help already, supervised by the squad and presumably on its payroll. The government opted to **create a new governmental agency** made up of former squad-employed workers, but still relying mostly on part-time employees. Sixth, many **volunteers felt fear and a suspicion of a doomsday** for their endeavors. However, the official statement of "reinforcing, not replacing" volunteers probably served to reassure volunteers of their place in the county's EMS system. However, old-timer Elmer Jeeter's question is haunting: "How are you going to pay ten and expect thirty to do it for nothing?"

PRACTICAL CONSIDERATIONS FOR VOLUNTEERS AND GOVERNMENT

Make A Distinction Between People And Their Positions _____

In many situations of great internal conflict, we have noticed that there is a tendency for some volunteer organizations to blur the distinction between a person and his or her position. There is a tendency for people to believe they own their positions. In a church congregation, when a member quits, his or her position in that congregation is lost, except in cases of leadership jobs. In volunteer emergency organizations, there needs to be sufficient formality such that when a person leaves, his or her position remains and the loss is not seen as irreparable.

If people are recruited into preexisting positions (including rank and file ones) the psychology of the organization may not respond with such doom and gloom when there is membership turnover. **A healthy view of the organization is that it exists independently of the people in it, and that leaders and members should at least act as if this were fact.**

There are a couple of corollaries to this idea of recruiting for positions, as opposed to people. The reader will recall that Chapter Three describes the psychological process of ego involvement as the volunteer is eventually socialized to become a chief (or a squad captain). First, if a member understands that he or she holds a distinct and predefined position among other positions, there may be a reduction of the amount of ego involvement of individuals who are inclined to overinvest their time, energy, and self-concept in the organization. Admittedly, this is somewhat speculative on our part, but it makes some sense in light of the nature of volunteer organizations that set virtually no limit on how much a member can give to the group. This "investment" phenomenon is a double-edged sword inherent in many all-volunteer organizations.

Second, all of us know that in any conflict situation, there may well be individuals so aggrieved for reasonable or unreasonable causes that they cannot be deterred from trying intentionally to damage the organization. If the organization has the view of itself as existing independently of the people in it, less weaponry is provided to the angry member or members. Further, it would seem these individuals would be less able to upset the majority.

Expand Structure, Mission, And Linkages To Other Organizations

In the face of change that seems to threaten the survival of a volunteer organization, the organization can, in a sense, remake itself into something that causes members to focus on the future instead of the past. Here, we are thinking of some strategic changes in the mission of the traditional volunteer EMS organization. Adding the mission of public safety and education along with programs aimed, for example, at children and/or the elderly, the organization can set itself on an expanded course that can result in invigorating the embattled and embittered volunteers.

Whether or not there is expansion of mission, a volunteer organization can make some simple internal structural modifications that can relieve some pressure on the membership. Brown (1993) and Fitch (1994) noted that positions could be created for non-medical needs of a volunteer squad, like administration, physical plant maintenance, fund-raising, and recruitment. Such a move would expand the recruit pool of potential volunteers, relieve time commitment and burnout, and generally redistribute a heavy workload.

A volunteer EMS organization can build linkages to other community organizations, especially hospitals. Since hospitals are the typical destination of emergency transports, it would seem fitting that squads

217

and hospitals become partners. (See, Perkins, Ballweg, and Dyer, 1993). In the future, these linkages to hospitals (and HMOs) may prove particularly helpful in the survival of volunteer squads.

Provide Financial Incentives To Volunteers

"How are you going to pay ten and expect thirty to do it for nothing?" is a relevant question. Clearly, the ethic of providing Good Samaritan service is a powerful motivator in the culture of volunteer EMS organizations. However, squad leaders and local government cannot expect the world to be the same for volunteers when the decision is made to have even a small paid service to augment a volunteer system.

In the face of a newly created paid EMS agency, volunteers almost always feel threatened. Financial rewards programs, such as an awards plan based on length of service, seem to us to be a concrete step a locality can take for volunteers. (See also Hudgins, 1988; Garza, 1991; National Volunteer Fire Council, 1993). One of the best known of such plans is sponsored by the Volunteer Firemen's Insurance Services, Inc. Essentially, this is a pension system where a volunteer earns credit toward a small retirement (often between $50 and $100 per month upon reaching age 55). There are numerous other financial incentives concerning recruitment we have already addressed in Chapter Six. But for now, let us say that if a locality really wants to see volunteers remain a significant part of an EMS service, it should consider a systematic financial program for volunteers.

One great advantage for leaders and government officials of a formalized monetary reward system is the leverage it can give toward accountability of volunteer organizations. All sorts of behavioral expectations can be tied to eligibility for rewards. In a sense, the adoption of a length of service rewards program can cause volunteers to rethink and remake their whole operation toward the future instead of dwelling on the past.

Insist On Leadership Training

Stittleburg (1994c), speaking about the National Volunteer Fire Council, strongly asserted that leadership is the key to a healthy volunteer organization. We agree. One can find the issue of the need for leadership training in almost every published article and research report about volunteer (and career) fire and EMS organizations. However, there seem to be barriers preventing many volunteer leaders from actually becoming "trained" in administration and management.

What we have to say begs the question of exactly what is leadership training. This is a question we feel is worth asking. Although a curriculum of leadership training is beyond the scope of this book, we do believe that a large portion of any training course should focus on the nature of volunteer organizations and their strategic planning. Such a curriculum should not be limited to incident command and response matters (Benoit, Richardson, Rees, and Holesworth, 1989).

Oddly enough, the virtuous element of democracy works against leadership training. Many leaders are elected who believe they already know enough about leading the organization. Since it is just a small volunteer group, how hard can it be? Therefore, blunder after blunder occurs until they are at the end of their term or an opposition group succeeds in voting them out. The unluckiest of organizations get civil rights lawsuits as a result of bad leadership and internal conflict, examples of which we presented in Chapter Four.

Democracy can often require term limits for all officers. In some volunteer organizations we have studied, there is a limit of two one-year terms. The most committed and open-minded leader would have to be unusually motivated to put much work in "leadership training" when he or she may only have one or two years in the position. In other organizations, like the Lexington squad, the captain apparently had been in his position for years, a situation that brings its own problems in finding a successor.[6] Leadership succession problems are common to all organizations, however, not just volunteer ones. We have noticed that leaders often do not train underlings to succeed them.

Perhaps one of the best ways to assure that persons undergo some sort of training in leadership (beyond incident command) is to build such a requirement into the duties of all the leadership positions. This, unfortunately for most organizations, might necessitate by-law changes. Of course, this is an internal political matter, practically untouchable by local government. **Although there are problems in instituting leadership training, it is a low-cost, high-yield strategy**.

Volunteers never like to be told by outsiders what they should do. So, if the county or local association of squad leaders and/or fire chiefs decided to have such a training exercise (and perhaps, better yet, to design it themselves) there might be some hope of good attendance.

---

[6] The reader is encouraged to consult Caplow's (1983) *Managing an Organization,* where he discusses leadership succession. Alvin Gouldner's (1954) *Patterns of Industrial Bureaucracy*, is a fine case study of problems of leadership succession.

Although, it does seem that much of the time of many similar associations is spent on county politics, renumbering apparatus, devising disaster plans, and planning for drills and competitions. Leadership training might not carry much priority. Perhaps, if a county has a volunteer coordinator, this would be a good opportunity for him or her to use his or her leadership skills and set leadership training in motion. In fact, a volunteer coordinator's effort at establishing a curriculum of leadership training would probably be seen as supportive of volunteers.

Government Should Make Clear What It Wants

One theme that was apparent from our interviews with fire service leaders was the importance of a government making a clear policy statement about what it wants the future of EMS and fire services to be. Given the nature of volunteer organizations to react, (and overreact), a government needs publicly and formally to declare its view of how volunteers fit into the future of the locality. If volunteers are to be the foundation of any system in the foreseeable future, then the government should state this in no uncertain terms. Failure to communicate a definition of the future role of volunteers will almost invariably lead to a volatile, politically charged situation. In a context of fighting for survival, volunteers in EMS and fire service can wield immense power over government, not to mention attract considerable media attention and even unwittingly damage public service.

We turn now to a consideration of probable future changes. These changes could very well be on a much greater scale than that of a government getting into the EMS business to help volunteers meet demand. At the very least, governments and volunteer emergency organizations need to know about these potential changes. Hopefully, what we have to say might stimulate planning. We admit that portraying the future for volunteer EMS service is an inexact science. There are many questions that are unanswerable now. Nevertheless, we are convinced that many volunteer EMS organizations are going to feel the impact of managed health care and the associated competition for EMS provision by private providers. How they position themselves will make a difference as to whether or not they survive.

THE FUTURE OF THE PUBLIC UTILITY MODEL OF EMS

Ultimately...HMOs will replace the government as the primary provider of EMS. And only EMS companies and organizations that can adapt will survive.[7]

---

[7] This is a quote from *EMS Insider*, October 1993.

Many volunteer EMS organizations exist with a high degree of autonomy from hospitals and government. The support they have from government is based on the premise that EMS is a public utility that should be provided some way, some how by government. Volunteers have been a godsend, and will very likely continue to be.

What we see ahead for many areas of North America is a shift away from the belief that local government is obliged to provide, or at least oversee, EMS provision (the public utility model) and toward an emphasis on hospital-based care. There certainly is now an increasing economic pressure for "migration" of these services toward the players in the managed health care scene. These players are mainly HMOs and private ambulance companies. **Fire departments of all types, which now own the greatest share of EMS, are highly vulnerable to the loss of EMS.** Our thinking has been informed by numerous sources from published articles and interviews with EMS and hospital officials. (See Lehto, 1994; Kuehl, 1994; Garza, 1994a; Ludwig, 1994; Benson, 1993; Criss, 1994; Gresham; 1994; and Page, 1990.)

From all indications, health care, which is based on payment in advance to an HMO by "enrollees" (see footnote 2), or their employers, seems to be the primary model for the future delivery of most medical services in the United States. The old method of insurance companies paying fees for services is rapidly diminishing (Stoline and Weiner, 1988). It has already institutionalized some large urban markets. Costs and utilization of emergency medical services fall squarely into the domain of health care that must be managed.

The growth of HMOs has led to the concept of "capitated" payments as a popular method of paying medical care. Capitation simply means funding care based on the number of individual subscribers who may, at any given time, seek services. In this sense, capitated payment is understood as a set fee paid in advance for future services that may be provided to "subscriber-patients." The transition from being an occasional patient to a subscriber has necessitated a keen interest by the HMO in reducing, as much as possible, the medical care sought by a subscriber. One question, we briefly examine below, is the problem of what organization will provide EMS to non-subscribers (non-enrollees) when health care is managed by an HMO. The chronic poor and the unemployed come to mind as not fitting into the ideal HMO arrangement.

An "emergency" for a subscriber in a managed care environment is something that cannot be left to chance, like many hospitals now do until the patient arrives. Under managed care, the quality and quantity of any pre-hospital care sets a kind of future cost trajectory that needs to be "managed." Economically, there is considerable pressure for the HMO to be involved at the front end of any medical situation of its subscribers. This is in contrast to the current model in many communities where the hospital has limited involvement prior to the patient arriving at its door.

Furthermore, the literature distinctly suggests that the role of the EMS provider (whether volunteer or paid, private or from a fire department) may well be undergoing a significant change in the location of where EMS may be delivered. This change is from the traditional system of quick response by EMTs and paramedics for stabilization and transport to a hospital to that of a primary care giver in the home or workplace **without** the costs associated with transport. This notion of the changing role of the paramedic is another facet of managed care that will likely have a large effect on EMS delivery. One veteran writer in the EMS field referred to this particular change as no less than a "paradigm shift" in how EMS is delivered (Garza, 1994a, 1994b).

As a summary and a clarification of these changes, we reproduce a chart, developed by Jack Stout of Laidlaw's Medical Transport Division, that suggests how EMS might look under managed health care.

HEALTH CARE REFORM AND EMS

	Now	Under Managed Care
Production Philosophy	Specialized, Limited	Flexible, Full-service
Geographic Scope	Mono Jurisdictional	Medical Trade Areas, National Contracts
Method of Funding	Fee-for-service	Capitated Contracts with Local Tax Subsidy
Career Evolution	Dual-role, Cross Firefighter/Paramedic	Dual-role, Cross-trained Paramedic/PA
Market Allocation	By Local Government Non-competitive	Managed Care General Contractor
Role of EMS Provider	Depends on System, Design, and Specialty	Quality Full Service, Customer Service, Economic Efficiency, and Assumption of Risk

Old Question: "What's a life worth?"
New Question: "Is this the best that can be done with the money we've got?"

FIGURE 9.1* Developed by Jack Stout (Laidlaw, Medical Transportation Division.) Supplied by Susan McHenry, Virginia Office of EMS

Let us assume, based on the economic facts of changes in health care, that EMS is indeed becoming an advance arm of a highly organized system of HMOs that stress cost effectiveness and accountability. If this is the case, local governments will have much less a desire to be directly involved with EMS, (at least in the United States), preferring, instead, to allow the medical industry to take prime responsibility. Clearly, given the thousands of local governments, there will be great variety in how EMS will be worked out. However, one cannot ignore the economic trends outlined above. We agree with Susan McHenry (1994), a former president of the National Association of EMS Directors and formerly the director of Virginia's Office of EMS, who stated: "It is clear that managed care is becoming the reality... In the long run, localities would be relieved of the responsibility to subsidize EMS, as it would be paid for as part of the managed care system."

Let us further assume, which seems safe to do, that suburban and even many rural areas will be affected by the trend toward managed care, along with more pre-hospital care given in the homes of subscribers by paramedics. What will be the fate of volunteer EMS organizations, including volunteer fire departments that provide this service? At the very least, the **status quo** as a model for the future is not likely to prevail. While paid government EMS agencies appear to be a threat to volunteers now, the future in many areas served by volunteers most likely will see private providers in the EMS marketplace competing for contracts.

ADAPTATION OF VOLUNTEER EMS ORGANIZATIONS

We could end our chapter here by saying that managed health care and private EMS providers spell doom for volunteers. We are not willing to do this for two reasons. First, change is seldom rational, linear, and knowledgeable of how long something will take to come to fruition, how widespread it might be, and what exact form it will take. As we have noted about the volunteer fire service, there is such local variation that no universal model is ever likely to be found in its pure form. We must acknowledge, however, that managed health care operates on a regional model, not staying within government jurisdictions. Second, **with enough warning and good leadership, many volunteer squads could remake themselves into highly competitive vendors.**

Before we consider some practical issues about survival, we should note two problem spots in the managed care scenario. These relate to who will serve non-subscribers to managed care organizations and what to do with current government employees.

We can only raise questions here. The picture so far is that everyone will eventually belong to an HMO. Of course, there will be poor, uninsured, unemployed people who will have emergencies but not be subscribers of an HMO. Does government retain a small public utility role to serve these people? Will private providers (or volunteer organizations) who are under contract to serve an exclusive HMO be allowed to take charity cases?

What does a government do with its paid EMTs and paramedics? Does the government get into the EMS vending business and offer itself as a competitor with private vendors? Does it claim the authority to define who will provide EMS for an HMO? Does it "downsize" and lay off its employees? Do volunteers reclaim the domain of fire protection with the paid people to get jobs with the HMOs and private transport services? The situation of governments likely shifting responsibility for EMS is not without a real human element, especially in areas that have paid government employees providing services. We have no good answers, only to say that government cannot afford to ignore the potential disruptiveness presented by changing health-care economies. If it believes that, for example, a combination paid and volunteer system is the best for its citizens, then it may have to take a stand against the pull of the HMO.

MORE PRACTICAL CONCERNS

Our two case examples presented earlier provide us with a starting point in addressing the problems of adaptation of volunteers to a system of EMS under managed health care. Problems of retention, because of internal conflict and daytime response due to increasing call load, were evident. These problems are widespread but are not insurmountable nor are they universal. There are numerous all-volunteer organizations that do not have these problems and are themselves outstanding models for any private company to imitate.

Much of what we said earlier about practical strategies for EMS organizations in the face of governmental involvement can be reemphasized here. These strategies were aimed at countering typical volunteer problems. Great internal conflict, retention problems, and lack of daytime response make a volunteer organization a plain liability for an HMO. **There is no way a volunteer organization can hope to survive in a managed health care environment with these problems out of control.** Only when these are under control can an organization turn its attention to adaptation to managed health care. A proactive stance, which is based on strategic planning, is a first step. Below are several ideas to aid in making an adaptation.

The famous sociologist, W. I. Thomas, said that if people define situations as real, the situations are real in their consequences. If a volunteer group defines the future as hostile and destructive to it, then the outcome is likely to be hostility and demise. Likewise, if the group defines the future as something in which it can survive, the group has made a big step in that direction. Problems become opportunities.

An informed leadership and membership is the first obvious condition necessary for any forward step. It is always better to have anticipated and prepared for change. Keeping in contact with local hospital officials would be helpful. Having pre-existing linkages to these organizations, where credibility has been established, can make open communication easier during a time of transition of managed health care. Subscriptions to and a study of major trade journals and national newsletters is a necessity.

It may sound trite, but a task force of volunteers and likely players from government and health care is a simple method of making sound decisions on how to compete for contracts. Business professionals should be enlisted on the committee to aid in proposal-writing exercises. The mere act of acknowledging the need for such a group begins to set in motion images of survival. The future becomes controllable.

The organization should initiate a thorough internal audit of what it perceives to be its assets and liabilities, whether they be human, fiscal, or material. This suggestion is worthwhile to do even if no change toward managed health care presented itself. However, since change in this direction appears to be coming for EMS organizations, the "leaner and meaner" one can **document** what the organization is, the better the position to compete with private services or any services that an HMO might plan of its own.

The development of a well-documented, attractively presented portfolio is a good idea. Admittedly, this is a self-serving endeavor for an organization that is devoted to being a Good Samaritan. However, one can rest assured that a private competitor will have a glowing portfolio. This portfolio will contain a mission statement, hard facts, and accurate descriptions of every dimension of the organization that could be of interest to an HMO. Response times at all hours of the day, personnel characteristics and individual resumes, debt, investments, capital value, and apparatus characteristics make up elements of a portfolio. Now, the Good Samaritan (that is, the volunteer EMS service) has to market itself.

The easiest method to begin to reshape a volunteer organization into a viable competitor is to find out what other groups are doing. Contact should be made with volunteer EMS organizations in areas undergoing the transition to managed care and who have beat out private providers. A delegation should be sent to view first-hand what the situation is like and to bring back ideas and documents. Members of the strategic planning committees will enjoy this assignment.

CONCLUSION

We have tried to treat the EMS dragon in as comprehensive a manner as possible. No doubt the reader has gotten the point that we see some interesting relations in the future between volunteers, government, and players in the health care industry. **We disagree with those who say that the days are numbered for volunteers providing EMS.** We would agree that some EMS organizations will have to give it up because they simply do not make the effort to survive and provide adequate service. But to make a sweeping generalization about decline of the volunteer EMS service as a whole is without merit.

THE FUTURE OF VOLUNTEER EMERGENCY ORGANIZATIONS

RETURNING TO THE TYPOLOGY

In Chapter Two, we introduced a typology to describe the kinds of volunteer emergency organizations we would be considering in this book. Part of the discussion of the typology included transition from the traditional rural volunteer department (Type 1) to other types. This approach has value also in this chapter. However, we wish to expand our typology to include fully career (fully paid) departments as well. Although fully career departments go beyond the scope of this book, they remain a logical possibility. Moreover, they do describe the typical structure of urban areas in the United States and Canada. Recall the typology described in Chapter Two as follows:

FIGURE 10.1 Type 6 is beneath Type 5 and Type 10 is beneath Type 9.

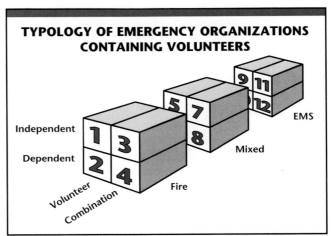

Let us expand this typology by adding fully career departments. Because we wish to remain consistent with the numbering of the original typology present in Chapter Two, we add the letter "c" to describe fully career departments.

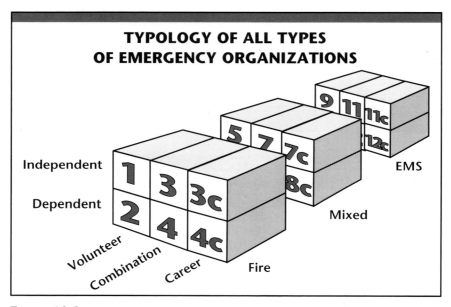

FIGURE 10.2 As before, Type 6 is beneath Type 5 and Type 10 is beneath Type 9. Now Type 8 is beneath Type 7 and Type 12 is beneath Type 11.

MAKING THE TYPOLOGY DYNAMIC

Now let us consider the following forces that alter an organization's position within the typology. The forces are:

- tax base growth or decline
- aging population
- avoidance of litigation
- cost reduction
- recruiting difficulties
- enhanced 9-1-1
- HMO-driven pre-hospital care
- closure of small semi-rural hospitals.

The direction of these forces is indicated in Figure 10.3 below:

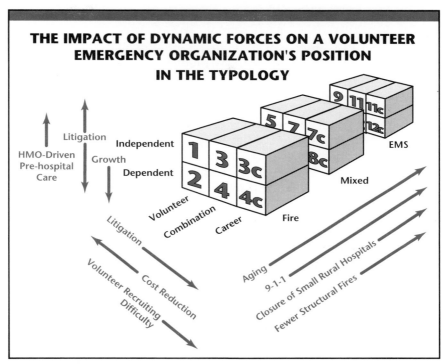

THE IMPACT OF DYNAMIC FORCES ON A VOLUNTEER
EMERGENCY ORGANIZATION'S POSITION
IN THE TYPOLOGY

FIGURE 10.3

Although we previously have elaborated upon many of the forces
that induce change in VEOs we have not done so in the context of the
new typology above. We will consider the forces in general (as shown
in Figure 10.3) and then consider how particular types of VEOs might
change.

First, let us consider the forces that affect the vertical axis that determines whether a VEO is independent from, or dependent upon, local government. One of these forces is community growth. Historically, as the community grows, the fire threat increases because there
are more buildings to burn. Also, the number of calls for service increases. Fortunately, the means to meet this demand is also available
because of an expanding tax base. Consequently, volunteer departments
become combination or fully career, therefore increasing the demand
for tax dollars. Inevitably, the department increases its dependence on
local government. However, not all communities grow and some even
decline in population. If the tax base shrinks, then local government

may spend less on fire services. If volunteers are introduced, then pressures to achieve independence from local government may develop. A second force is the impact of HMO-driven pre-hospital care; it works in the opposite direction of growth. We predict that HMOs will not want local government interference in affiliated rescue/EMS services, particularly if the HMO is making a major financial contribution. Local governments may only be too happy to let HMOs take over what they hitherto have funded. The money saved will either be used elsewhere, or it will lower the tax rate. Either way, local government wins. However, the cost of winning is to surrender any control it once had over the VEO. Thus, the VEO reduces its dependence on local government. Finally, the third force is the impact of litigation; its effect is ambiguous. On one hand, to avoid a lawsuit a local government might choose to distance itself from the VEO, therefore reducing that VEO's dependence on local government. On the other hand, if the local government has no faith in this strategy, then it may seek greater control in order to employ a risk management strategy reducing the probability and/or the consequences of a lawsuit. Since the arguments cancel each other out, the reader might argue that we should ignore litigation. However, the impact of litigation is so great, we ignore it at our peril.

Second, let us examine the horizontal axis shown in Figure 10.3 that is the continuum from volunteer, to combination, to career personnel in a VEO. The first force is litigation. Once again, the impact of litigation is ambiguous. Nearly all VEOs that have faced a lawsuit tended to become more combination or career in form. This is particularly true if the local government sought to hire personnel to gain more control. Conversely, many local governments might have chosen to distance themselves from VEOs by encouraging volunteering, which leads us to the second force, cost reduction. The effect of fiscal restraint within local government is much clearer. Local governments paying for fully career departments may want to encourage volunteering so as to reduce personnel costs. However, this serves to evoke the third force, volunteer recruiting difficulty. We have already seen the difficulty that arises when recruiting. The inability to recruit sufficiently reliable, responding volunteers is what often precedes the conversion of a volunteer department into a combination department.

Finally, the "diagonal" dimension is the continuum from essentially a fire service, to a mix of fire and EMS service, to essentially an EMS service. Here, the forces are uniformly moving in the direction of an increased EMS role. An aging population demands EMS. Enhanced 9-1-1 makes a prompt EMS service more possible, as well as other technical improvements, such as computerized defibrillation.[1] The closure of small rural hospitals (due to fiscal restraints) increases the need for patient transport and lengthens the time from calling the service to arriving at the emergency ward, producing a need for greater pre-hospital care by the EMTs. Lastly, fire prevention has reduced the number of structural fires (largely through improved construction). The resulting down time, as well as the fiscal pressures, have encouraged many types of fire departments to diversify by including EMS.

Let us consider some of the current positions of emergency organizations and trace the effect of these pressures toward certain outcomes. We have already examined the traditional rural department (Type 1) in Chapter Two, so let us now consider an all-career urban local government fire department (Type 4c). The principal pressure for change will be the fiscal austerity of the city government. Many small cities suffering the loss of a manufacturing plant are particularly vulnerable to sudden financial shocks. Since employee compensation is the largest budget expenditure item, these cities will begin to press for the establishment of a force of volunteer auxiliaries to supplement the career force (Types 4c to 4). Probably, attrition of the career force will occur as volunteers will be used to replace retiring career firefighters. Such an outcome will face resistance from the local union. Part of this resistance will arise from the real, or perceived, threat to layoff firefighters, and part may arise from the city's reluctance to announce a no layoff policy. Although the city might very well wish to announce such a policy, it may fear bearing this risk because future provincial or state revenues are uncertain. Another less expected form of resistance may arise from the volunteers themselves. Perhaps few of them would volunteer to serve as replacements for career firefighters.

One way to avoid this scenario is to diversify by expanding the EMS role, bowing to the demographic pressure of an aging population (Types 4c to 8c). Offering more service by using the available time of career firefighters ensures that their value increases, which makes them less vulnerable to layoffs. As we have already seen, the number of calls will rise dramatically. In addition to an actual increase in service, citizens are more likely to anticipate needing EMS as opposed to fire pro-

---

[1]Although definitive studies have not been published, it seems that defibrillation will increase cardiac survival rates only if the response time is small (usually under five minutes). Enhanced 9-1-1 reduces response time by about 30 seconds by speeding dispatch.

tection. Consequently, the existing department is able to maintain job security. However, the transition to EMS delivery is costly (vehicles must be purchased and training must be acquired). Thus, the department may be forced into cost-saving by using volunteer auxiliaries (Types 4c to 8c to 8). The introduction of volunteer auxiliaries raises the specter of career layoffs. Nevertheless, this fear may be reduced by the fact that career firefighters are also serving as EMTs.

On the opposite (left) side of the typology, we have already noted that community growth may induce difficulties when recruiting volunteers and may require the hiring of a core of career firefighters to address daytime response. Furthermore, that change may result in greater local government control as the proportion of revenue that is provided by the local government's grant increases (Type 1 to 3 to 4). Part of this community response is also a form of risk management as fears of litigation drive this trend.

SOME TENTATIVE OBSERVATIONS

Recognizing the processes of change outlined in the scenarios above, a few tentative observations can be made:

1. In response to the pressures listed above, fire departments will diversify by offering EMS delivery. (This may or may not include patient transport.)

2. In response to the pressure of insufficient volunteers, many volunteer departments will become combination.

3. In response to local government fiscal pressure, many career departments will become combination.

As we "combine" these predictions, the combination department offering a mix of fire and EMS services becomes most likely. Thus, Types 1, 2, 3, 4, 3c and 4c alter themselves to become Type 7 or Type 8, or combination and mixed, that is either dependent or not dependent on local government.

If a voluntary emergency organization begins as a fire service, is Type 8 inevitable? That is, is a combination department offering a mixed fire/EMS service dependent on local government an inevitable form for fire departments? From what we have predicted about the rise of combination departments and the increasing conversion from a fire service to a mixed fire/EMS service, the answer seems to be "yes." However, the reader may note that we are silent on the inevitability of increasing dependence on local government. Re-examination of Figure

10.3 reveals contradictory forces, some increasing dependence on local government, others reducing dependence on local government.

To elaborate further, growth may very well increase the tax base of a local government allowing for larger budgets for volunteer emergency organizations. Nevertheless, growth is not inevitable. Some parts of the United States and Canada have experienced population growth; other parts have faced decline. Even where population has remained stable, the fiscal trends we have discussed earlier suggest that many local governments will be providing less money than in the past. Since money is a source of power, then the lack of it (eventually at least) reduces the local government's power on volunteer emergency organizations, thus, increasing the independence of the volunteer emergency organizations.[2] Baltic (1992) has reported on the effect of a tax base decline on small cities or large towns. Often the major decline is abrupt because a multinational corporation closes a local manufacturing plant that results in a direct loss of industrial assessment and an even greater indirect loss through loss of employment.

Finally, as Chapter Four demonstrates, local governments' concerns over litigation arising from tortuous behavior by volunteer emergency organizations is well founded. What is not clear is whether increasing dependence or independence is the best solution. Perhaps the safest prediction (but the least satisfactory one) is to say that the powerful emotional and political events related to a particular case will determine unique outcomes. In other words, one should "flip a coin" to predict whether dependence or independence will increase. Therefore, we conclude that volunteer emergency organizations that are Types 1, 2, 3, 4, 3c or 4c are likely to evolve to Type 7 or Type 8.

Now let us examine the back of the typology, where volunteer emergency organizations deliver EMS. Does it follow that all EMS services will also modify themselves to become Type 7 or Type 8? That is: Will EMTs learn to become firefighters and will combination departments be likely? We do not consider this trend to be nearly so likely. First of all, EMS providers are already responding to high call volume. Indeed, as we have seen in Chapter Nine, emergency medical practitio-

---

[2]Paradoxically, as local government considers reducing its fire department budget, it typically has **more** power over the volunteer emergency organization. This is because the VEO depends on the money and has yet to reduce its need, or find the funds elsewhere. Of course, it tends to redouble its efforts to "sell" its service to the local government, but this strategy usually fails. Once the decision is made to cut the funding, then any additional power, recently gained by local government, is lost.

ners are trying to lower that volume already. Providing primary care may be a solution, but, if this is so, it will require even more education. Increased demand for education and increased demand for training time and study time may well be a disincentive for many volunteers who have paid work to complete. Second of all, in the United States the health maintenance organizations have a financial interest in providing emergency medical service to their own subscribers. As such, it is unlikely that volunteers will be attached to the service because:

1. HMOs will want even greater control over volunteer behavior than local governments want. Recognizing that this control cannot be obtained, HMOs will want to pay their own EMTs.

2. Potential volunteers are less likely to volunteer for a large private organization than for a local government or independent non-profit organization.

Thus, we cautiously conclude that where population density is high enough to make an HMO profitable volunteer rescue squads are vulnerable, whether they are independent or dependent on local government. Some volunteer rescue squads might strike a deal with the local decision makers who represent an HMO, but this will only be likely if the HMO has a high degree of confidence in the effectiveness and accountability of the volunteer rescue squad.

Ironically, this option will preserve the integrity of some volunteer rescue squads. In effect, low population density means too few calls to provide revenue in order to pay the salaries. The HMO might want to control pre-hospital care, but not if the price is too high. In the absence of control, cooperation is desirable. Recall that the HMO, as a private corporation with "deep pockets," cannot appeal to sovereign immunity. Thus, it will prefer a legally separate volunteer rescue squad.

What population density makes a career EMS organization profitable? We are unaware of any answer to this question. On one hand, we suspect that the low population densities in the rural areas of plain and mountain states might be too low to be profitable. On the other hand, the rural areas east of the Mississippi (except Appalachia and the North Woods) will contain population densities high enough to generate a profitable call volume. Should Canada privatize its health care delivery system (at this time, the trend is unclear), then nearly all of rural Canada will contain low, unprofitable population densities, allowing EMS delivery by volunteers to continue.[3]

---

[3]The exceptions are southern Ontario and the St. Lawrence lowlands in Quebec, where rural population densities are similar to those of the eastern United States.

In general, we feel that reasonable predictions can be made about the future of a large number of volunteer emergency organizations. If they are, or were, exclusively fire services, then we can safely say:

1. Many career fire services will become combination and diversify to include EMS response; and

2. Many volunteer fire services will become combination and diversify to include EMS response.

These predictions are most likely to hold in suburban areas, but we should expect some career departments in large cities to change. We should also expect some rural and small town volunteer fire departments to diversify and become combination.

THE DRAGONS BREATHE FIRE

The reader will note that we believe these predictions describe a large number of volunteer emergency organizations. Any particular fire or rescue chief or any particular local government CAO might wonder: Does this prediction apply to my department or local government? Ambiguously, the answer is a "definite maybe." As the preceding chapters have often indicated, the dragons are far too wily to permit easy prediction. Let us consider this further.

The legal dragon often pounces with an actual or potential court case. The searing emotional battle usually leaves all parties (except the legal professionals) scarred by the experience. The resulting decisions are so unique that the only reasonable prediction is to expect that a volunteer emergency organization will become more accountable. However, whether increased accountability will also lead to increased stability is unclear.

The standards dragons depend on the resolution of national issues beyond the scope of any one local government or department. Granted, representative bodies, such as the International Association of Fire Chiefs, the National Volunteer Fire Council, or the International Association of Fire Fighters, can be lobbied, but the effect of any one department or local government is weak. The recruitment dragon suggests an outcome that enhances a combination department; nevertheless, many rural areas might be sufficiently successful in convincing employers to permit time off, in order to improve a weekday, day-time response. For example, if a volunteer fire department were to recruit salaried professionals, then much of the lost work time would be made up in unpaid overtime. Thus, the employer would have no, or little, disincentive to permit responding to alarms during work hours.

The body of the consolidation dragon, as the case studies indicate, is incredibly convoluted (to mix metaphors, it is a "can of worms"). Thus, any attempt at **specific** prediction for an individual department or local government is doomed to fail. Nevertheless, whatever the consolidation scenario, the **general** prediction of diversification of service and combination, at least so that career and volunteer firefighters interact more with each other, is highly likely. What is equally likely as the combination dragon "rears its ugly head" is that conflict between career and volunteer firefighters will increase, unless that conflict is prevented or effectively managed.

Finally, the EMS dragon is so complex that the beginning of the conflict among the contending parties, let alone the end of the conflict, is unclear. At this stage, we can only provide intelligent speculation about the interests of such parties as the various HMOs or the major ambulance companies. Clearly, more research is needed to clarify this, but even then, some research cannot even begin. There is little point in interviewing the CEO of an HMO about his or her position on volunteer rescue squads if that CEO has never even thought about the issue. All we can be confident about is that that same CEO will think about the issue within the next few years.

RELATIVE POWER

There is, however, a principal lesson we wish to convey: "Volunteer emergency organizations and local governments need to cooperate and coordinate but not necessarily control each other." If you have read most of this book, we hope that this lesson will be evident. On one hand, local government almost always has money and legitimacy needed by volunteer emergency organizations. On the other hand, the volunteer emergency service almost always recruits and socializes the volunteers who provide the principal resource needed to offer an emergency service.

To emphasize this point further, if you are a CAO and you think you have power over volunteer fire/rescue departments, you probably have less power than you think you have. If you are a fire/rescue chief and you think you have power over local government, you probably have less power than you think you have. Since neither the fire/rescue chief nor the CAO can control the outcome of fire/rescue service delivery without taking into account the other party, then it makes sense to:

Consult

Cooperate

Coordinate.

The last few paragraphs might leave the reader with an unsettling feeling: "You mean after ten chapters and a couple of hundred pages you still don't know?!" Nevertheless, that is precisely the point for reading the book. The complexities of individual and organizational motivation, the complexities of an increasing number of inter-organizational relationships and the increasing rate of change, all induce turbulence into the environment of the volunteer organization. As Dorothy said in *The Wizard of Oz* after being lifted by the tornado: "We're not in Kansas anymore, Toto."

The complex dynamic environment of the current volunteer emergency organization is such a sharp contrast to that of a generation ago that we should not be surprised that successful adaptation will be necessary. Beyond the generalizations listed earlier, the fact that this book cannot give simple rules demonstrates the turbulence of that environment. Nevertheless, when an environment is complex and dynamic, an appreciation of complexity can still lend itself to reasonable organizational adaptation ... if skill, patience, luck, and motivation are present.

THE DRAGON'S APPENDIX: RESEARCH METHODS

This book arose from the passionate interest both authors have in the volunteer fire service. The book also arises from the professional training of both authors who are sociologists. It is our hope that we have been able to convey some of the insights of social science in application to the issues we have addressed in this book.

The fact that one author is American and the other author is Canadian has brought a comparative perspective to the book. Also, the fact that the two systems of government are very different at the national level allows this comparative approach to be used. Nevertheless, the reader should not be misled. Despite the national differences at the state/province and federal levels, local governments, at least in rural areas and small towns, are very similar. Moreover, many of the volunteer emergency organizations are very similar. Indeed, one fact which has impressed both authors is that the volunteer fire departments in Virginia and Nova Scotia (the authors' homes) are more similar to each other than Nova Scotia's are to its sister province, New Brunswick, or Virginia's are to its sister state, North Carolina.

This book began from a conversation in the fall of 1993; however, the specific nature and issues were not identified until June of 1994 when our publisher was identified and a multi-page proposal was written. In August of 1994, a general agreement with Fire Protection Publications was reached (represented by Gene Carlson). Over the fall of 1994, Ken began to research and write. Also, at this time, Don Flinn agreed to take a role in the preparation of the Montgomery County Fire/Rescue case study in the chapter on combination departments (Chapter Eight). By the winter of 1995, John was able to take on his share of the project. In January, the following principles evolved through constant but enjoyable conversation:

1. Most chapters should be organized using the following:

    a) a case that is to illustrate issues of interest (such as inter-organizational conflict in Queen County or department/politician relations in Blucherville);

b) a set of specific questions and answers that the reader might have (particularly if the reader is a volunteer chief or a CAO or a mayor). Alternatively, these might be lessons.

2. Chapters Two and Three are to concentrate on describing volunteer fire departments and local government and the power relationship between them. These chapters set the context where specific issues are addressed.

3. Chapters Four through Nine are to address the specific issues which affect volunteer emergency organizations, local governments, and their relation to each other. As each chapter was drafted, it became apparent that issues should proceed from obvious to subtle. Thus, Chapter Four, "The Legal Dragon," is a problem evident to both volunteer emergency organizations and local governments. Conversely, the diversification of services to include EMS found in Chapter Nine is seen by most as a solution when in reality it is a complex problem as well as a solution.

4. The concluding chapter is to attempt to "predict" the future of volunteer emergency organizations based on the likely trends addressed in earlier chapters.

5. The hero, villain, and dragon metaphors are to be used. (We have a weakness for the dramatic.)

Naturally, a book of this sort is not written without prior research. Several sources have informed our writing. Perhaps the most important is a series of interviews with a number of "opinion leaders" in volunteer emergency services and local governments in Canada and the United States. Both authors have been extremely grateful for the time granted by the interviewees. In all, 82 persons were interviewed or surveyed (69 interviews, 13 surveys); each interview lasted an average of 1½ hours. In several instances, more than one interview was granted as new issues arose. In particular, Chapter Five, "The Standards Dragons," required more than one interview with some interviewees because issues on standards were changing from month to month. Indeed, our fear was that circumstances would force us to act as reporters. Knowing that this issue was bound to change in the time between the final submission to the publisher and when this book would be read, we feared that the chapter would be dated, as indeed some of it is bound to be.

As many of the issues we present are controversial, the issue of confidentiality arose. We were caught in a dilemma. If we did not assure confidentiality, then some of what we were told would not have been said. Conversely, if we did not identify our sources, then the reader might wonder how much of what is written is a figment of the overactive imaginations of the authors. We resolved this dilemma as follows:

1. At the beginning of each interview, the interviewees were told that their remarks were not going to be attributed to them unless they agreed otherwise.

2. Nevertheless, each interviewee would be named in the appendix of the book so the reader is able to assess the authors' sources overall.

All the interviewees agreed to these conditions.

Some of the stories used in this book identify real organizations. In particular, the identification appears where the documented story is a matter of public record, such as a legal case. Correct identification helps the reader who may wish to do further legal research. Nevertheless, most stories have fictional names of persons and organizations so as to ensure confidentiality. Despite this, we assure the reader that every story is a true story, which has occurred to someone, or some organization, somewhere at sometime.[1] This assurance may be insufficient for the sceptical reader. If so, all we can suggest is to contact a few of the interviewees. Undoubtedly, you will hear a familiar story if you have read the book carefully.

Our other formal sources are the published documents found in the bibliography.

Finally, the book arises from the cluttered memories of the authors who have different but practical roles with the volunteer fire service. Ken's experience as a volunteer firefighter and member of the Board of Directors of the Prospect Volunteer Fire Department informs this book in various ways. Similarly, John's teaching and administrative experience dealing with the Fire Service Administration Program and the Volunteer Fire Service Leadership program informs this book. Finally, Don Flinn's long tenure with the Montgomery County Fire/ Rescue Service has been a contribution.

---

[1] The exception is the fictitious conversation that introduces Chapter Five.

List of Interviewees

Individuals Interviewed and or Surveyed

(* indicates surveyed only)

Lou Amabili, Executive Director, Delaware State Fire School, Dover, Delaware.

*Steve Austin, Aetna Hose, Hook and Ladder Company, Newark, Delaware.

Jack Ball, Emergency Services Coordinator, Louisa County, Virginia.

Georges Bastarache, Fire Chief, Dieppe Fire Department, Ville de Dieppe, New Brunswick.

Peter Beals, Fire Chief, Oromocto Fire Department, Oromocto, New Brunswick.

*John H. Beatty II, Director, National Volunteer Fire Council, West Virginia State Firefighters' Association, West Virginia.

Garry Briese, Executive Director, International Association of Fire Chiefs, Fairfax, Virginia.

Rohn Brown, Recruitment and Retention Coordinator, Office of EMS, Richmond, Virginia.

*Reade Bush, TriData Corporation, Arlington, Virginia.

Howard Campbell, Chief, Prospect Volunteer Fire Department, Prospect, Virginia.

Gene Carlson, IFSTA, Oklahoma State University, Stillwater, Oklahoma.

Hugh Carwile, Chairman, Board of Supervisors, Prince Edward County, Farmville, Virginia.

*Doug Chappell, Alternate Director, National Volunteer Fire Council, Illinois Firefighters' Association, Illinois.

*Jack Condon, First Vice President, National Volunteer Fire Council, Oregon.

Robert Cormier, Fire Marshal, Halifax, Nova Scotia.

Jeff Crawford, Past President, IAFF Local 2598, Prince William County, Virginia.

Larry Davis, Chairman, The Alliance for Fire and Emergency Management, Hartford, Connecticut.

*Warren Deemer, Alternate Director, National Volunteer Fire Council, Louisiana.

Dave Doehler, Past President, IAFF Local 2598, Prince William County, Farmville, Virginia.

Walter Drinkard, Treasurer, National Volunteer Fire Council, Alabama.

"Bubs" Dupplessis, Deputy Fire Chief, Miramichi Fire Department, Miramichi City, New Brunswick.

Michael Eddy, Fire Chief, Sackville Fire Department, Halifax County, Nova Scotia.

Marcel Ethier, Executive Director, Canadian Association of Fire Chiefs, Ottawa, Ontario.

Donald Flinn, Volunteer Coordinator, Montgomery County Fire and Rescue Commission, Rockville, Maryland.

Steve Foley, Executive Secretary, Fire Service Section, National Fire Protection Association, Quincy, Massachusetts.

Jim Forgo, Past President, IAFF Local 2598, Prince William County, Virginia.

Mike Frees, Director, National Volunteer Fire Council, California State Firefighters' Association, California.

Burt Fusk, Fire Chief, Fredericton Fire Department, Fredericton, New Brunswick.

Harry Gaudet, Chief Administrative Officer, City of Charlottetown, Charlottetown, Prince Edward Island.

*Myron L. George, Director, National Volunteer Fire Council, Ohio State Firemen's Association, Ohio.

Billy Goldfeder, Director Fire/Rescue Services, Loudoun County, Leesburg, Virginia.

Gary Greene, Fire Chief, Dartmouth Fire Department and President, Canadian Association of Fire Chiefs, Dartmouth, Nova Scotia.

Elsworth Greer, Director, National Volunteer Fire Council, Texas.

*Joseph Guyotte, Director, National Volunteer Fire Council, Maine.

Doug Hamer, Fire Chief, Riverview Fire Department, Riverview, New Brunswick.

Susie Hampton, County Administrator, Prince Edward County, Farmville, Virginia.

Ken Harding, Town Clerk/Development Officer, Town of Woodstock, Woodstock, New Brunswick.

Wayne Harper, President, IAFF Local #2779, Sydney Fire Department, Sydney, Nova Scotia.

Bill Hewitt, Fire Chief, Saskatoon Fire Department, Saskatoon, Saskatchewan.

Terry Dawn Hewitt, Lawyer, Calgary, Alberta.

*Norman Hoeft, Alternate Director, National Volunteer Fire Council, Nebraska.

William Hogan, Fire Inspector/Administration Officer, Charlottetown Fire Department, Charlottetown, Prince Edward Island.

A. Pierre Jackson, Attorney-at-Law, Farmville, Virginia.

Brian Jenson, Deputy Fire Chief, Rothsay Fire Department, Rothsay, New Brunswick.

Bobby Joyner, Director, National Volunteer Fire Council, North Carolina State Firemen's Association, North Carolina.

David Keating, Fire Chief, Miramichi Fire Department, Miramichi City, New Brunswick.

Lew Lewis, California State Firefighters' Association, California.

Charles MacDonald, Fire Education Officer, Department of Advanced Education and Training, Province of New Brunswick, Fredericton, New Brunswick.

Jim MacDougall, Fire Safety Officer, Victoria General Hospital, Halifax, Nova Scotia.

Bernie MacKinnon, Director of Fire Services, Regional Municipality of Cape Breton, Sydney, Nova Scotia.

Norman MacPhee, Fire Chief, North River Volunteer Fire Department, North River, Prince Edward Island.

Gerry Mallais, Chief Administrative Officer, Ville de Dieppe, Dieppe, New Brunswick.

*John McAuliffe, Alternate Director, National Volunteer Fire Council, Connecticut, Massachusetts.

Sue McCauley, Librarian, EMS Clearing House, Florida.

James McDavid, Dean, Faculty of Public Administration, University of Victoria, Victoria, British Columbia.

Susan McHenery, Director, Office of EMS, Richmond, Virginia.

Robert McKeen, Chairman, National Volunteer Fire Council.

*J. Allen Metheny, Alternate Director, National Volunteer Fire Council, Delaware.

Mary Beth Michos, Director, Fire/Rescue Services, Prince William County, Mannassas, Virginia.

Carl Milofsky, Department of Sociology, Bucknell University, Lewisburg, Pennsylvania.

*Jerry Moen, Director, National Volunteer Fire Council, Minnesota.

Bruce Morrison, Fire Chief, Moncton Fire Department, Moncton, New Brunswick.

Alan Moye, Reference Librarian, T.C. Williams School of Law, University of Richmond, Virginia.

David Muise, Municipal Clerk/Solicitor, Cape Breton County, Sydney, Nova Scotia.

Harold Pennington, Fire Chief, Coxheath Volunteer Fire Department, Regional Municipality of Cape Breton, Cape Breton, Nova Scotia.

Ed Rees, Executive Director, Nova Scotia Firefighters School, Waverley, Nova Scotia.

Harold Richardson, Instructor, Nova Scotia Firefighters School, Waverley, Nova Scotia.

Gordon Routley, Senior Partner, TriData Corporation, Alexandria, Virginia.

Philip Schaenman, President, TriData Corporation, Arlington, Virginia.

Howard Seter, Fire Chief, Surrey Fire Department, Surrey, British Columbia.

Al Siegel, Secretary, National Association of County Administrators; Commissioner, Montgomery County Maryland Fire and Rescue Commission, Rockville, Maryland.

Jim Stith, Fire Marshal, Province of New Brunswick, Fredericton, New Brunswick.

Glen Tait, Fire Chief, Saint John Fire Department, Saint John, New Brunswick.

*W. H. Templar, Alternate Director, National Volunteer Fire Council, Nebraska State Volunteer Firefighter Association, Nebraska.

Raymond Therrien, Director Fire Service, Verdun, Québec, Former Fire Chief, Montréal Fire Department, Montréal, Québec.

Sandy Thompson, Department of Economics, Vassar College, Poughkeepsie, New York.

Bernie Turpin, Coordinator of Fire Services, Municipality of the County of Halifax, Halifax, Nova Scotia.

Donna Waddell, Chief Administrative Officer, Community of West Royalty, West Royalty, Prince Edward Island.

Rob Weiderhold, Hazardous Material Instructor, National Fire Academy, Emmitsburg, Maryland; Chief, Sterling Virginia Volunteer Fire Rescue Department.

Gus Welter, Alternate Director, National Volunteer Fire Council, Minnesota.

Bernie White, Municipal Clerk, Regional Municipality of Cape Breton, Sydney, Nova Scotia.

Jack Winkler, Secretary-Treasurer, Wayne Township Fire Department, Inc., Indianapolis, Indiana.

Individuals Who Provided Special Help

Larry Allen, Firefighter, Prospect Volunteer Fire Department, Prospect, Virginia.

A. Pierre Jackson, Attorney-at-Law, Farmville, Virginia.

Sue McCauley, Librarian, Florida EMS Clearing House, Tallahassee, Florida.

Alan Moye, Reference Librarian, T.C. Williams School of Law, University of Richmond, Virginia.

Agencies Which Provided Information

EMS Clearing House, Tallahassee, Florida.

Institute for Leadership and Volunteer Development, Virginia Polytechnic Institute and State University, Blacksburg, Virginia.

National Fire Academy, Emmitsburg, Maryland.

TriData Corporation, Arlington, Virginia.

Virginia Division of EMS, Richmond, Virginia.

Wayne Township Fire Department, Wayne Township, Indiana.

Organizations Which Provided Financial Support

Henson College, Dalhousie University, Halifax, Nova Scotia.

Longwood College, Farmville, Virginia.

BIBLIOGRAPHY

Abner, David. "NFPA 1500 - Are You Compliant?" *Health and Safety*, September 1994, pp. 7, 12.

Adams, J. Stacey. "Inequality in Social Exchange." Leon Berkowitz (ed.) *Advances in Experimental Social Psychology*. New York: Academic Press, 1965.

Adams, Rich. "Rural Responders." *Firehouse*, May 1995, p.14.

Alliance for Fire and Emergency Management. *201 Performance Standard for Volunteer Fire Department Suppression Personnel*. Ashland, MA: Alliance for Fire and Emergency Management, 1995a.

Alliance for Fire and Emergency Management. *502 Performance Standard for Incident Scene Safety Officer*. Ashland, MA: Alliance for Fire and Emergency Management, 1995b.

Alliance for Fire and Emergency Management. *601 Performance Standard for Demonstrator*. Ashland, MA: Alliance for Fire and Emergency Management, 1995c.

Alliance for Fire and Emergency Management. *602 Performance Standard for Educator*. Ashland, MA: Alliance for Fire and Emergency Management, 1995d.

Alliance for Fire and Emergency Management. *603 Performance Standard forTrainer*. Ashland, MA: Alliance for Fire and Emergency Management, 1995e.

Alliance for Fire and Emergency Management. *2001 Volunteer Fire Department Organization and Operation*. Ashland, MA: Alliance for Fire and Emergency Management, 1995f.

Baltic, Scott. "The Combination Transition." *Fire Chief*, August 1992, pp. 60-64.

Bard, Steve. "Union: Don't Work at County Stations." *Potomac News*. July 17, 1994a.

Bard, Steve. "Spending by Volunteers Comes Under Fire." *Potomac News*. July 19, 1994b.

Bard, Steve. "Board Puts Fire Out with Compromise." *Potomac News*. July 20, 1994c.

Benoit, John. "The Fire Service Volunteers: Their Image and Their Reality." James Rice (ed.) *Canadian Volunteers*. Ottawa: Secretary of State for Canada, 1990.

Benoit, John. "The Triumph of Managerial Capitalism in a Composite Fire Department: Getting Them to Scorn 'The Base Degrees by Which They Did Ascend'." Paper presented to the Southern Sociological Society, New Orleans, LA, 1992.

Benoit, John and J. Roger MacMillan. *Fire Officers' Project: A Training Needs Survey of Fire Officers in the Maritime Provinces*. Halifax, NS: Institute of Public Affairs, Dalhousie University, 1984.

Benoit, John, Harold Richardson, Ed Rees, and Jack Holesworth. *Volunteer Fire Service Leadership*. Halifax, NS: Henson College, Dalhousie University, 1989.

Bentivoglio, John. "OSHA Compliance." *Firehouse*, May 1995, pp. 58-61, 90.

Benson, Katy. "A Direction For Tomorrow: Emergency's Advisors' Predictions for What EMS Might Be In 1999." *Emergency*, December 1993, p. 28.

Bingham, William. "Managing the Sexual Harassment Issue." *Fire Engineering*, February 1995, pp. 56-59.

Black's Law Dictionary, 6th Edition. St. Paul, MN: West Publishing Co., 1990.

Blau, Peter. *Exchange, Power and Social Life*. New York: Wiley, 1964.

Boyd, David R. "The History of Emergency Medical Services (EMS) Systems in the United States of America." In David Boyd, R. R. Edlich and S. Micik (eds.) *Systems Approach to Emergency Medical Care*. Norwark, Connecticut: Appleton-Century Crofts, 1983, pp. 1-82.

Brown, Rohn. "Volunteer Programs That Work." *Emergency*, June 1993, p. 42.

Bruno, Hal. "New Congress Means New Challenges for Fire Service." *Firehouse*, January 1995a, p. 10.

Bruno, Hal. "The Power Shifts in Washington." *Firehouse*, February 1995b, p. 10.

Bruno, Hal. "Congress Asks To Settle Career - Volunteer Issue." *Firehouse*, March 1995c, p. 10.

Bruno, Hal. "Welcome News for the Fire Service." *Firehouse*, May 1995d, p. 10.

Bruno, Hal. "Lessons from Oklahoma City." *Firehouse*, June 1995e, p. 10.

Buckman, John. "Training Volunteers, Part 2." *Fire Engineering*, February 1995, pp. 10-13.

Byrne-Walsh, Michelle and Karen Wojcik. "Coping With NFPA 1500." *Fire Chief*. February 1990, pp. 44-47.

Caplow, Theodore. *Managing An Organization*. New York: Holt, Rinehart and Winston, 1983.

Carlson, Gene. "Partnerships With Local Industry." *Fire Engineering*, March 1995a, pp. 12-14.

Carlson, Gene. "What Happened To Our Budget?" *Fire Engineering*, July 1995b. pp. 10-12.

Carlson, Gene. "Recruiting and Retaining Volunteers." Unpublished document, 1995c.

Coleman, James. *Foundations of Social Theory*. Cambridge, MA: The Belknap Press of Harvard University Press, 1990.

Coleman, Ronald E. *Implementation of NFPA 1500: A Case Study of North Port, Florida*. Report for Executive Fire Officer Program, National Fire Academy, Emmitsburg, MD, 1994.

Colestock, Michael. "Personnel Accountability." *Fire Engineering*, January 1994, pp. 10-15.

Criss, Elizabeth. "Unlocking The Future: EMS Must Choose a Path." *Journal of Emergency Medical Services*. December, 1994, p. 23.

Crozier, Michel. *The Bureaucratic Phenonmenon*. Chicago, IL: University of Chicago Press, 1964.

Davis, Larry. *Industrial Emergency Response for the '90s, 1st Edition*. Ashland, MA: Industrial Fire and Emergency Management Training Association, 1993.

Davis, Larry. *The Volunteer Fire Chief's Guide to Avoiding the Hot Seat*. Ashland, MA: The Alliance for Fire and Emergency Management, 1994.

Davis, Larry. "The Need for Volunteer Fire Department Standards." *Firefighter's News*. June/July 1995, pp. 62-64.

Delaware State Fire School. *Course Catalog*. Dover, DE: Delaware State Fire School, 1995.

Eisner, Harvey. "Urban Search and Rescue: A New Era." *Firehouse*, June 1995, p. 7.

EMS Insider. Jems Communications, October 1992.

Federal Emergency Management Agency. *A Handbook on Women in Firefighting: The Changing Face of the Fire Service*. Madison, Wisconsin: Women in the Fire Service, 1993.

Festinger, Leon. *A Theory of Cognitive Dissonance*. Stanford, CA: Stanford University Press, 1957.

Fire Engineering. "The rural fire service: issues and challenges." *Fire Engineering*. December 1994, pp. 49-53.

Fire Service Planning Committee. *Report on the Amalgamation of the Charlottetown, Parkdale and Sherwood Fire Departments*. Charlottetown, PEI: Fire Marshal's Office of PEI, 1994.

Fitch, Joseph. "Volunteers." In Alexander E. Kuehl (ed.) *Prehospital Systems and Medical Oversight, 2nd Edition*. St. Louis, MO: Mosby-year, 1994, pp. 316-320.

Fritz, Mark. "U.S. Firefighters Working to Save Their Livelihood: They're Battling Corporations for Paramedic Work." *Richmond Times-Dispatch*, October 1994.

Garza, Marion Angell. "Money Talks, Nobody Walks: Financial Incentives For Volunteers." *Journal of Emergency Medical Services.* February, 1991, p. 8.

Garza, Marion Angell. "Treatment Without Transport: Expanded-Scope Concept Gains Momentum." *Journal of Emergency Medical Services* April 1994a, p. 75.

Garza, Marion Angell. "From Mom and Pop to Big Business: The Ambulance Industry Consolidates. "*Journal of Emergency Medical Services.* April 1994b, p. 44.

Goldfeder, William. "Retaining and Recruiting Members." *Fire Engineering.* May 1992, p. 10.

Goldfeder, William. "Redirecting Behavior." *Fire Engineering*, December 1994, pp. 12-13.

Goodwyn, M.W. "Calls For Help Now Always Answered: Despite Progress Dinwiddie's EMS System is Ailing." *Richmond Times-Dispatch*, November 27, 1994a.

Goodwyn, M.W. "Change Key to Curing EMS Ills." *Richmond Times-Dispatch.* November 28, 1994b.

Gouldner, Alvin W. *Patterns of Industrial Bureaucracy: A Case Study of Modern Factory Administration.* New York: The Free Press, 1954.

Graham, John. *Royal Commission on Education, Public Services and Provincial-Municipal Relations, Vol. II.* Halifax, NS: Queen's Printer, 1974.

Granito, John. "Some bad news never changes." *NFPA Journal*, July/August 1994, pp. 111, 112.

Grant, Nancy and David Hoover. *Fire Service Administration.* Quincy, MA: National Fire Protection Association, 1994.

Gresham, Ryan. "Does EMS Belong in the Fire Service?" *Emergency Medical Services.* March 1994, p. 47.

Hall, John Jr. "Fiddling while Rome burns...and other myths about fire." *Fire Engineering.* November/December 1994, pp. 67-72.

Hampden-Turner, Charles. *Creating Corporate Culture.* Don Mills, ON: Addison-Wesley, 1990.

Harwood, Doug. "Squad Squabbles Cause Resignations." *The Rockbridge Advocate*. October 1994.

Hayward, C. William. *Interim Report of the Municipal Reform Commissioner: Halifax County (Halifax Metropolitan Area)*. Halifax, NS: Department of Municipal Affairs, 1993.

Heider, Fritz. *The Psychology of Interpersonal Relations*. New York, NY: Wiley, 1958.

Hewitt, Terry-Dawn. *Fire Loss Litigation in Canada*. Toronto, ON: Carswell, 1995.

Hewitt, William. *Recreating the Fire Service*. Ottawa, ON: Kendall Publications, 1995.

Hodge, Gerald and Mohammed Qadeer. *Towns and Villages in Canada*. Toronto, ON: Butterworths, 1983.

Hoetmer, Gerard. "Alternative Delivery Systems." In Ronny Coleman and John Granito (eds.) *Managing Fire Services 2nd Edition*. Washington, DC: International City Management Association, 1988.

Homans, George. *Social Behavior: Its Elementary Forms*. New York: Harcourt, Bruce and World, 1961.

Hudgins, Edward. "Volunteer Incentives: Solving Recruitment and Attrition Problems." *Journal of Emergency Medical Services*. June 1988, p. 58.

International Society of Fire Service Instructors. *Training of Industrial Fire Brigade Apparatus Operators, 1992 Edition*. Ashland, MA: International Society of Fire Service Instructors, 1992.

Justice Institute of British Columbia/Fire Academy. *Risk Management for the Fire Service*. Vancouver, BC: Justice Institute of British Columbia, 1988.

Keeton, W. Page. *Prosser and Keeton on the Law of Torts, Fifth Edition*. St. Paul, MN: West Publishing Co., 1984.

Kochanek, K.D. and B.L. Hudson. "Advance Report of Final Mortality Statistics, 1992." *Monthly Vital Statistics Report. Vol. 43, No.6, Supplement*. Hayattsville, MD: National Center for Health Statistics, 1994.

Kuehl, Alexander. "Not EMS — Pre-Hospital Medicine." *Rescue — EMS Magazine*. May/June 1994, p. 22.

Lawrence, Cortez. "Company Staffing: The Proof is in Your Numbers." *Fire Engineering*. April 1995, pp. 61-64.

Lehto, Eric. "EMS Relationships With Managed Care." *Ambulancy Industry Journal*. March/April 1994, p. 8.

Leschak, Peter. "Taking the Heat: Volunteer Fire Chiefs Confront a New Age." *Firehouse*. March 1995, pp. 76-78, 94.

Lion, Douglas. "Physical Performance and Conditioning." *Fire Fighting in Canada*. November 1994, pp. 63, 74.

Ludwig, Gary. "The Crossroads of EMS." *9-1-1 Magazine*. November/December 1994, p. 40.

MacDonald, Bruce. *NFPA 1500 - It's Impact on Small Town Fire Departments*. Report for Executive Fire Officer Program. Emmitsburg, MD: National Fire Academy, 1994.

Manning, Bill. "Labor Ruling in Maryland Opens Pandora's Box." *Fire Engineering*. March 1994, p. 6.

Manning, Bill. "A 'New' Player in the Standards Game." *Fire Engineering*. September 1994, p. 6.

Manning, Bill. "Readers Respond to Standards Survey." *Fire Engineering*. January 1995a, pp. 47-54.

Manning, Bill. "Make Standards A Win-Win for the Fire Service." *Fire Engineering*. February 1995b, p. 6.

Manning, Bill. "Miscellaneous Fictions." *Fire Engineering*, March 1995c, pp. 6-8.

Marinucci, Richard A. "Setting Recruitment Standards," *Fire Engineering*. December, 1989, p. 8.

Marlatt, F. Patrick and Bruce Walz. "Training and Professional Development." In Ronny Coleman and John Granito (eds.). *Managing Fire Services 2nd Edition*. Washington, DC: International City Management Association, 1988.

Marshall, Steve. "Pagers and Politicians." *Firehouse*. March 1995, pp. 74-75.

Masuch, Michael. "Vicious Circles in Organizations." *Administrative Science Quarterly*. 30, 1985, pp. 14-33.

McDavid, James. "Part-Time Firefighters in Canadian Municipalities: Cost and Effectiveness Comparisons." Canadian Public Administration. 29, 1986, pp. 377-387.

McHenry, Susan. "Managed Health Care and EMS." Unpublished working document. Richmond, Virginia: Office of Emergency Medical Service, 1994.

Monigold, J. "Education in the Fire Service." *The NFP/A Journal*. January/February 1995, pp. 61-65.

Morris, Gary, Nick Brunacini and Lynn Whaley. "Fireground Accountability: The Phoenix System." *Fire Engineering*. April 1994, pp. 45-61.

Murphy, Dennis. "Throw Away the Rule Book." *Journal of Emergency Medical Services*. June 1986, p. 57.

Murtagh, Matthew. "Fire Department Promotion Tests: A New Direction." *Fire Engineering*. December 1994, pp. 54-57.

Mustalish, Anthony C. and Carl Post. "History." In Alexander E. Kuehl (ed.) *Prehospital Systems and Medical Oversight, 2nd Edition*. St. Louis, MO: Mosby-Year, 1994.

Nadeau, John. *Diminishing Fire Department Volunteerism: One Community's Approach*. Report for Executive Fire Officer Program. Emmitsburg, MD: National Fire Academy, 1990.

National Fire Protection Association. *NFPA 1401: Recommended Practice for Fire Service Training Reports and Records*. Quincy, MA: National Fire Protection Association, 1989.

National Fire Protection Association. *NFPA 36: Solvent Extraction*. Quincy, MA: National Fire Protection Association, 1992a.

National Fire Protection Association. *NFPA 211: Chimneys, Fireplaces, Vents*. Quincy, MA: National Fire Protection Association, 1992b.

National Fire Protection Association. *NFPA 472: Hazardous Materials Responder Professional Competencies.* Quincy, MA: National Fire Protection Association, 1992c.

National Fire Protection Association. *NFPA 600: Industrial Fire Brigades.* Quincy, MA: National Fire Protection Association, 1992d.

National Fire Protection Association. *NFPA 1001: Fire Fighter Professional Qualifications.* Quincy, MA: National Fire Protection Association, 1992e.

National Fire Protection Association. *NFPA 1021: Fire Officer Professional Qualifications, 1992 Edition.* Quincy, MA: National Fire Protection Association, 1992f.

National Fire Protection Association. *NFPA 1403: Live Fire Training Evolutions.* Quincy, MA: National Fire Protection Association, 1992g.

National Fire Protection Association. *NFPA 1500: Fire Department Occupational Safety and Health Program.* Quincy, MA: National Fire Protection Association, 1992h.

National Fire Protection Association. *NFPA 1582: Medical Requirements for Fire Fighters.* Quincy, MA: National Fire Protection Association, 1992i.

National Fire Protection Association. *NFPA 1901: Pumper Fire Apparatus.* Quincy, MA: National Fire Protection Association, 1992j.

National Fire Protection Association. *NFPA 1583: Recommended Practices for Fire Fighter Physical Performance and Conditioning Program.* Quincy, MA: National Fire Protection Association, 1995a.

National Fire Protection Association. *NFPA Standards and You: Understanding and Participating in the NFPA Standards Making System.* Quincy, MA: National Fire Protection Association, 1995b.

National Volunteer Fire Council. *Retention and Recruitment in the Fire Service: Problems and Solutions.* Washington, DC: National Volunteer Fire Council, U.S. Fire Administration and Federal Emergency Management Agency, 1993.

O'Brien, Allan. *Municipal Consolidation in Canada: Its Alternatives.* Toronto, ON: Intergovernmental Committee on Urban and Regional Research, 1993.

Office of Rural Health Policy. *Success and Failure: A Study of Rural Emergency Medical Services*. National Rural Health Association. Washington, DC. May 1990.

O'Nical, Denis. "In response to the demand for fire department cutbacks." *Fire Engineering*. August 1993, pp. 45-64.

Orsborn, J. *Actions Against Municipality Asserting Negligence of Volunteer Fire Department With Resulting Loss of Property*. St. John's, NF: Supreme Court of Newfoundland, Trial Division, 1995.

Page, James. "Emergency Medical and Rescue Services." In Ronny Coleman and John Granite (eds.). *Managing Fire Services 2nd Edition*. Washington, DC: International City Management Association, 1988.

Page, James O. "Spotting Hot Trends In Fire Service EMS." *Journal of Emergency Medical Services*. December 1990, p. 42.

Parker, John. "What the 'Contract with America' Means for the Fire Service and Fire Safety." *NFPA Journal*. May/June 1995, pp. 46-50.

Parsons, Talcott. *The Social System*. New York, NY: The Free Press, 1951.

Penwell Publications. *Directory of Fire Departments*. Tulsa, OK: Penwell Publications, 1993.

Perkins, Kenneth B. *Volunteer Firefighters in the United States: A Sociological Profile of America's Bravest*. Report to the National Volunteer Fire Council, Farmville, VA: Longwood College, 1987a.

Perkins, Kenneth B. "Volunteer Fire Departments: Community Integration, Solidarity and Survival." *Human Organization*. 46: 4, 1987b, pp. 342-348.

Perkins, Kenneth B. "Volunteer Firefighters in the United States: A Descriptive Study." *Non-profit and Voluntary Sector Quarterly*. 18:3, 1989, pp. 269-277.

Perkins, Kenneth B. "Volunteer Fire and Rescue Corporations: Structure, Process and Survival." *Non-profit and Voluntary Sector Quarterly*. 19: 4, 1990, pp. 359-370.

Perkins, Kenneth B. "Government Co-Production With the Rural Volunteer Emergency Services Corporation: An Analysis of a Dual Love-Hate Relationship." Paper presented to the Association for Research on Non-profit Organizations and Voluntary Action, Toronto, ON: 1993.

Perkins, Kenneth B., John Ballweg and Del Dyer. *An Exploration of a Partnership Concept for Staffing Rural Emergency Medical Squads*. Institute for Leadership and Volunteer Development. Blacksburg, Virginia: Virginia Tech, 1993.

Perkins, Kenneth B. and Darryl Poole. "Oligarchy in a Voluntary Association: An Analysis of its Functions for Democracy and Adaptation to Mass Society." *Non-profit and Voluntary Sector Quarterly*. 25: 1996, pp. 73-88.

Perry, Dale. "Fire Suppression Rating Schedule." *Fire Engineering*. June 1995, pp. 10-14.

Pittard, Floyd (ed.). *A Systematic Approach to Functional Consolidation and Merger: A Fire Service Case Study and Outline for Implementation, 3rd Edition*. Beaverton, Oregon: Tualatin Valley Fire and Rescue, 1992.

Schneid, Thomas. "Is your department ready for OSHA reform." *Fire Engineering*. August 1993, p. 139.

Siegel, David. "The ABCs of Local Government: An Overview." In Dale Richmond's and David Siegel's (eds.). *Agencies, Boards and Commissions in Canadian Local Government*. Toronto, ON: The Institute of Public Administration of Canada, 1994.

Selznick, Philip. *TVA and the Grass Roots*. New York: Harper and Row, 1966.

Sorkin, Alan L. *Health Care and the Changing Economic Environment*. Lexington, Massachusetts: Lexington Books, 1986.

Staff. "CAFS Mini-pumper Does the Job." *Fire Fighting in Canada*. November 1993, p. 8.

Staff. "The Rural Fire Service: Issues and Challenges." *Fire Engineering*. December 1994, pp. 49-53.

Staff of the Municipality of the County of Cape Breton. *A Municipal Employee Response To Regional Government in Cape Breton County*. Municipality of the County of Cape Breton, 1994.

Stittleburg, Philip. "Standards, Who Needs Them?" *NFPA Journal*. May/June 1992, pp. 36-37.

Stittleburg, Philip. "Leaders Set the Tone for Members." *NFPA Journal*. July/August 1993a, p. 83.

Stittleburg, Philip. "The Future of Fire Service Funding." *NFPA Journal*. September/October 1993b, p. 120.

Stittleburg, Philip. "Recruitment and Retaining Volunteers." *NFPA Journal*. March/April 1994a, p. 20.

Stittleburg, Philip. "Pride Helps Keep Morale High." *NFPA Journal*. May/June 1994b, p. 18.

Stittleburg, Philip. "Change is the Key to Survival." *NFPA Journal*. July/August 1994c, pp. 20, 110.

Stittleburg, Philip. "Title?" *NFPA Journal*. July/August 1995.

Stoline, Anne and Jonathan P. Weiner. *The New Medical Marketplace: A Physician's Guide to the Health Care Revolution*. Baltimore: Johns Hopkins Press, 1988.

Stout, Jack and American Ambulance Association. *Contracting for Emergency Ambulance Services*. Sacramento, CA: American Ambulance Association, 1994.

Sullivan, Thomas. *Creation of Career Officer Positions Within the Chain of Command of a Volunteer Fire Department*. Report for Executive Fire Officer Program. Emmitsburg, MD: National Fire Academy, 1993.

Thompson, Alexander. "Volunteers and Their Communities: A Comparative Analysis of Volunteer Firefighters." Working Paper #24. Department of Economics. Poughkeepsie, NY: Vassar College, 1992.

Thompson, Alexander M. III. "Latent Cosmopolitan and Local Orientation Among Rural Emergency Service Volunteers." *Non-profit and Voluntary Sector Quarterly*. 24: 2, 1995, pp. 103-116.

Tomsho, Robert. "Ambulance Companies Fight Municipalities for Emergency Market." *The Wall Street Journal*. December 27, 1994.

Toqueville, Alexis de. *Democracy in America*. New York, Vintage Press, 1945.

TriData Corporation. *Final Report for Fire and Rescue Services Study*. Prepared for Board of County Supervisors, Prince William County, Virginia. Arlington, VA: TriData, 1994.

Vidich, Arthur and Joseph Bensman. *Small Town in Mass Society*. Princeton: Princeton University Press, 1968.

Weber, Max. *Theory of Social and Economic Organization*. Trans. By A. Henderson and T. Parsons. Glenco, IL: The Free Press, 1947.

Weeks, John R. *Population: An Introduction to Concepts and Issues.* Belmont, CA: Wadsworth, 1989.

Williams, R.M. "National Health Care Reform and Emergency Medicine." *Annals of Emergency Medicine.* 22: 1, 1993, pp. 123-131.

Windisch, F.C. "Influencing change with a new culture." *Fire Engineering.* April 1995, pp. 12-16.

Wolff, Barak. "An Expanded Vision for EMS." *Emergency.* June 1994, p. 9.